Evidence-based practice for information professionals
a handbook

Evidence-based practice for information professionals
a handbook

Edited by
Andrew Booth and Anne Brice

facet publishing

© The compilation: Andrew Booth and Anne Brice 2004
The articles: the contributors 2004

Published by
Facet Publishing, 7 Ridgmount Street,
London WC1E 7AE
www.facetpublishing.co.uk

Facet Publishing is wholly owned by CILIP: the Chartered Institute of Library
and Information Professionals.

First published 2004
Reprinted 2004

British Library Cataloguing in Publication Data
A catalogue record for this book is available from the British Library.

ISBN 1-85604-471-8

Typeset from editors' disks by Facet Publishing in 11/13 pt Elegant Garamond
and Humanist 521.
Printed and made in Great Britain by MPG Books Ltd, Bodmin, Cornwall.

Contents

Foreword

Librarians working in healthcare in the late 1990s had the considerable privilege, and indeed pleasure, of witnessing and participating in a revolutionary paradigm, which was to place information management, its associated skills and technologies at centre stage of the delivery of appropriate and effective care. That paradigm, variously identified as 'evidence-based medicine', 'evidence-based healthcare' or 'evidence-based practice' placed a premium on the retrieval of rigorous and reliable evidence to inform clinical decision making.

Had this been the full impact of this new model for ongoing discovery and lifelong learning then you, the reader, probably working in an information sector outside healthcare, would have no need even to open this edited book on evidence-based information practice. The fact that you *have* opened this book bears testimony to the migration of the 'evidence-based' model to other sectors including education, social work and management. It also attests to an increasing interest in the evidence base for our own practice. Although much of the trail has been blazed from within the healthcare sector, and is necessarily represented as such in this book, we contend (and many colleagues agree) that this model is equally valid for the sector within which you are working. What is required is the *application* of the tools and techniques to your specific area of practice, be it in libraries, museums or archives, and its sensitive *adaptation* to your local culture and environment.

Each Part of the book employs a different approach according to its subject content:

- Part 1 contains comprehensive overview chapters, which represent state-of-the-art thinking in relation to evidence-based practice with a special focus on the implications for information work. Each chapter is comprehensively referenced to allow access to writings from the wider paradigm.
- Part 2 comprises practically oriented how-to-do-it chapters outlining the process of evidence-based information practice from initiation to evaluation and review.

- Part 3 explores each of the six domains of evidence-based librarianship identified by Crumley and Koufogiannakis, to demonstrate the application of
evidence-based information practice to a practical decision-making context.
Each chapter begins by reviewing the types of question that might inform each
area of professional practice. It then reviews sources of evidence to be used to
answer these questions before proceeding to identify some major study-types
in each domain. These chapters cover generic topics of interest to those working in information work in general with an emphasis on the most rigorous
study-types. One or more illustrative chapters containing a special topic follows each chapter that dicusses one of the six domains, to provide practical
examples of the application of evidence-based principles and methods.

We, the editors, would like to invite you to examine this model with an open mind
and to attempt to identify its potential usefulness within your specific context. As
you do so, we would encourage you to challenge, to criticize and even to com-
bat! 'No stimulation without irritation' has long been a rallying cry from Muir
Gray, one of the leading proponents of evidence-based practice. In producing the
light that only the generation of heat can occasion, we believe that the cause of
evidence-based practice will be better advanced than through some uneasy and
artificial consensus.

We would like to take this opportunity to thank both our spouses and families for their patience, forbearance and encouragement as we oversaw the progress
of this work from idea to realization.

Andrew Booth and Anne Brice

Editors and contributors

Catherine Beverley is Senior Information Officer/ HTA Information Unit Manager at the School of Health and Related Research (ScHARR), University of Sheffield. Previously, she worked as a research assistant at Community Health Sheffield NHS Trust. Her main area of interest is providing information support to systematic reviews. She is also undertaking a part-time PhD on the health and social care information needs of people with a visual impairment.

Andrew Booth has twenty years' experience as a health information professional, since 1994 at the School of Health and Related Research (ScHARR), University of Sheffield as Director of Information Resources and Senior Lecturer in Evidence Based Healthcare Information. His current brief is to support evidence-based healthcare within the University of Sheffield and Trent Region. Andrew is an experienced trainer of end-users and NHS Librarians in literature searching and critical appraisal. He has developed and delivered the ADEPT course on applying evidence-based principles to literature searching in six NHS regions. Andrew attended the first ever UK Workshop in Teaching Evidence Based Medicine in Oxford and has subsequently tutored at three of the equivalent Northern and Yorkshire Evidence Based Practice Workshops in Durham.

Andrew is on the editorial boards of *Evidence Based Healthcare* and *Health Information and Libraries Journal* (formerly *Health Libraries Review*). He chairs the Health Libraries Group Research Working Party and, in this role, contributes the quarterly Using Research In Practice column to the *Health Information and Libraries Journal (HILJ)*. Together with colleagues in the Information Resources Section at ScHARR he organized the first Evidence Based Librarianship Conference in Sheffield in September 2001. In June 2003 he chaired the International Programme Committee for the second Evidence Based Librarianship Conference in Edmonton, Canada. He co-edited (with Jonathan Eldredge) a special issue of *HILJ* on Evidence Based Health Information Practice to coincide with this latter conference. Andrew owns the www.eblib.net domain, an international gateway to resources in evidence-based information practice.

Alison Brettle is Research Fellow (Information) at the Health Care Practice R&D Unit (HCPRDU), University of Salford. She began her health information career as Information Manager at the UK Clearing House on Health Outcomes, Nuffield Institute for Health. She moved to the North West R&D Unit for Nurses and Therapists, establishing a research information service. At HCPRDU she is responsible for providing information support and advice to research staff, teaching information skills and research into information issues relevant to evidence-based practice. She is interested in effective searching for systematic reviews and the effectiveness of information skills training.

Anne Brice is currently Head of Knowledge and Information Sciences, in the Public Health Resource Unit, Oxford. Anne is seconded to the National electronic Library for Health, where she is responsible for the development of the Specialist Libraries programme, building knowledge networks and communities of practice around specialist healthcare domains. She is also contracted for one day a week as a health knowledge management consultant to the Acting Director of Knowledge Management, NHS Modernisation Agency.

After qualifying in 1983 Anne worked at the Royal Postgraduate Medical School, followed by a post at Queen Mary College, both part of the University of London. Following six years as Regional Librarian in the Borders Health Board, Scotland she was appointed in 1995 as Librarian at the Institute of Health Sciences, University of Oxford. She moved to the post of Assistant Director of the Health Care Libraries Unit, University of Oxford in 1996 with responsibility for co-ordinating and facilitating training, networking and co-operation among the member libraries of the Health Libraries and Information Network. She transferred to her current post in 2002. Anne's current professional interests include e-learning in evidence-based healthcare, mentoring and professional development, knowledge harvesting and communities of practice, and evidence-based librarianship.

Cindy Carlson joined the Learning and Development Team at the Public Health Resource Unit in Oxford in September 2002. She previously worked as Senior Lecturer and Programme Leader for the MSc in Public Health at Oxford Brookes University, having designed the course and taught on it for three years. Before her foray into academia, she worked as a senior manager for several international development organisations, based firstly in Africa and latterly in the UK. Her interests range widely, from supporting public health training and development in the UK to sexual health concerns and the effects of conflict on health in Africa, to mobilizing social capital in her local community. Her current work at PHRU includes public health practitioner development, mentor training, facilitating international courses in Poverty Reduction Strategies, facilitating action learning sets and teaching a variety of public health-related subjects. Cindy is also a founding member and treasurer of CASP International Network, as well as a founding member of the Oxford Development Partnership.

Lynette Cawthra is Information and Library Service Manager at the King's Fund, an independent charitable foundation whose goal is to improve health, especially in London. Its library is open to the public, and contains a unique collection of material on UK healthcare policy and management. She is joint project manager of the National electronic Library for Health's specialist library for management, and current Chair of the Consortium of Independent Health Information Libraries in London (CHILL). Previous posts include Information Manager at Age Concern England, and bibliographic researcher for an art foundation.

Ellen Crumley is the Clinical Librarian with the Department of Pediatrics at the University of Alberta, Canada. She is currently completing the Master of Science in Clinical Epidemiology and is Co-Chair for the 2003 EBL Conference. Her research interests include quality of librarianship research, systematic reviews, education and evidence-based practice. Ellen conducted two reviews about where and how to search for trials for systematic reviews and is currently completing comprehensive searches for the AHCDC about Hemophilia and von Willebrand's Disease. Ellen was previously the Editor of the Canadian Health Libraries Association journal (2001–2). She has published numerous articles and presented research at national events.

Dr Jonathan Eldredge holds the position of Assistant Professor in the School of Medicine and Coordinator of Academic and Clinical Services in the Health Sciences Library and Informatics Center at the University of New Mexico.

Dr Eldredge created the Medical Library Association's continuing education course in 1998 and has taught it 15 times in the US, Canada and the UK. He has published 14 articles on evidence-based librarianship (EBL). Dr Eldredge received both the MLA Research Award and the MLA South Central Chapter's Research Award during 2002. His current research focuses upon the innovative applications of the cohort design and the randomized controlled trial to answering important questions facing our profession.

Dr Paul Genoni is teaching with the Department of Media and Information at Curtin University of Technology, Perth, Western Australia. His previous position was as Law Librarian at the University of Western Australia, and he has extensive general experience in academic libraries. His current teaching and research interests include collection management, in particular aspects of co-operation between research libraries. He has also published numerous articles related to professional development for librarians, with an emphasis on mentoring.

Maria J. Grant is a Research Fellow (Information) at the Salford Centre for Nursing, Midwifery and Collaborative Research (SCMNCR), University of Salford. Maria has a background in information science and provides literature-searching support to SCNMCR members developing research bids or undertaking projects. Maria also contributes to systematic reviews of health interventions. Her research interests include enhancing practice through the investigation of optimal database searching, and investigating the effectiveness of literature-searching training provision. Maria is Chair of IFM Healthcare, a charitable organization committed to improving the provision of information in enhancing healthcare management and delivery.

Dr Gaby Haddow is currently working as a Research Project Officer for the Western Australia Centre for Evidence Based Nursing and Midwifery, a collaborating centre of the Joanna Briggs Institute. The Joanna Briggs Institute is an international collaboration involved in producing and disseminating evidence-based practice information for health professionals. Gaby's previous experience includes teaching in library and information science (LIS) and managing the research center of the United States Information Service in Western Australia. Her research interests are the communication of research to practice in LIS and health science, the quality of health information on the internet, and the role of publications within a discipline.

Alison Hill is Programme Director of the South East Region Public Health Observatory which is a joint initiative between the Public Health Resource Unit and the University of Oxford, providing and brokering public health information in the south east region. She is also Director of the Public Health Resource Unit, which is an NHS unit at the Institute of Health Sciences Oxford, supporting public health education, intelligence, service development and professional development. Before this she was Director of Public Health in Buckinghamshire. She has been actively involved in the Critical Appraisal Skills Programme since it began in 1993. Her major areas of interest are public health and health service development, professional development and getting research into practice. Her background is in hospital medicine and medicine in the developing world; she worked in a rural hospital in Transkei, South Africa, between 1979 and 1981.

Jennie Kelson is Library Services Manager at Stoke Mandeville Hospital, Buckinghamshire Hospitals NHS Trust. She worked initially at King Edward Memorial Hospital for Women, Perth, to set up a women's health information service providing consumer health information to the public of Western Australia. Since relocating to Britain, she has been involved in supporting evidence-based practice, research and knowledge management projects within the Trust. Her main areas of interest are evidence-based librarianship and teaching critical appraisal skills.

Robert Kiley is Head of Systems Strategy at the Wellcome Library for the History and Understanding of Medicine. In this role he is responsible for directing the operation and development of the Library's automated systems and digital resources, with particular responsibility for strategic planning and co-ordination. Robert describes himself as a 'net enthusiast', and is author of *Medical information on the Internet: a guide for health professionals* (Churchill Livingstone, 3rd edn, 2003 ,www.medinfolinks.com/), the *Patient's Internet Handbook* (RSM, 2002, www.patient-handbook.co.uk/) and the *Doctor's Internet Handbook* (RSM 2000, www.rsmpress.co.uk/bkkiley.htm/). Prior to joining the Wellcome Trust, Robert worked as an NHS librarian at Frimley Park Hospital NHS Trust, Camberley. Robert is a qualified librarian and a Chartered Member of CILIP: the Chartered Institute of Library and Information Professionals.

Denise Koufogiannakis is Collections Manager at the John W. Scott Health Sciences Library, University of Alberta, Canada. Denise began her health sciences librarianship career in 1997, after graduating from the School of Library and Information Studies, University of Alberta, where she is now a sessional lecturer. She is interested in finding practical ways in which librarians can make their everyday decisions more evidence-based.

David Peacock is Knowledge Services Manager at the Northern England Workforce Development Confederation. He began his library career in the public sector, working for Northumberland County Council. He then moved to Sunderland University, and then the University of Northumbria at Newcastle, where he managed the nursing libraries in a number of local hospitals. Since 1998 he has worked in the NHS, initially as the Regional Librarian (Information Management & Technology) for the old Northern and Yorkshire region. He has been involved in the National Core Content Working Group.

Ann Ritchie is employed with the Royal Australian College of General Practitioners as the Project Officer for the National Standing Committee, Education. Ann's librarian background was in medical libraries, and her professional interests are in continuing education, particularly in evidence-based healthcare and mentoring. She is the current holder of the Professional Development portfolio, Health

Libraries Australia, and chair of the IFLA section Continuing Professional Development and Workplace Learning.

Dr Christine Urquhart is Programme Director of the distance learning Health Information Management MSc programme, at the Department of Information Studies, University of Wales, Aberystwyth. She teaches information systems methodologies on the undergraduate and postgraduate programmes at UWA, and has research interests in the field of information behaviour, information systems and services evaluation, and health services research. Currently she is directing a JISC-funded project on the use and provision of electronic information services by staff and students in further and higher education institutions, and a project concerned with the evaluation of collaborative partnerships developing 'virtual outreach services' for health professionals and consumers. Previous projects include GIVTS (Getting Information to Vocational Trainees), EVINCE (Establishing the Value of Information to Nursing Continuing Education) and the Value project.

Alison Winning is Clinical Effectiveness Information Specialist, Doncaster and Bassetlaw Hospitals NHS Trust, Doncaster. Alison's career in health information began in 1999, supporting the research activities of NHS staff in Trent through the Trent Institute for Health Services Research at the School of Health and Related Research (ScHARR), University of Sheffield. Her main interests are the use of research to support clinical practice and clinical librarianship. Having taken up a new post in 2002 she is currently supporting the clinical governance agenda within an NHS trust through the provision of a clinical effectiveness information service.

1

Why evidence-based information practice?

Andrew Booth and Anne Brice

Introduction

Evidence-based practice is rightly described as one of the 'success stories of the 1990s' (Trinder, 2000). Its growth in popularity is demonstrated by its spread from medicine to related health fields and, more importantly, by its migration to other disciplines and professions.

This chapter begins with a discussion of evidence-based practice, outlining the political and social context within which it has developed as a major part of public policy (Weiss, 1998; Nutbeam, 2001). It then moves to consider evidence-based information practice in particular, and concludes by discussing some of the strengths and weaknesses of the evidence-based practice paradigm as they apply to information practice.

Scenario

You are a member of a city-wide action group set up by the Education and Leisure Services to tackle concerns regarding the city's 14–16 year olds. There is an increasing perception that this age group is not being addressed by local facilities and amenities and, rightly or wrongly, this lack is being linked to a high prevalence of vandalism, drug use and teenage pregnancy. Working in a subgroup involving representatives of school, public, educational charity and further education college libraries, you are devising an action plan focusing on the specific contribution libraries might make.

You decide to look for evidence from the research literature to inform your decision making. A search on the internet, complemented by bibliographic databases, identifies work funded by the UK organization Museums, Libraries and Archives Council (then Resource) as part of the 'Start with the child' initative. A research report reviews primary and secondary research and is usefully subdivided by age group. Each section models the child's world, then identifies the needs and motivations of that age group before outlining the implications for services.

On the basis of this evidence the subgroup devises an action plan which includes the following strategies:

- to provide a more welcoming atmosphere with a more sophisticated ambience and a variety of dedicated spaces – quiet, loud and chill-out
- to involve young people in the design and in staffing and interfacing
- to broaden content to reflect popular/contemporary/commercial culture, including music and fashion
- to allow young people to plug their own music into workspaces, through headphones and listening posts.

One year after implementing the action plan you will evaluate it and look to identify any unresolved issues.

What you are doing is practising 'evidence-based practice'! You have harnessed existing research evidence in support of a practical decision. Admittedly you might have come to a similar solution by 'brainstorming' from the group's experience or by conducting a local survey. However, by using a review of the literature you have minimized your chance of overlooking something or trying something that is known not to work. Your task is easier in this case because a synthesized report of the evidence exists, but the process would be essentially the same if you had to identify evidence from primary research.

Why evidence-based practice?

Regardless of whether you work in education or social services, government or healthcare, you are likely to have encountered 'evidence-based practice'. For many information professionals their first encounter is in the context of *supporting* evidence-based practice, that is to say facilitating the use of research by their users, readers or clients. Typically this starts with the application of traditional skills in information retrieval, organization and management but with an added sense of urgency, not to say purpose, injected by the need to support day-to-day decision making. This new sense of purpose is often accompanied by an increasing awareness and understanding of the barriers and biases that have impeded the application of research into practice, and to which the traditional role of libraries has contributed in many ways. It may also involve the identification and acquisition of new 'evidence-based' resources and the need to promote these and to

enable users to exploit them through instruction and training. Finally, supporting evidence-based practice may also include the application of new skills such
as formulating the question (Booth, 2000a), filtering the literature (Paisley, 2000)
and critically appraising studies (Dorsch et al., 1990) to assess whether their
results are valid, reliable and applicable. This may lead naturally to consideration of appropriate ways of summarizing, interpreting and disseminating
information to assist the adoption of research findings to practice.

Evidence-based medicine first appeared from fairly specialized beginnings as
'clinical epidemiology' (Sackett et al., 1991), i.e. the application of research findings from studying a group (or 'population') to the management and care of the
individual patient. In 1992, rebadged as 'evidence-based medicine' (Evidence-
Based Medicine Working Group, 1992), it was promoted as a model of practice
for practitioners and policy makers, as opposed to the exclusive domain of academics and students. From here its adoption, either under the generic banners
of 'evidence-based healthcare' or 'evidence-based practice' or under speciality specific labels such as 'evidence-based pathology', has been pervasive (Sackett et al.,
1996). As Trinder (2000) observes: 'Over the last few years evidence-based
approaches have been developed in most health fields, including evidence-based
dentistry, nursing, public health, physiotherapy and mental health'.

Perhaps more surprising has been the migration of the key concepts of evidence-
based practice to non-health disciplines or professions. Trinder (2000) continues:
'Progress has not stopped there: uniquely it would appear that an approach
originating in medicine is being advocated and adopted in more distant fields of
professional activity, including social work, probation, education and human
resource management'.

Trinder's use of the phrase 'professional activity' is significant. In truth, the
arguments for basing professional practice on the evidence are compelling – the
concept of professionalism requires that a practitioner remains in constant contact with the knowledge base that determines the content, nature and impact of
their day-to-day activities. Implicit, or tacit, knowledge acquired from years of experience must be informed, and indeed complemented, by explicit knowledge, or
evidence, derived from more formal recorded sources (Moody and Shanks, 1999).
This evidence not only has to be reliable, valid and applicable but, importantly,
must also be the 'best-available' from the perspectives of both access and currency.

The stimuli for such an approach are, at the same time, pre-emptive and
defensive. Concerns with the ineffectiveness of traditional mechanisms for transferring information through basic and continuing education have led to increasing
recognition of the importance of skills for 'lifelong learning' (Shin et al., 1993).
Such skills, encapsulated in the Chinese proverb 'Give a man a fish and you feed
him for a day, teach him to fish and you feed him for a lifetime' (Haynes, 1998)
are increasingly promoted by government (DFEE, 1998; DoH, 2001), academic

and professional bodies. Traditional models of publishing, models for which librarians have, to some extent, been gatekeepers, have also been mainly concerned with transferring knowledge between researchers, rather than between researchers and practitioners.

The knowledge base itself has been growing at an unparalleled rate, as have the new technologies and treatments available at the point of healthcare decision making. The imperative to increase the capacity and delivery of healthcare systems has grown, yet, at the same time, as Trinder (2000) observes, the imperative for risk management, driven by the emergence of an increasingly litigious society, has required that professionals demonstrate their ongoing competence. Initially, emphasis was upon detecting the aberrant individual, embodied in the 'Bolam Principle' in medicine where 'reasonable care' is defined as that standard of care deemed appropriate by a respected body of one's peers (Fenwick and Beran, 1997; Coiera, 1997). However, the realization that such a principle, based on an 'averaging' or relative effect, does little to counter a general shortfall in quality of practice has led to a requirement for a more exacting and absolute authority for performance. Thus it has been proposed that reference be made to an external body of evidence, the so-called 'Cochrane principle' (named after a database of best available evidence for treatments and other interventions, the Cochrane Library), as a more rigorous, if less forgiving standard.

Finally, the changing attitude of society to the role and status of the professional, allied to the increase in accessible information, has changed the relationship between patient and practitioner, and forced practitioners to examine more closely their abilities and skills in managing the knowledge so crucial to their performance and professionalism.

The political context

In an era when evidence-based practice has thrived, almost regardless of the political power in the ascendancy, this particular model of professional self-regulation has had much to recommend it. During the late 1980s the preoccupation of monetarist governments with 'value for money' had done much to alienate professionals such as teachers, doctors and nurses who prefer to focus on quality of service. Within the health service, for example, cost-cutting managers were ranged against clinical 'champions' for public standards. Shifting the emphasis from *economy* (i.e. cost-effectiveness) to *effectiveness*, while not completely circumventing the cost debate, served to unite managers and professionals in pursuit of a common goal. At a time when concern with the performance of public employees was high, and self-regulation of performance by peer-review had not yielded the intended results, evidence-based practice was seen as a way of introducing explicit standards into professional activity.

Admittedly many of the targets were 'soft', focusing on disinvestment from practices proven to be ineffective ('start-stopping') or delaying the introduction of practices not yet proven to be effective ('stop-starting'). Nevertheless, where debates over resources had raged for many years, for example on 'class size' for optimal teaching performance, there was at least the possibility of an additional option, i.e. referral to an independent assessment based on the body of published evidence. Of course, such an approach carries no guarantees of success as neither party need necessarily abide by the verdict should it not conform to their chosen stance. The way in which this model has transformed the operation of public service management is chronicled by the book, *What Works? Evidence-based policy and practice* (Davies et al., 2000).

The pervasive effect of evidence-based practice has also been seen in government. There was increasing recognition that if the Government was to utilize this rational model of decision making as a control on the professional performance of those in the public sector, then it could also be used as a guide for the performance of policy makers. In 1999, a White Paper on *Modernising Government* observed: 'The Government expects more of policy makers. More new ideas, more willingness to question inherited ways of doing things, better use of evidence and research in policy making and better focus on policies that will deliver long-term goals' (Cabinet Office, 1999).

The social context

In the 1990s, more populist approaches to government were reflected in an increasing consumer dimension to evidence-based practice. Allied to an imperative for public sector research to yield results in the form of guidance on how to make society better, rather than merely increase our understanding of it, consumers were to be involved in every stage of the research process. This so-called 'utilitarian turn in research' (Solesbury, 2001; Solesbury, 2002) meant that research projects should address priorities of importance to users of services, specifically focusing on questions identified by them or their representatives. Users should be involved in the conduct of the research and in the appropriate dissemination of its findings. Finally, and most importantly, in the context of the practitioner (as opposed to the more specialist 'doer' of research) the findings from any research study should be mediated and moderated by the views, preferences and values of the community within which the evidence is to be implemented.

Such a utilitarian perspective on research is further seen in the popularization of the systematic review method. Systematic reviews may be viewed as a particular type of secondary research which seeks 'to exploit more fully existing data and existing research findings'. As Solesbury (2001) observes: 'Both systematic reviews and secondary analysis of data depend on an awareness of previous research so skills in searching for existing data or findings are also important.' For the first time, in modern history at least, the skills of the information worker had become recognized as pivotal to the conduct of practical and useful research, and its impact on improving the quality of health and healthcare.

This brings us to another crucial feature of the social context that has impacted on the development of evidence-based practice. The so-called 'Information Society' has seen technologies for the access and delivery of information placed at the disposal of the average man, woman and, indeed, child. Nowhere is the impact of this technology more apparent than in the domain of evidence-based practice. Indeed, within healthcare, evidence-based medicine was the first paradigm to coincide with the development of the world wide web. International collaborations such as the Cochrane Collaboration are able to share information and data across boundaries. To a large extent, the period since the early 1980s has seen an increasing globalization of research with emphasis on generalizability (will it work elsewhere?) in preference to applicability (why did it work here?). It is within this context of increasing access to the evidence, sharing of research across international boundaries, and the globalization and popularization of research that this work on evidence-based information practice belongs.

So what is evidence-based information practice?

As several commentators have observed, the model of evidence-based practice is fundamentally one of information management. In fact it addresses two information 'pathologies' (Booth, 1998) namely 'information overload' and the slow dissemination of research findings into routine practice. Similarities with information management become even more apparent when we examine the five stages of evidence-based practice (Sackett et al., 1997):

1   identification of a problem or question
2   finding, as efficiently as possible, the best evidence to answer the question
3   appraising the evidence for validity and usefulness
4   applying the results to a specific population
5   evaluating the outcome of the intervention.

Although stages one and two of this process are those most obviously associated with information practice, it is immediately apparent that judging information quality (stage three), judging relevance (stage four) and evaluating the outcome of information provision (stage five) are all integral to good information management.

Several commentators have observed, therefore, that it would be perverse if a profession that has done so much promulgate the importance of information management were to miss the opportunity to apply these principles to their own professional practice (Booth, 2000b) – that is, in failing 'to model what they teach' (Ritchie, 1999). We may also be tempted to ask why those acting as intermediaries between the research base and the users, or potential users of research, did not act more quickly or proactively to address these issues. For many information professionals, involvement in evidence-based practice has led variously to an epiphany-like realization or, more commonly, to a nagging awareness that they too should be *practising* evidence-based practice.

Even in its relatively short existence (1997 onwards) there have been three attempts to define 'evidence-based librarianship' (EBL). Eldredge (2002) defines EBL thus: 'Evidence-Based Librarianship (EBL) seeks to improve library practice by utilising the best available evidence in conjunction with a pragmatic perspective developed from working experiences in librarianship. The best available evidence might be produced from quantitative or qualitative research designs, although EBL encourages more rigorous forms over less rigorous forms of evidence when making decisions'.

Crumley and Koufogiannakis (2002) revert to the stages of the evidence-based practice process in supplying their definition: 'Evidence-based librarianship (EBL) is a means to improve the profession of librarianship by asking questions, finding, critically appraising and incorporating research evidence from library science (and other disciplines) into daily practice. It also involves encouraging librarians to conduct research', while, somewhat uncharacteristically, Booth (2000b) ducks the challenge and, instead, provides minor modifications to an existing definition of evidence-based practice (McKibbon et al., 1996). That definition does, however, have the advantage of being coined by a librarian, Anne McKibbon from McMaster University, the spiritual home of evidence-based medicine: 'Evidence-based librarianship (EBL) is an approach to information science that promotes the collection, interpretation and integration of valid, important and applicable user-reported, librarian-observed, and research-derived evidence. The best available evidence, moderated by user needs and preferences, is applied to improve the quality of professional judgements'.

Elsewhere, Booth (2002) argues that attempts to invent a speciality labelled 'evidence-based librarianship' might be considered retrograde when compared with the advantages of allying ourselves to the already established movement of evidence-based practice. There are inherent weaknesses in defining the speciality only in terms of its differences from, rather than its similarities to, other domains of evidence-based practice. More importantly, such an approach misses parallel developments in the area of information systems that are closely related to those in evidence-based librarianship (Atkins and Louw, 2000). Furthermore, the label 'evidence-based librarianship' leads, as Crumley and Koufogiannakis (2002) recognize, to an inevitable confusion between librarians *supporting* evidence-based practice and librarians *practising* evidence-based practice. Such confusion becomes increasingly unhelpful as the distinction between these becomes blurred.

Evidence-based information practice is thus our preferred term for the approach championed within this work. The first recorded occurrence of this term was, to the best of our knowledge, in an editorial written by our respected colleague, Margaret Haines, then NHS Library Adviser, in June 1995. Commenting on the newly emergent phenomenon of 'Evidence-based Purchasing' she wrote: 'What I find particularly appealing about the (Anglia and Oxford Librarian of the 21st Century) programme is that it will not only help librarians to support evidence-based practice of their users but it will also develop their *own evidence-based information practice* (italics added) which should result in more cost-effective and higher quality information support to the NHS' (Haines, 1995).

Subsequently the term has appeared in research statements such as the (US) Medical Library Association's *Using Scientific Evidence to Improve Information Practice* (1995) and the (US) Special Libraries Association's *Putting OUR Knowledge to Work* (2001).

Our choice of label stems from our shared dissatisfaction with the limitations of 'evidence-based librarianship' as recorded above. We wish to acknowledge the wider context of information science that will inform our approach, and that of our contributors, throughout the book. More importantly, by including 'information' within the already recognized phrase 'evidence-based practice' we aim to focus on the commonality of issues and methods within the domain of information practice with those that have emerged from the origins of the generic paradigm. Evidence-based information practice is evidence-based practice with information as both its subject and its object.

The strengths and weaknesses of evidence-based information practice

Such a philosophy is immediately seen to be appropriate as we discuss the strengths and weaknesses of evidence-based information practice. It is useful to consider criticisms of evidence-based information practice (EBIP) within the framework by which Straus and McAlister (2000) respond to attacks on evidence-based healthcare (EBHC). We can thus divide such criticisms into:

- those that arise from misunderstandings of the process of EBIP
- those that apply to all forms of information practice and are not, therefore, exclusive to EBIP
- those that are specific to EBIP.

Although much of the debate around EBIP is common to that which surrounded evidence-based healthcare, we shall focus on four principal objections encountered in championing EBIP among information professionals.

Misunderstandings

'But what about qualitative research which comprises by far the largest part of the information science literature?'

EBIP does not assume the innate superiority of any particular research design. Instead it echoes the advocates of evidence-based medicine in reasoning that the selection of an appropriate study design will be determined by the nature of the question being asked (Sackett and Wennberg,1997). In fact, the centrality of the user perspective to many information contexts will immediately recommend more qualitative research approaches. Nevertheless the compatibility of naturally occurring teaching groups to more deterministic and quantitative designs such as cohort studies, or even randomized controlled trials, together with the plentiful nature of routine observational data, means that EBIP will draw on the widest possible variety of evidence sources.

Objections common to information practice

'But I don't have the time'

Such pleas are difficult to sustain when placed alongside demands on other busy professional groups such as doctors and teachers. A wise commentator once observed: 'It is never true to say that you don't have time for something when, in effect, you mean that it is not high enough up your list of priorities'. Any form of service evaluation takes time (e.g. a questionnaire will require time for design, administration, distribution and analysis). The alternative is to run the risk of wasting valuable time by persevering with some intervention that the evidence might demonstrate to be ineffective. Indeed a search of the relevant literature will find immediate examples of existing, under-utilized research that highlights ineffective practices that consume large amounts of information professionals' time and resources. Despite their skills in information retrieval, information professionals do not systematically search their own knowledge base for evidence with which to support their decisions. As the Special Library Association's research statement (2001) charitably puts it: 'Like other professional groups, librarians tend to be action-oriented, relying on our own experience and professional judgment to make decisions. Both the need to make decisions quickly and the lack of a clear connection between much library and information science research and the day-to-day problems faced by librarians make seeking and applying our own knowledge base a challenge'.

Objections unique to EBIP

'But the evidence is of such poor quality/quantity'

Granted such an observation may prove true but what such critics usually mean is that they have not bothered to search and examine the evidence. The evidence base for information practice will not be derived merely from library and information science databases but will be found in management, computing, social science and education databases (Booth, 2002). Even though such evidence may not be plentiful, a practitioner will usually find some item of research that may be used to address a specific focused question.

'I don't have the skills or resources to practise EBIP'

Many information workers have developed new skills in supporting evidence-based practice. The fact that they have done so demonstrates that not only is this feasible but that this is seen as a worthwhile goal. The application of evidence-based approaches to our own professional practice is no less worthy an aspiration. This book will aim to provide you with many of the skills and resources required for EBIP. In truth, however, many of the models and tools that you will require are already available within the broader context of evidence-based practice.

Conclusion

This chapter has explored some of the background to evidence-based practice clearly locating EBIP within the broader paradigm (EBMWG, 1992). It has discussed the political and social context for the emergence of a preoccupation with practical and useful research findings. It has anticipated objections to the concept of EBIP, employing a framework designed to counter similar concerns expressed by critics of evidence-based healthcare. These and other issues will be further developed throughout the subsequent pages of this work.

References

Atkins, C. and Louw, G. (2000) Building Bridges: constructing a framework for evidence-based information systems, *Health Informatics Journal*, **6**, 121–6.
Booth, A. (1998) How to Search for the Evidence, *Bulletin of the Royal College of Pathologists*, **103**, 44–57.

Booth, A. (2000a) Formulating the Question. In Booth, A. and Walton G. (eds), *Managing Knowledge in Health Services*, London, Library Association Publishing, 197–206.

Booth, A. (2000b) *Librarian Heal Thyself: evidence based librarianship, useful, practicable, desirable? Proceedings of the 8th International Congress on Medical Librarianship, held between July 2 and 5, 2000,* London, UK, www.icml.org/tuesday/themes/booth.htm.

Booth, A. (2002) From EBM to EBL: two steps forward or one step back?, *Medical Reference Services Quarterly,* **21** (3), 51–64.

Cabinet Office (1999) *Modernising Government*, London, Stationery Office, Cm 4310, www.cabinet-office.gov.uk/moderngov/whtpaper/index.htm.

Coiera, E. (1997) *Guide To Medical Informatics, The Internet and Telemedicine*, London, Chapman & Hall Medical.

Crumley, E. and Koufogiannakis, D. (2001) Developing Evidence Based Librarianship in Canada: six aspects for consideration, *Hypothesis,* **15**, 9–10.

Crumley E. and Koufogiannakis, D. (2002) Developing Evidence-Based Librarianship: practical steps for implementation, *Health Information and Libraries Journal,* **19** (4), 61–70.

Davies, H. T. O, Nutley, S. M. and Smith, P. C. (eds) (2000) *What Works? Evidence-based policy and practice in public services*, Bristol, Policy Press.

DFEE (1998) *The Learning Age: a renaissance for a new Britain*, London, HMSO.

Department of Health (2001) *Working Together, Learning Together: a framework for lifelong learning in the NHS*, London, DoH.

Dorsch, J. L., Frasca, M. A., Wilson, M. L. and Tomsic, M. L. (1990) A Multidisciplinary Approach to Information and Critical Appraisal Instruction, *Bulletin of the Medical Library Association,* **78** (1), 38–44.

Eldredge, J. D. (2002) Evidence-based Librarianship: what might we expect in the years ahead?, *Health Information and Libraries Journal,* **19** (2), 71–7.

Evidence-Based Medicine Working Group (1992) Evidence-Based Medicine: a new approach to teaching the practice of medicine, *JAMA,* **268** (17), 2420–5.

Fenwick, P. and Beran, R. G. (1997) Informed Consent: should Bolam be rejected?, *Medicine and Law,* **16** (2), 215–23.

Haines, M. (1995) Librarians and Evidence Based Purchasing, *Evidence Based Purchasing*, (8), 1.

Haynes, H. A. (1998) What Do Medical Students Need and What Do They Want?, *Arch Dermatol,* **134** (6), 731–2.

McKibbon, K. A. et al. (1996) *The Medical Literature as a Resource for Evidence Based Care*, http://hiru.mcmaster.ca/hiru/medline/asis-pap.htm.

Medical Library Association Research Task Force (1995) *Using Scientific Evidence to Improve Information Practice*, Chicago, Medical Library Association, http://mlanet.org/research/science1.html.

Moody, D. and Shanks, G. (1999) *Using Knowledge Management and the Internet to Support Evidence Based Practice: a medical case study. Proceedings of the 10th Australasian Conference on Information Systems*, Wellington, New Zealand, 660–76.

Nutbeam, D. (2001) Evidence-based Public Policy for Health: matching research to policy need, *Promotion & Education*, **2** (Special supplement), 15–19.

Paisley S. (2000) Filtering the literature. In Booth, A. and Walton, G. (eds), *Managing Knowledge in Health Services*, London, Library Association Publishing.

Ritchie, A. (1999) Evidence-based Decisionmaking, *incite Magazine*, (December), www.alia.org.au/incite/1999/12/appraisal.html.

Sackett, D. L., Haynes, R. B., Guyatt, G. H. and Tugwell, P. (1991) *Clinical Epidemiology: a Basic Science for Clinical Medicine*, Boston, Little, Brown and Company.

Sackett, D. L., Rosenberg, W. M., Gray, J. A., Haynes, R. B. and Richardson, W. S. (1996) Evidence Based Medicine: what it is and what it isn't, *BMJ*, **312** (7023), 71–2.

Sackett, D. L. and Wennberg, J. E. (1997) Choosing the Best Research Design for Each Question, *BMJ*, **315** (1636).

Sackett, D.L. et al. (1997) *Evidence-based Medicine: how to practise and teach EBM*, Edinburgh, Churchill Livingstone.

Shin, J. H., Haynes, R. B. and Johnson, M. E. (1993) Effect of Problem-based, Self-directed Undergraduate Curriculum on Lifelong Learning, *Canadian Medical Association Journal*, **148**, 969–76.

Solesbury, W. (2001) *Evidence Based Policy: whence it came and where it's going*, (Working Paper 1), London, ESRC UK Centre for Evidence Based Policy and Practice (October), 10pp.

Solesbury, W. (2002) The Ascendancy of Evidence, *Planning Theory and Practice*, **3** (1), 90–6.

Special Library Association (2001) *Putting OUR Knowledge to Work: A new SLA research statement. The role of research in special librarianship* (June).

Straus, S. E. and McAlister, F. A. (2000) Evidence-based Medicine: a commentary on common criticisms, *Canadian Medical Association Journal*, **63** (7), 837–41.

Trinder, L. (2000) Introduction: The Rise of Evidence-based Practice. In Trinder, L. (ed.), with Reynolds, S., *Evidence-based Practice: a critical appraisal*, Blackwell Science.

Weiss, C. H. (1998) *Evaluation: methods for studying programs and policies*, 2nd edn, London, Prentice Hall.

2

A brief history of evidence-based practice

Anne Brice and Alison Hill

Introduction

This chapter reviews the growth of evidence-based practice. It does not offer a comprehensive history of the relationship between research and practice, but highlights the main landmarks and initiatives, initially in healthcare, but also in such areas of practice as education, social care, and policy. It describes the significant effect the evidence-based healthcare movement has had on the role and practice of librarians, focusing on the UK in particular.

Although single events may appear to be major catalysts of change, in retrospect any trend is a composite of diverse and complex social, political and technological change. The current context as it affects further development of evidence-based practice will be discussed.

Definitions and debates

There are many definitions of evidence-based practice in the literature (Critical Appraisal Skills Programme, 2003). The one that we feel best encapsulates the core concepts of evidence-based clinical practice states that it is 'an approach to decision making in which the clinician uses the best evidence available, in consultation with the patient, to decide upon the option which suits the patient best' (Gray, 2001).

The evidence-based movement was based on the concept that practice should be based on up-to-date, valid and reliable research. It is difficult to argue with such a simple and direct message. The term 'evidence-based' was adopted deliberately to challenge prevailing practice at the time and to provoke practitioners into proving that they were up-to-date with research evidence, and incorporating that evidence into their practice (Gray, 2001). The term is now accepted and in universal usage, but at the start it met with negative reactions from the medical establishment, and generated ridicule and controversy (Feinstein and Horwitz, 1997; Grahame-Smith, 1995; Isaacs and Fitzgerald, 1999; *Lancet* Editorial, 1995; Molesworth, 1998; Sackett, 1995). Criticism ranged from evidence-based medicine being 'old hat' to it being a dangerous innovation, a threat to clinical autonomy, aimed at rationing healthcare and suppressing clinical freedom through 'cook book' medicine (Sackett et al., 1996).

Underlying factors that explain why practitioners utilize interventions shown to be ineffective, or worse, harmful are (Haynes et al., 1997; Reynolds and Trinder, 2000):

- the poor quality of existing research
- difficulties of generalizing what evidence exists to individual patients
- information overload
- lack of skills to distinguish between good and poor quality research and to put evidence into practice
- limited time and resources both to learn and apply.

Much has been done to overcome these barriers. In the UK, research prioritization has become more systematic and is tied into the strategic and operational needs of the National Health Service. Systematic reviews of research literature are now accepted as major contributors to the evidence base. The last decade has seen a new industry of secondary publications, such as the evidence-based journals and the publication *Clinical Evidence* (www.clinicalevidence.com/), which appraise and make available research papers that are valid and relevant. Much more is known about effective learning, and evidence-based practice is being incorporated into the undergraduate curriculum. Post-registration clinical staff have opportunities for learning evidence-based practice, and systematic reviews and critical appraisal are increasingly recognized as legitimate activities in postgraduate education (Alderson et al., 2003).

Milestones in evidence-based practice

In Chapter 1, evidence-based healthcare was described as a product of its time (Reynolds and Trinder, 2000). Several factors helped to ensure that the time was right for its development and dramatic spread as a global movement.

The father of evidence-based practice is Archie Cochrane. His powerful and engaging book *Effectiveness and Efficiency: random reflection on health services* (Cochrane, 1972) argued that, since healthcare resources will always be limited, services must be based on effectiveness. Although randomized controlled trials as a methodology had been around for many years, Cochrane's clarion call was that they were not being utilized to inform practice, and should be the foundation for evaluating treatments, saying: 'it is surely a great criticism of our profession that we have not organised a critical summary, by specialty or subspecialty, adapted periodically, of all relevant randomised controlled trials' (Cochrane, 1979).

While this appeal was read and promoted by many, Cochrane's challenge was not taken up until a decade later, when two parallel developments got underway.

Systematic reviews

The first was the movement to bring together the results of research studies, through systematic reviews and meta-analysis. Iain Chalmers, who started his research career in maternity care, wanted to overcome the problem that many research studies were of insufficient size and power to be able to demonstrate an effect. He began to explore the techniques of systematic reviews in maternal and perinatal care. The publication of *Effective Care in Pregnancy and Childbirth* (Chalmers et al., 1989) brought together evidence from randomized controlled trials for different interventions and synthesized and summarized them. The book pushed maternity care to the forefront of evidence-based practice.

Iain Chalmers went on to create the first Cochrane Centre in Oxford, UK, in 1992. He then instigated what was to become an extraordinary global phenomenon, the Cochrane Collaboration, in 1993. This has resulted in international agreement on principles and processes for systematic reviews (Booth, 2001; Dickersin et al., 1994; Fitzpatrick, 2000; Lefebvre, 1994; Whyte, 1999), and a global resource called the Cochrane Library (www.update-software.com/cochrane/). The Cochrane Collaboration logo reflects its origins in perinatal care, depicting how the individually inconclusive results of individual trials of steroids in preterm labour could be synthesized into a decisive 'bottom line'.

Clinical epidemiology

A parallel development saw changes in medical education pioneered by McMaster University in Ontario, Canada. The new curriculum emphasized self-directed and problem-based learning, integrating research and practice. This discipline was called 'clinical epidemiology' and another milestone in evidence-based practice was the publication of *Clinical Epidemiology: a basic science for clinical medicine* (Sackett et al., 1985). Research papers at the time were written primarily for researchers rather than for clinicians wishing to put research into practice. This influential book set out how clinicians can apply research findings from a study population to the management and care of the individual patient. It identified tools and techniques to find and make sense of the scientific literature.

The principles of clinical epidemiology were increasingly recognized as fundamental to clinical practice and a working group of international experts set out to develop resources to support practitioners. After toying with the term 'scientific medicine', the group decided on 'evidence-based medicine' and the Evidence-Based Medicine Working Group was formed in 1992. This group created the evidence-based medicine user guides, beginning in 1993 in the *Journal of the American Medical Association* (JAMA) and subsequently published as a manual (Guyatt and Rennie, 2001) and online (www.cche.net/usersguides/main.asp). These were promoted as a model of practice for practitioners and policy makers.

Implementing research evidence

While the concepts and tools became well developed, no real attempts were made to embed these into practice. Consequently, Muir Gray, Director of Research and Development for the Anglia and Oxford health region, invited David Sackett to Oxford in 1994 to set up The Centre for Evidence-Based Medicine. This significant development helped create the environment for the widespread uptake of evidence-based concepts and practice. Centres for evidence-based practice in other disciplines, for example in child health, nursing and mental health, soon followed. These helped spread expertise throughout the country, and the programme of short and postgraduate courses offered in many locations promoted capacity building and skills development.

A spin-off from the burgeoning evidence-based practice movement was evidence-based policy making. Evidence-based healthcare, the use of best current knowledge as evidence in decision making about groups and populations, gained considerable momentum in the UK (Gray, 2001). Developments in the UK National Health Service in the early 1990s were the catalyst. Evidence of effectiveness emerged as the most important criterion for assisting decision making. In the Oxford region two initiatives helped those purchasing healthcare to understand how to interpret evidence and get it into practice (Gray, 2001).

The Critical Appraisal Skills Programme (www.phru.org.uk/~casp/casp.htm) was set up in 1993, to support those involved in purchasing healthcare. The programme involved half-day workshops to help people make sense of the scientific literature, based on the *JAMA* user guides checklists (Guyatt and Rennie, 2001). The programme aimed to help create an evidence-based culture, by cascading training to develop champions of evidence-based decision making throughout the NHS. No formal evaluation of this aim has been undertaken, but the success of the programme is attested by its continued existence more than ten years later, and the development of an international movement called CASP International (Bradley and Hill, 2001).

The other pioneering initiative in the Oxford region was the GRiPP (Getting Research into Practice and Purchasing) Project, which set out to identify gaps between research and clinical practice and to establish, through case studies, the steps in getting research into practice (Gray, 2001). This project paved the way for an England-wide project call PACE (Promoting Action on Clinical Effectiveness) which consolidated the work of GRiPP and established a set of tasks that were prerequisites to changing policy and practice (Dunning et al., 1999).

By the late 1990s few were questioning that policy should be based on high quality research evidence. The Department of Health in England adopted the concepts and began funding support to decision makers and generating evidence-based policy.

Why EBP is a product of its time

The demographic, social, political and technological trends influencing the development of evidence-based librarianship are described in Chapter 1. The development of evidence-based practice was closely linked with several separate yet parallel evolutions in society which created the context for its development (Reynolds and Trinder, 2000).

The risk society and the audit society

Dramatic social change has occurred over the last two decades. Society has a heightened sense of risk, which ranges from what we eat through to the post-September 11 fear of external terror attacks. This has been described as the 'risk society', informed by the work of Giddens (1994). Society puts in place contingencies to control and limit risk, with the need for trust in expert systems. Evidence-based practice is a manifestation of expert systems, where science can find solutions to major problems.

The last two decades have also seen the emergence of managerialism, with its emphasis on effectiveness, accountability and transparency, and the associated need for value for money. This societal change, coined the 'audit society' (Power, 1997) has gone hand-in-hand with increased awareness of risk and diminution of trust in experts, transferring trust to audit and regulation. Evidence-based practice focuses on effectiveness and its consequent processes, such as identifying evidence, critically appraising the research, incorporating research into guidelines, and evaluating practice.

The information society

The explosion of medical information was key to the development of evidence-based practice. Before electronic bibliographic databases it was simply not possible to obtain rapid access to research evidence to inform practice. Evidence-based librarianship started here: accessing and searching databases initially required international phone calls, and after that the purchase of stacks of CD-ROMs. Access to these required the expert skills of librarians. The next revolution was the internet and global electronic communication, which radically changed the nature of access to databases and therefore the role of librarians. Librarians, finding users not so dependent on their help to access databases, adopted the role of guide and expert, helping users find appropriate sources and undertake precise and efficient searches. The internet has also enabled the development of systems such as the Cochrane Collaboration, with its requirements for international co-operation in finding and synthesizing the evidence.

The consumer society

There have been two strands of consumerism within healthcare. Both have influenced developments in evidence-based practice. One is shared decision making with its requirement for evidence-based health information to enable patients to make informed choices. Evidence-based practice puts patient values at its heart, as patient preferences, concerns and expectations must be integrated into clinical decisions (Sackett et al., 2000). Patients (and other service users) require evidence-based information to help them make informed choices, and clinicians find themselves having to change radically the way they relate to their patients.

The other strand is the participation of public and patients in policy development, planning and evaluation of healthcare. This has evolved rapidly over the last decade, and an outcome of this has been pressure to meet the requirements of lay people to access and understand research in order to influence service development.

Evidence-based everything

The concept of evidence has moved a long way from its origins in randomized controlled trials. Evidence comes not only from research but also from the views of the providers or users of services, the routine statistics with which professionals monitor service delivery, and even the 'one-off' critical incident. Preferred forms of evidence may vary from sector to sector, or even within a single sector (Wavell et al., 2002), e.g.:

- public libraries rely heavily on quantitative measures, such as performance indicators, issue statistics, headcounts and questionnaire surveys; although more qualitative data, from focus, consultative and user groups, are also collected.
- museums, while using 'traditional' data collection tools, such as questionnaire surveys and face-to-face or telephone interviews, also utilize more unusual methods, such as note diaries, video recording and the use of photographic evidence.
- less is known about evaluation methods and results in archives, with fewer than 15% of projects having been formally evaluated.

The important issue is not the inherent qualities of evidence, but the ability of that evidence to answer a particular type of question. In client-centred disciplines such as nursing and social services, where little evidence is available from randomized controlled trials, the acceptance that patient values are central to decision making has helped to counter criticisms about the evidence-based movement. With its strong emphasis on management, policy and consumer involvement, the movement has broadened out into many other areas, most notably education and social sciences. A sibling organization to the Cochrane Collaboration, the Campbell Collaboration, was formed in 1999, with the aim of bringing together and evaluating the best available evidence for the effectiveness of social interactions in crime and justice, education and social welfare (Davies and Boruch, 2001).

The collaboration was named for the late Donald T. Campbell, an influential psychologist and evaluation theorist. Robert Boruch of the University of Pennsylvania was the counterpart to Iain Chalmers. Just as randomized clinical trials are the gold standard for Cochrane systematic reviews, randomized field experiments are the gold standard for the Campbell systematic reviews (Schneider, 2002).

The role of the librarian

Librarians have played a central and critical role in the evidence-based movement, and equally the movement has created crucial influences and challenges to the role of health librarians. A significant barrier to putting research into practice is the nature and availability of information published in the public domain. Early experience in the development of evidence-based healthcare identified several negative influences perpetrated by librarians, albeit unknowingly. These included poor quality indexing, inadequate resourcing leading to uncritical purchasing, information retrieval based on unsystematic methods and a lack of understanding of the many biases inherent in the accepted publishing models of the time.

Challenges

Finding evidence is key to evidence-based practice. Clinicians became increasingly keen to access the evidence for themselves. Some librarians were not happy to relinquish the role of custodian and gateway, and were concerned with the quality of user-performed searches.

Lack of understanding of the needs of adult learners required the acquisition of teaching and learning skills. Librarians also needed to help their users differentiate between the broader process of developing search strategies, and that of acquiring technical skills in searching individual databases. Lack of familiarity with research methods exacerbated this problem.

The profession also shared a reluctance to adopt open, reproducible and transparent methods to filtering information using explicit, rather than subjective and intuitive, methods. Since the advent of evidence-based approaches, librarians have required an increasing array of skills, translating into a need for continuing professional development. Responses to these demands included the Anglia and Oxford Librarian of the 21st Century Programme (Palmer, 1996; Palmer, 1997; Palmer et al., 1997; Palmer and Streatfield, 1995), the University of Sheffield ADEPT Programme (Hicks et al., 1998) and the West Midlands Project Apple (Whittlestone et al., 1999).

These and other initiatives have helped to place high quality information and knowledge management skills in the centre of developments in secondary publications, review methodologies, information literacy and improved teaching and learning. One group that has put these skills into practice is librarians involved in supporting systematic review activities. The requirement to conduct searches to a high standard and to engage with research teams in explaining and defending search methods is a stimulating context within which to hone research skills. The librarians at the Cochrane Centres, the NHS Centre for Reviews and Dissemination, and universities such as Sheffield, Southampton, Salford and Birmingham, have moved from a primarily supporting role to developing research-based search methods and conducting systematic reviews in their own right (Booth and Haines, 1998; Boynton et al., 1998; Brettle and Long, 2001; Helmer et al., 2001; White et al., 2001). Such activities have been mirrored worldwide in the collaboration of librarians working for national health technology assessment agencies within such networks as the HTAi (Health Technology Assessment international) and the Cochrane Collaboration (Booth and Haines, 1998; Brettle and Long, 2001; White et al., 2001). This has culminated in a proposed Information Retrieval Methods Group within the Cochrane Collaboration (Pritchard and Weightman, 2003).

Librarians are thus in a key position actively to encourage and support practitioners and managers to ask the right questions, find the evidence and appraise the papers that they identify. Opportunities to work with professionals in new ways, to develop new skills and rediscover old ones, are emerging. Indeed, librarians are poised to move to centre stage in the policy arena, to bring the user focus to the forefront of all policy areas and, of course, to transfer skills and approaches to their own setting.

Conclusion

The success of the evidence-based practice movement has resulted in a new paradigm, which has stimulated a shift in policy and practice worldwide. It remains to be seen whether the information profession is able to position itself to capitalize fully on the opportunities and potential that such a shift might offer.

References

Alderson, P., Gliddon, L. and Chalmers, I. (2003) Academic Recognition of Critical Appraisal and Systematic Reviews in British Postgraduate Medical Education, *Medical Education*, **37** (4), 386.

Booth, A. (2001) Will Health Librarians and Related Information Workers Ever Work Together to Create an International Network?, *Health Libraries and Information Journal*, **18** (1), 60–3.

Booth, A. and Haines, M. (1998) Room for a Review?, *Library Association Record*, **100** (8), 411–12.

Boynton, J., Glanville, J., McDaid, D. and Lefebvre, C. (1998) Identifying Systematic Reviews in MEDLINE: developing an objective approach to search strategy design, *Journal of Information Science*, **24** (3), 137–54.

Bradley, P. and Hill, A. (2001) Critical Appraisal Skills Programme International Network: making sense of the evidence, *European Journal of Public Health*, **11** (2), 238.

Brettle, A. J. and Long, A. F. (2001) Comparison of Bibliographic Databases for Information on the Rehabilitation of People with Severe Mental Illness, *Bulletin of the Medical Library Association*, **89** (4), 353–62.

Chalmers, I., Enkin, M. W. and Keirse, M. J. N. C. (1989) *Effective Care in Pregnancy and Childbirth*: Volumes 1 and 2, Oxford, Oxford University Press.

Cochrane, A. (1972) *Effectiveness and Efficiency: random reflections on health services*, London, Nuffield Provincial Hospitals Trust.

Cochrane, A. L. (1979) *1931–1971: A critical review, with particular reference to the medical profession*, London, Office of Health Economics.

Critical Appraisal Skills Programme (2003) *Evidence-based Health Care Open Learning Resource*, 2nd edn, Oxford, Critical Appraisal Skills Programme.

Davies P. and Boruch R. (2001) The Campbell Collaboration, does for public policy what Cochrane does for health, *BMJ*, **323**, 294–5.

Dickersin, K., Scherer, R. and Lefebvre, C. (1994) Identifying Relevant Studies for Systematic Reviews, *BMJ*, **309** (6964), 1286–91.

Dunning, M., Abi-Aad, G., Gilbert, D., Hutton, H. and Brown, C. (1999) *Experience, Evidence and Everyday Practice. Creating systems for delivering effective health care*, London, King's Fund.

Feinstein, A. R. and Horwitz, R. I. (1997) Problems in the 'evidence' of 'evidence-based medicine', *American Journal of Medicine*, **103** (6), 529–35.

Fitzpatrick, R. B. (2000) The Cochrane Library and Cochrane Collaboration, *Medical Reference Services Quarterly*, **19** (4), 73–8.

Giddens, A. (1994) Living in a Post-Traditional Society. In Beck, U, Giddens, A. and Lash, S. (eds), *Reflexive Modernisation*, Cambridge, Polity.

Grahame-Smith, D. (1995) Evidence Based Medicine: Socratic dissent, *BMJ*, **310**, 1126–7.

Gray, J. A. M. (2001) *Evidence-based healthcare*, 2nd edn, London, Churchill Livingstone.

Guyatt, G. H. and Rennie, D. (2001) *Users' Guides to the Medical Literature: essentials of evidence-based clinical practice*, Chicago, AMA Press.

Haynes, R. B., Sackett, D. L., Guyatt, G. H., Cook, D. J. and Gray, J. A. (1997) Transferring Evidence from Research into Practice: 4. Overcoming barriers to application, *ACP J Club*, **126** (3), A14–A15.

Helmer, D., Savoie, I., Green, C. and Kazanjian, A. (2001) Evidence-based Practice: extending the search to find material for the systematic review, *Bulletin of the Medical Library Association*, **89** (4), 346–52.

Hicks, A., Booth, A. and Sawers, C. (1998) Becoming ADEPT: delivering distance learning on evidence-based medicine for librarians, *Health Libraries Review*, **15** (3), 175–84.

Isaacs, D. and Fitzgerald, D. (1999) Seven Alternatives to Evidence Based Medicine, *BMJ*, **319**, 1618.

Lancet Editorial (1995) Evidence-based Medicine, in its Place, *Lancet*, **346**, 785.

Lefebvre, C. (1994) The Cochrane Collaboration: the role of the UK Cochrane Centre in identifying the evidence, *Health Libraries Review*, **11** (4), 235–42.

Molesworth, N. (1998) Down with EBM!, *BMJ*, **317** (7174),1720a–21.

Palmer, J. (1996) Skills for the Millennium: the librarian of the 21st century, *Librarian Career Development*, **4** (1), 13–17.

Palmer, J. (1997) Skills for a Virtual Future, *Bibliotheca Medica Canadiana*, **19** (2), 62–5.

Palmer, J., Ashwell, S., Miles, D., Johnson, D. and Forsyth, E. (1997) The Twenty-first Century is Here, *Library Association Record*, **99** (6), 315–7.

Palmer, J. and Streatfield, D. (1995) Good Diagnosis for the Twenty-first Century, *Library Association Record*, **97** (3), 153–4.

Power, M. (1997) *The Audit Society: rituals of verification*, Oxford, Oxford University Press.

Pritchard, S. J. and Weightman, A. L. (2003) Towards a Cochrane Information Retrieval Methods Group: a progress report, *Health Information and Libraries Journal*, **20** (Suppl 1), 69–71.

Reynolds, S. and Trinder, E. (2000) *Evidence-Based Practice: a critical appraisal*, Oxford, Blackwell Science.

Sackett, D. L. (1995) Evidence Based Medicine, *Lancet*, **346**, 1171–2.

Sackett, D. L., Haynes, R. B., Guyatt, G. H. and Tugwell, P. (1985) Clinical *Epidemiology: a basic science for clinical medicine*, Boston, Little, Brown and Company.

Sackett, D. L., Rosenberg, W. M., Gray, J. A., Haynes, R. B. and Richardson, W. S. (1996) Evidence Based Medicine: what it is and what it isn't, *BMJ*, **312** (7023), 71–2.

Sackett, D. L., Straus, S. E., Richardson, W. S., Rosenberg, W. and Haynes, R. B. (2000) *Evidence-Based Medicine: how to practise and teach EBM*, 2nd edn, London, Churchill Livingstone.

Schneider, E. (2002) The Campbell Collaboration: preparing, maintaining, and promoting the accessibility of systematic reviews of the effects of social and educational policies and practices, *Hypothesis*, **16** (3), 1–13.

Wavell, C., Baxter, G., Johnson, I. and Williams, D. (2002) *Impact Evaluation of Museums, Archives and Libraries: available evidence project*, London, Resource.

White, V. J., Glanville, J. M., Lefebvre, C. and Sheldon, T. A. (2001) A Statistical Approach to Designing Search Filters to Find Systematic Reviews: objectivity enhances accuracy, *Journal of Information Science*, **27** (6), 357–70.

Whittlestone, R., Low, B. Y. M. and Pope, A. (1999) Partnerships for the New NHS, *Library Association Record*, **101** (12), 704–5.

Whyte, R. (1999) Reviews and Systematic Reviews: the place of the Cochrane Collaboration, *Bibliotheca Medica Canadiana*, **21** (1), 253.

3

Evidence-based information practice: a prehistory

Jonathan Eldredge

Introduction

Although the contribution of evidence to information practice has only been recognized in recent years, librarianship has a long pedigree in practitioner-based research. The first known cohort study in health librarianship was reported in 1946 and other health librarians adapted the basic cohort design to answer important questions during the 1950s and early 1960s. The first randomized controlled trial (RCT) in health librarianship took place during the late 1970s. A small but identifiable stream of such studies continued during the early 1990s (see Box 3.1).

Thus, health librarians can point to use of research designs such as cohort studies or RCTs even before 'evidence-based medicine' was first reported.

This chapter charts the development of practitioner-led research as a fundamental platform for evidence-based librarianship (EBL) and the broader, evidence-based information practice (EBIP). It considers where EBIP has come from, examines major historical developments, and highlights a few individual contributions in our search for the early origins of EBIP.

In the beginning . . .

. . . was a question. Evidence-based information practice (EBIP) existed as a concept long before it became a label. A long time ago someone working in a library asked, 'Is this *really* the best way to do this?' Or, perhaps they wondered, 'Why don't we try doing this a new way instead of the way we have always done it?' Or, perhaps they asked, 'Why don't more people use our library?' What happened next probably depended upon how their manager (or some other person in

---

Box 3.1   Some candidate randomized controlled trials in information practice

Haynes, R. B, Johnston, M. E., McKibbon, K.A., Walker, C. J. and Willan, A. R. (1993) A program to enhance clinical use of MEDLINE. A randomized controlled trial, *Online J Curr Clin Trials*, May 11; Doc No 56: (4005 words; 39 paragraphs).

Haynes, R. B., Ramsden, M. F., McKibbon, K. A. and Walker, C. J. (1991) Online access to MEDLINE in clinical settings: impact of user fees, *Bull Med Libr Assoc*, **79** (4), (October), 377–81.

McKibbon, K. A., Haynes, R. B., Johnston, M. E. and Walker, C. J. (1991) A study to enhance clinical end-user MEDLINE search skills: design and baseline findings, *Proc Annu Symp Comput Appl Med Care*, 73–7.

Wolffing, B. K. (1990) Computerized literature searching in the ambulatory setting using PaperChase, *Henry Ford Hosp Med J.*, **38** (1), 57–61.

Marshall, J. G., Neufeld, V.R. (1981) A randomized trial of librarian educational participation in clinical settings, *J Med Educ.*, **56** (5), (May), 409–16.

Verhoeven, A. A., Boerma, E. J. and Meyboom-de Jong, B. (2000) Which literature retrieval method is most effective for GPs?, *Fam Pract*, **17** (1), (February), 30–5.

Villanueva, E. V., Burrows, E. A., Fennessy, P. A., Rajendran, M. and Anderson, J. N. (2001) Improving question formulation for use in evidence appraisal in a tertiary care setting: a randomised controlled trial [ISRCTN66375463], *BMC Med Inform Decis Mak*, **1** (1), 4.

Foust, J. E., Tannery, N. H. and Detlefsen, E .G. (1999) Implementation of a Web-based tutorial, *Bull Med Libr Assoc.*, **87** (4), 477–9.

Erickson, S. and Warner, E. R. (1998) The impact of an individual tutorial session on MEDLINE use among obstetrics and gynaecology residents in an academic training programme: a randomized trial, *Med Educ*, **32** (3), (May), 269–73.

Johnson, E. D, McKinin, E. J., Sievert, M. E. and Reid, J. C. (1997) An analysis of objective quality indicators on Year Book citations: implications for MEDLINE searchers, *Bull Med Libr Assoc*, **85** (4), (October), 378–84.

Balas, E. A, Stockham, M. G., Mitchell, J. A, Sievert, M. E, Ewigman, B. G. and Boren, S. A. (1997) In search of controlled evidence for health care quality improvement, *J Med Syst*, **21** (1), (February), 21–32.

---

authority) reacted to their questioning of conventional wisdom. The identity of that first librarian is lost to the obscurity of time.

Early EBIP antecedents

The roots of EBIP pre-date the modern international movement and may be traced in the histories of the profession and biographies of noted librarians, professional 'ancestors' who exhibited, at times, one or more of its defining characteristics. Surveying the past 5500 years, however, historian James Thompson (Thompson, 1977) makes the humbling observation that: 'The development of libraries and librarianship has not been some kind of evolutionary process whereby these have grown better and better'. Sometimes, inferior newer methods replace older, superior methods without question; existing and incompetent practices meanwhile continue unchallenged. Perhaps progress in the past is attributable to the extent that librarians of the past have been prototypical evidence-based practitioners?

Librarianship has only recently become a legitimate profession, beginning about 1876. Prior to this 'librarians' ranged from technically competent slaves to famous scholars but few had any apparent professional consciousness. The profession began to emerge with the formations of the American Library Association (1876) and the Library Association (1877). Professional journals and formal library education soon followed. Social and political movements such as Progressivism (McCrimmon, 2001) and Populism (Goodwyn, 1978) exerted a strong influence upon the emergence of the values of the US library profession. These same values later diffused to other countries. More importantly for EBIP, another philosophy profoundly influenced early librarianship: Pragmatism (Pratt, 2002). Evidence-based medicine clearly owes much of its philosophical heritage to Pragmatism and many EBIP characteristics and values share these origins.

Two US librarians stand out for their advancement of EBIP principles and were probably, at the time, identified as pragmatists. John Shaw Billings (1838–1913), developed the Library of the Surgeon General of the United States Army. Billings was a catalyst in transforming a modest-sized military library into the National Library of Medicine and his innovative approaches to librarianship exhibit early traces of an EBIP perspective. His descriptive research article on the US medical literature offers many insights into the medical journals of his time which he condemns for lack of scientific validity: 'Many articles intended to be practical, are far from being such, although the authors would probably be surprised and indignant to hear them termed otherwise . . . Their productions read curiously, like the literature of the last century, and are to be classed with old women's advice; amusing generally; practically suggestive sometimes; clear, scientific, and conclusive, never' (Billings, 1876).

Billings' career led him to serve as director for the fledgling New York Public Library where he came into brief contact (Kingdon, 1940) with another early ancestor of the EBIP movement, John Cotton Dana. John Cotton Dana (1856–1929) exhibited many prototypical EBIP qualities. Throughout his career, Dana refused to accept the familiar boundaries of conventional wisdom. He advocated a style of library management open to experimentation, flexibility, and the constant questioning of fundamental assumptions. He thought that librarianship had an inherently rigid outlook, and he tried to discourage any hint of this tendency in those around him (Eldredge, 1992).

Dana was a prolific writer as well as innovator. In the preface to one of his books published in 1916 he wrote: 'the wise librarian will keep his mental manners plastic and his professional methods flexible . . . the most essential attribute of the librarian, if he would be forever helpful and never an obstacle, is a profound belief that the end is not yet, that new conditions arise daily and that they can be wisely met only after a confession of ignorance, a surrender of all doctrine and careful and unprejudiced observations' (Dana, 1916).

Dana condemned conventional wisdom throughout his career, much to the chagrin of more complacent contemporaries. In his 1896 inaugural speech as President of the American Library Association he shocked his colleagues by stating: 'A collection of books gathered at public expense does not justify itself by the simple fact that it is' (Dana (1916) in Thornton (ed.), 1957).

One biographer depicted him as 'the experimenting librarian' and reported: 'His experiments in his first years as a librarian began a revolution throughout the entire field of library practice' (Kingdon, 1940). Dana referred to this approach as 'Bibliothecal scepticism' (Dana, 1905).

The professionalization of librarianship led to the establishment of formal library education. From their beginnings, library schools have reflected EBIP concerns with merging theoretical and practical orientations (Davis, 1994). It is only in recent decades, however, that library education has demonstrated a concern for applied research.

Melvil Dewey pioneered the famous decimal classification system that bore his name, helped form the American Library Association, and founded the first library school in the US. Yet, research reveals that Dewey exhibited a decidedly anti-EBIP rigidity toward the profession, frequent reversion to conventional thinking (Beck, 1996), and a tendency toward codification over scepticism (Wiegand, 1996). Fortunately, library and informatics schools in recent years have encouraged applied research and have valued research-based evidence. It is likely that such activities have likely influenced the formation of the current EBIP movement.

The observational research era

Library research continues to favour descriptive, rather than observational or experimental, research methods (Eldredge, 2000). Such tendencies echo those of early researchers in medicine who employed mostly descriptive or anecdotal research methods. Medical textbooks and journals from the period between 1880 and 1980 attest to this predominance. While some famous observational studies, principally cohort studies, occurred prior to the 1980s, they constituted only a small percentage of published medical research.

William D. Postell inaugurated the observational era in library research during the 1940s when he began the first known cohort study (Postell, 1946) to question the practice of using recommended books and titles from 'authoritative lists' to guide selection decisions. This practice, still common and far more codified today (Hague, 2000; Hill and Stickell, 2001), is unsupported by published evidence (Plutchak, 2003). Postell employed a cohort design to determine how those journals most highly ranked on a list of recommended journals compared to journals actually used by his clientele (Eldredge, 2003a). Postell found that usage of journals correlated somewhat with the quality ranking opinions of the physiology faculty at Columbia University but did not correlate with two previous citation analyses. The cohort study thus became a new method for predicting likely future use, with Postell heralding the significance of this development, noting: 'It is most interesting to observe the evidence . . . '(Postell, 1946).

Frederick G. Kilgour at the Yale Medical Library wished to identify the most popular journals in his reading room so as to display only the most heavily used titles from the much larger overall journals collection. He supplemented his cohort study of usage with a citation analysis, based upon references found in recent Yale faculty publications. His cohort study measured use for a five-year period through an analysis of old charge slips. Heaviest usage of journals occurred within the first year of publication and 40 journals alone accounted for nearly 50% of total journals use (Kilgour, 1953). In 1962, he published the results of a subsequent cohort study (Kilgour, 1962a; Kilgour, 1962b). During 1964, Kilgour teamed up with his counterpart at Columbia University, Thomas Fleming, to compare subsequent cohort studies for journal collections at two sites (Fleming and Kilgour, 1964).

During 1954 another cohort study of journals usage reported on the 50 most heavily used titles for a four-year period, but also revealed extensive use of the library's other 900 current journal subscriptions. The same report described a second cohort study on interlibrary loan requests of relative frequency for 116 journal titles not owned by the library. Subsequent interlibrary loan cohort study analysis led to the library purchasing subscriptions to 64 frequently requested journal titles (Morse et al., 1954).

Later, a larger cohort study of interlibrary loan requests involved 77,698 users of medical libraries who, during the calendar year 1959, made interlibrary loan requests, via 1780 medical libraries, to the National Library of Medicine. This large cohort study noted that 6.9% of 4347 journal titles at NLM accounted for 53% of filled interlibrary loan requests (Kurth, 1962).

The diffusion (Rogers, 1995) of such innovative early cohort study designs deserves further inquiry beyond the scope of this book chapter. We can note, however, that Thomas E. Keys of the Mayo Clinic Library in his book *Applied Medical Library Practice* (a candidate for EBIP ancestor status for using such a title!) discusses the cohort study for determining the patterns of journals collection use as if it was commonplace (Keys, 1958). During the 1970s both types of cohort (journal use and interlibrary loan request analysis) studies were commonly employed by medical libraries yet rarely published in peer-reviewed journals.

The 1960s and 1970s saw gravitation towards a prototypical EBIP orientation. A biographical sketch of Frank Bradway Rogers noted that 'He demanded evidence and written analysis with data to substantiate the position being taken' (Braude, 1998a). Meanwhile in the late 1970s the Medical Library Association was starting to articulate a serious need for higher standards in applied research regarding health librarianship practice (Love, 1980).

Staudt, Halbrook and Brodman conducted a third type of cohort study during the 1970s to evaluate a Clinical Medical Librarian service (CML). Medical residents 'exposed' to the CML service tended to request more library services. Anticipating a then long-distant systematic review (Winning and Beverley, 2003), the authors observe: 'As other libraries report their evaluations, thus providing data from a larger number of cases than any one library can provide, a generalized evaluation of the entire clinical librarian concept may be possible' (Staudt et al., 1976).

The article ends in lamenting the inadequacy of *this* particular research design: 'The worth of clinical librarians' programs has not yet been proved quantitatively or unequivocally . . . ' (Staudt et al., 1976).

This lament carries an unspoken appeal for more sophisticated research methods or, perhaps, a recognition that the cohort design was not the least biased research design for answering their particular question.

The experimental research era

In attempting a further evaluation of a CML programme in the late 1970s, Joanne Gard Marshall and her colleague Victor Neufeld made EBIP history by utilizing the Randomised Controlled Trial (RCT) research design to answer their specific question on the programme's efficacy (Marshall and Neufeld, 1981). In contrast to the ambiguous results of Staudt, Halbrook and Brodman, Marshall and Neufeld's RCT provided robust evidence.

The 1970s had witnessed a tremendous increase in the number and popularity of pharmaceutical RCTs. The proliferation of hundreds of new drugs between the 1950s and 1970s led the US Food and Drug Administration (FDA) to encourage pharmaceutical firms to use RCTs to demonstrate the efficacy of the many new drugs competing for approval (Meldrum, 2000). Although the RCT design originated during the 1940s in the UK (Medical Research Council, 1948), it became widely utilized only following endorsement by the FDA.

Notwithstanding the respective contributions of the UK and the US, it was a Canadian, Joanne Marshall, who introduced RCTs to health librarianship. Subsequently, further teams of Canadians conducted RCTs in search of evidence concerning online searching (Haynes et al., 1991; McKibbon et al., 1991). Eventually, health librarians in the US and UK respectively began to utilize the RCT research design (Eldredge, 2003b).

In 1982 former MLA President Erika Love guided the formation of the MLA Research Section (Braude, 1998b). The MLA Research Section produced three noteworthy contributions to the formation of the EBIP movement. In 1987 it began the newsletter *Hypothesis*, a major communication vehicle and focus for researchers within health librarianship. Secondly, the Research Task Force developed a research policy for MLA entitled 'Using Scientific Evidence to Improve Information Practice'. This new policy hinted at the concept of EBIP in the language used in two passages (Medical Library Association, 1995). Thirdly, the Research Section established the MLA Research Award in 1996. Competition for this annual award has acted as a powerful incentive to conduct and present research projects that have utilized higher levels of EBIP evidence (Eldredge, 2002a).

As early as 1996, the Research Section of MLA ran a session entitled 'Evidence based practice for librarians: practical examples of usable research' (Anonymous, 1996). Then, during her inaugural speech, an incoming MLA President made passing reference to 'evidence-based practice' (Anderson, 1998). This stimulated an article outlining what EBL might actually encompass (Eldredge, 1997). The MLA Continuing Education Committee convinced the author to flesh out his ideas about EBL in an MLA continuing education course.

Meanwhile, in the UK, the concept of EBIP had been fermenting for some time. In 1995 passing reference was made to 'evidence-based libraries' (Roddham, 1995). During 1998, members of the Health Libraries Group Research Working Party speculated on the feasibility and reality of evidence-based practice (Farmer et al., 1998). The following year, writers in the same column asked, 'Is information work evidence-based?' (Farmer and Williams, 1999).

Despite this synchronicity of ideas on both sides of the Atlantic, neither US nor UK writers cited one another, which suggests they were unaware of each others' work. In 1999, the Chair of the Health Libraries Group Research Working Party took the MLA's EBL continuing education course and enthusiastically reported his experience to colleagues in the UK. Transatlantic co-operation was crystallized at the 2000 joint MLA/CHLA Annual Meeting in Vancouver, Canada which featured a popular programme on EBL, leading to further networking between UK, Canadian and US colleagues. A leading UK evidence-based practitioner became a member of the *Hypothesis* editorial board and a column editor for its 'International Research Reviews' feature. The Evidence-Based Librarianship Implementation Committee (EBLIC) began an international collaborative search for the most relevant research questions facing our profession (Evidence-Based Librarianship Implementation Committee, 2001). Further international EBL collaboration led to recommendations for structured abstracts and practice guidelines (Bayley, 2001; Bayley, Wallace and Brice, 2002; Booth et al., 2001). The first International EBL Conference held in Sheffield during 2001 included attendees from the UK, Canada, the US, Sweden, and Norway (Eldredge, 2001). Two systematic reviews, reported as work in progress at the conference, constitute further significant landmarks (Brettle, 2003; Winning and Beverley, 2003).

The first International EBL Conference (Eldredge, 2001) also included two speakers from the UK Library and Information Research Group, a wider research group drawn mainly from the academic and public library constituencies. Established in 1977 to develop and maintain links, within the profession and elsewhere, between all who have an interest in library and information research and investigation, this Group had seen an increasing preoccupation with practitioner-based research as witnessed by its LIS-LIRG discussion group and its quarterly journal *Library and Information Research* (formerly *Library and Information Research News*).

Consequently, by the beginning of the 21st century the core characteristics of the international movement (Booth, 2002) variously called 'evidence-based librarianship' or 'evidence-based information practice' were seen to emerge:

- a process beginning with a clearly formulated question with relevance to our practice, a search for the evidence to address this question, the critical appraisal of the existing evidence (Booth, 2000; Booth and Brice, 2001), and the weighing of that evidence-based upon practical experience
- the recognition that appropriate answers for different types of question require different types of evidence
- scepticism about the validity and reliability of evidence due to the risks of introducing bias into research
- an international collaboration to ensure a widespread sharing of methodologies and evidence, aimed at improving professional practice (Eldredge, 1997; Farmer et al., 1998; Farmer and Williams, 1999; Eldredge, 2000; Eldredge, 2002b).

The next steps

Evidence-based information practice (EBIP) continues to unfold as this book goes to press. The publication of this book, a special issue of *Health Information and Libraries Journal* devoted to EBIP, and the second International EBL Conference in Edmonton, Alberta, Canada suggest that many more EBIP landmarks remain before us.

In going back in time, one risks misinterpreting or exaggerating 'evidence' for early traces of EBIP. How accurately can we detect faint antecedents of EBIP in the utterances and writings of colleagues long ago? Are we truly detecting an EBIP approach in their actions or were these colleagues influenced by other mind frames quite foreign to what we now call EBIP? Yet a different risk pertains to portraying EBIP as a new movement divorced from historical context. Even now, Billings, Dana, Postell, Love and Marshall attest to an EBIP orientation within our profession's history. Clearly, EBIP did not spontaneously generate within the past decade in response to the EBM movement as some simplistically try to argue. The values and experiences of our professional 'ancestors' have shaped what we now call EBIP.

References

Anderson, R. K. (1998) Presidential address. Proceedings of the 98th Annual Meeting, *Bulletin of the Medical Library Association*, **87** (1), (Jan), 1999, 112–5.

Anonymous (1996) Section papers and poster session abstracts, *Hypothesis* (Summer), 6.

Bayley, L., Wallace, A. and Brice, A. (2002) Evidence-based Librarianship Implementation Committee: Research Results Dissemination Task Force recommendations, *Hypothesis*, **16** (1), (Spring), 6–8.

Bayley, L. (2001) Evidence-based Librarianship Implementation Committee: Report of the Research Results Dissemination Task Force, *Hypothesis*, **15** (2), 6–7.

Beck, C. (1996) A 'Private' Grievance Against Dewey, *American Libraries*, **27** (1), 62–4.

Billings, J. S. (1876). A Century of American Medicine 1776–1876. IV. Literature and Institutions, *American Journal of the Medical Sciences*, **72**, 439–80.

Booth, A. and Brice, A. (2001) Research, *Health Information and Libraries Journal*, **18** (4), 175–7.

Booth, A. (2002) Evidence-based Librarianship: one small step, *Health Information and Libraries Journal*, **19** (2), 116–19.

Booth, A. (2000) Research, *Health Libraries Review*, **17** (4), 232–5.

Booth, A., Harris. M., McGowan, J. and Burrows, S. (2001) Submitted on behalf of the Evidence-Based Librarianship Implementation Committee Task Force on Practice Guidelines Recommendation/Position Statement, *Hypothesis*, **15** (2), 7

Braude, R. M. (1998a) A Medical Librarian's progress, *Bulletin of the Medical Library Association*, **86** (2), 157–65.

Braude, R. M. (1998b) The Research Section of the MLA: the first fifteen years 1982–1997, *Hypothesis*, **12** (2), 9–16, http://gain.mercer.edu/mla/research/hypothesis.html.

Brettle, A. (2003) Information Skills Training: a systematic review of the literature, *Health Information and Libraries Journal*, **20** (Suppl 1), 3–9.

Dana, J. C. (1905) A Helpful State of Mind, *Public Libraries*, **10**, 178–9.

Dana, J. C., Dana Looks at Librarians ('Hear the other side'). In Thornton, J. L. (ed.) (1957) *Classics of Librarianship: further selected readings in the history of librarianship*, London, The Library Association, 131–2.

Dana, J. C. (1916) *Libraries: addresses and essays*, New York, The H. W. Wilson Company, vii–viii.

Davis, D. G. (1994) Education for Librarianship. In Wiegand, W. A. and Davis, D. G. (eds), *Encyclopedia of Library History*, New York, Garland Publishers, 184–6.

Eldredge, J. (1992) Hear the Other Side: John Cotton Dana, *Wilson Library Bulletin*, **66** (8), (April), 48–9.

Eldredge, J. (1997) Evidence-Based Librarianship, *Hypothesis*, **11** (3), 4–7.

Eldredge, J. D. (2000) Evidence-Based Librarianship: an overview, *Bulletin of the Medical Library Association*, **88** (4), 289–302.

Eldredge, J. (2001) First Evidence-Based Librarianship (EBL) Conference, *Hypothesis*, **15** (3), 1, 3, 8–11.

Eldredge, J. D. (2002a). Evidence-based Librarianship: levels of evidence, *Hypothesis*, **16** (3), 10–14.

Eldredge, J. D. (2002b) Evidence-based Librarianship: what might we expect in the years ahead?, *Health Information and Libraries Journal*, **19** (2), 71–7.

Eldredge, J. D. (2003a) SCC Milestone in EBL History. South Central Connection, *MLA/SCC Chapter Newsletter*, **13** (2), 10, 14.

Eldredge, J. D. (2003b) The Randomized Controlled Trial Design: unrecognized opportunities for health sciences librarianship, *Health Information and Libraries Journal*, **20** (Suppl 1), 34–44.

Evidence-Based Librarianship Implementation Committee (2001) The Most Relevant and Answerable Research Questions Facing the Practice of Health Sciences Librarianship, *Hypothesis*, **15** (1), (Spring), 9–15, 17.

Farmer J, Booth A, Madge B, Forsythe E (1998). What is the Health Libraries Group Doing about Research?, *Health Libraries Review*, **15** (2), 133–41.

Farmer, J. and Williams, D. (1999) Research into Practice?, *Health Libraries Review*, **16** (2), 137–40.

Fleming, T. P. and Kilgour, F. G. (1964) Moderately and Heavily Used Biomedical Journals, *Bulletin of the Medical Library Association*, **52** (1), 234–41.

Goodwyn, L. (1978) *The Populist Moment: a short history of the agrarian revolt in America*, New York, Oxford University Press.

Hague, H. (comp.) (2000) *Core Collection of Medical Books and Journals 2001*, 4th edn, London, Medical Information Working Party.

Haynes, R. B., Ramsden, M. F., McKibbon, K. A. and Walker, C. J. (1991) Online Access to MEDLINE in Clinical Settings: impact of user fees, *Bulletin of the Medical Library Association*, **79** (4), 377–81.

Hill, D. R. and Stickell, H. N. (2001) Brandon/Hill Selected List of Print Books and Journals for the Small Medical Library, *Bulletin of the Medical Library Association*, **89** (2), 131–53.

Keys, T. E. (1958) *Applied Medical Library Practice*, Springfield, IL., Charles C. Thomas Publisher, 29, 389–93.

Kilgour, F. G. (1953) *Annual Report of the Yale University Medical Library 1952/1953*, New Haven, CT, Yale University.

Kilgour, F. G. (1962a) Use of Medical and Biological Journals in the Yale Medical Library. Part I: frequently used titles, *Bulletin of the Medical Library Association*, **50** (3), (July), 429–43.

Kilgour, F. G. (1962b) Use of Medical and Biological Journals in the Yale Medical Library. Part II: moderately used titles, *Bulletin of the Medical Library Association*, **50** (3), (July), 444–9.

Kingdon, F. (1940) *John Cotton Dana, a life*, Newark, The Public Library and Museum, 79.

Kurth, W. H. (1962) *Survey of the Interlibrary Loan Operation of the National Library of Medicine*, Bethesda, MD, National Library of Medicine.

Love, E. (1980) Research: the third dimension in librarianship, *Bulletin of the Medical Library Association*, **68** (1), (Jan), 1–5.

Marshall, J. G. and Neufeld, V. R. (1981) A Randomized Trial of Librarian Educational Participation in Clinical Settings, *Journal of Medical Education*, **56** (5), 409–16.

McCrimmon, B. (2001) Philosophies of Librarianship. In Stamm, D. H. (ed.) *International Dictionary of Library Histories*, Volume 1, London, Fitzroy Dearborn Publishers, 494–8.

McKibbon, K. A., Haynes, R. B., Johnston, M. E. and Walker, C. J. (1991) A Study to Enhance Clinical End-User MEDLINE Search Skills: design and baseline findings, *Proceedings of the Annual Symposium on Computer Applications in Medical Care*, 73–7.

Medical Library Association. Research Task Force (1995) *Using Scientific Evidence to Improve Information Practice*, Chicago, Medical Library Association, http://mlanet.org/research/science1.html.

Medical Research Council (1948) Streptomycin Treatment of Pulmonary Tuberculosis, *British Medical Journal*, **ii** (4582), 769–82.

Meldrum, M. L. (2000) A Brief History of the Randomized Controlled Trial: from oranges and lemons to the gold standard, *Hematology/Oncology Clinics of North America*, **14** (4), 745–60.

Morse, E. H., Beatty, W. K. and Hodge H. M. (1954) Annual Report on the Library, *Transactions and Studies of the College of Physicians of Philadelphia*, **21** (4), 138–50.

Plutchak, T. S. (2003) The Art and Science of Making Choices, *Journal of the Medical Library Association*, **91** (1),1–3.

Postell, W. D. (1946) Further Comments on the Mathematical Analysis of Evaluating Scientific Journals, *Bulletin of the Medical Library Association*, **34** (2), 107–9.

Pratt, S. L. (2002) *Native Pragmatism: rethinking the roots of American philosophy*, Bloomington, Indiana University Press.

Roddham, M. (1995) Responding to the Reforms: are we meeting the need?, *Health Libraries Review*, **12** (2), (June), 101–114.

Rogers, E. M. (1995) *Diffusion of Innovations*, 4th edn, New York, The Free Press, 1995.

Staudt, C., Halbrook, B. and Brodman, E. (1976) A Clinical Librarians' Program – an attempt at evaluation, *Bulletin of the Medical Library Association*, **64** (2), (April), 236–8.

Thompson, J. (1977) *A History of the Principles of Librarianship*, London, Clive Bingley, 10.

Wiegard, W. (1996) Dewey Declassified: a revelatory look at the 'irrepressible reformer', *American Libraries*, **27** (1), 54–60.

Winning, M. A. and Beverley, C. A. (2003) Clinical Librarianship: a systematic review of the literature, *Health Information and Libraries Journal*, **20** (Suppl. 1), 10–21.

4

How good is the evidence base?

Jonathan Eldredge

Introduction

Identifying research evidence relevant to answering EBIP questions poses an initial challenge. How good is the evidence base? How well does it answer our EBIP questions? Once we have identified and obtained this research then we have to evaluate its relevance and quality, a second major challenge (Chapter 9).

This chapter identifies the types of research that may be used to answer important questions for our practice and outlines how an understanding of research types helps in matching an appropriate research type to a specific question. The chapter ends with an appraisal of the overall evidence base.

Identifying the evidence base

The evidence base for information practice is located within three main search domains: (1) the library and informatics literature; (2) the so-called 'grey literature' for our field; and, (3) the literatures outside our field with functional relevance to the question such as the literatures of the social, behavioural, education or management sciences.

The library and informatics literature

Issues of index coverage

The first of these, the library and informatics literature, poses several unexpected challenges for the searcher. To illustrate from within the health sector, the major journals in our field include *Health Information and Libraries Journal*, *Journal of the Medical Library Association* and *Medical Reference Services Quarterly*. Less prominent journals include *Bibliotheca Medica Canadiana*; *Hypothesis* and *Journal of Hospital Libraries*. While PubMed is available to all searchers, commercial databases are likely to be too expensive for some professionals to access. The databases selected in any search for the contents of the major journals will yield different retrieval. Tables 4.1–4.3 illustrate uneven coverage amongst three databases. From Table 4.1 one notes that PubMed appeared to offer the most complete access, for the years 2001 or 2002, to the contents of *Journal of the Medical Library Association* (JMLA): (51 [2001] and 66 [2002] references compared to the Library Literature database's 32 and 42 respectively). For 1998, however, Library Literature provided access to 93 versus PubMed's 74 references to the same journal. Within the field, Library Literature is used extensively when searching for the evidence needed to make decisions. Yet, for the years 1998–2002, Library Literature did not index *any* contents for *Health Information and Libraries Journal* or its predecessor *Health Libraries Review*.

Cumulative Index to Nursing and Allied Health Literature (CINAHL) and PubMed both offer access to *Health Information and Libraries Journal*. Table 4.2 illustrates discrepancies, however, between the two databases during the years 1999–2002. Table 4.3 points to more complete coverage of *Medical Reference Services Quarterly* by the Library Literature database when compared to PubMed or CINAHL. Coverage of any journal by one of these databases might suggest that the database with the most complete coverage represents the better choice. Yet, discrepancies across different years as illustrated by Table 4.1, plus inconsistent coverage of any one journal within a single database makes it difficult to recommend any one database to the busy practitioner. Only the time-consuming approach of searching multiple databases maximizes the probability of complete access to the needed evidence within our core library and informatics literature.

Table 4.1   Index coverage for the *Journal of the Medical Library Association**

Year	PubMed	CINAHL	Library Literature
1998	74	52	93
1999	61	64	52
2000	50	41	60
2001	51	45	32
2002	66	46	42

Notes:
*Formerly the *Bulletin of the Medical Library Association* between 1998 and 2001. Searches conducted in referenced databases on December 3 and 9, 2002. CINAHL accessed via Ovid; Library Literature accessed via FirstSearch (OCLC).

Table 4.2   Index coverage for *Health Information and Libraries Journal**

Year	PubMed	CINAHL	Library Literature
1998	37	41	0
1999	26	40	0
2000	19	42	0
2001	38	28	0
2002	30	17	0

Notes:

*Formerly *Health Libraries Review* for the years 1998 to 2000.

Searches conducted in referenced databases on December 3 and 9, 2002. CINAHL accessed via Ovid; Library Literature accessed via FirstSearch (OCLC).

Table 4.3   Index coverage for *Medical Reference Services Quarterly*

Year	PubMed	CINAHL	Library Literature
1998	26	31	41
1999	29	30	32
2000	34	34	39
2001	31	31	43
2002	23	15	51

Notes:

Searches conducted in referenced databases on December 3 and 9, 2002. CINAHL accessed via Ovid; Library Literature accessed via FirstSearch

Issues regarding labelling of research designs

Filtering online for the best evidence from a database search poses another major obstacle for the library literature. Authors of original research articles in the clinical medicine literature have become increasingly conscientious in correctly labelling their research methods, thereby facilitating accurate indexing of their contents on databases. Searchers can filter randomized controlled trials or systematic reviews from an otherwise overwhelming set of references because of such authors' efforts *and* the additional efforts of the National Library of Medicine in accurately indexing MeSH study design terms. Filtering innovations in the PubMed database, or more specifically its subset MEDLINE, capitalize on such accurate MeSH indexing. Busy practitioners can limit their searches routinely to randomized controlled trials, where desired.

Information practitioners have no such option for filtering the best evidence for their own literature searches. Authors of articles in the library literature are notorious for not labelling their methods correctly. Even the author of this chapter, now a commentator on rigorous research designs in librarianship, can confess to past misdemeanours in failing to label a cohort study (Eldredge, 1998)! The information profession must become more aware of the usefulness of describing research methods succinctly and accurately with phrases such as 'randomized controlled trials' or 'cohort study'. Even if authors were to label their research methods correctly this would be no guarantee that appropriate indexing terms for study designs would be available within the structure of a database such as Library Literature. Availability of indexing terms will no doubt improve as awareness grows about the importance of proper labelling of research methods and individual authors implement a practice already common in medicine. At this time, hand-searching is the only reliable way to find articles that have used requisite research designs. In other words, the Library Literature database has no structural equivalent to the 'Publication Type' field in PubMed.

Issues regarding specialized versus generic research questions

What the data given in Tables 4.1–4.3 above does not convey is that the Library Literature database will yield access to resources sometimes overlooked by librarians when searching for evidence: journals from the university, college, health, special, and public library *specialities*. Many decisions facing information professionals working within health might be better addressed by research conducted by academic, special or public librarians, and vice versa. Topics such as negotiating publisher and vendor contracts or teaching web evaluation skills may be more comprehensively researched within other sectors. As evidence-based information practice becomes more common it is to be hoped that practitioners will become more aware of the differential coverage of the research themes of different sectors.

Issues regarding less influential journals

Access to the less influential journals in information practice poses perhaps even greater challenges in the search for needed evidence. Again illustrating from within the health sector, PubMed does not even cover three less influential journals: *Bibliotheca Medica Canadiana (BMC)*, *Hypothesis* or *Journal of Hospital Librarianship*. CINAHL has covered *Bibliotheca Medica Canadiana (BMC)* for 1984 to 2003. CINAHL lists 359 references from *Bibliotheca Medica Canadiana (BMC)* in its database (March 2003). CINAHL very selectively covers *Hypothesis* for the years 1998 to 2003. The author reviewed the 44 *Hypothesis* references covered by CINAHL for this period and, encouragingly, found that even some abstracts for research award winners had been covered. CINAHL covers *Journal of Hospital Librarianship* from its first issue in 2001. CINAHL lists 83 references to *Journal of Hospital Librarianship* (March 2003). The Library Literature database does not cover any of these three less influential, yet nevertheless significant, health librarianship journals.

The 'grey literature'

'Grey literature' constitutes a major portion of our overall knowledge base, with conference papers and posters comprising a large percentage of literature within the LIS profession. One study indicates that 22% of our published literature cites the grey literature (Alberani and Pietrangeli, 1995). We can hypothesize that members of the LIS profession have far more incentives to present papers or posters at conferences than to publish research results in peer-reviewed professional journals. A librarian wanting to benefit educationally from attendance at a professional conference may feel hampered by the financial cost of attendance. The likelihood of receiving full or partial funding for conference attendance from their parent institution is greater if they are presenting a paper or poster. Conversely, many might view the additional time and motivation necessary to prepare a manuscript based on the same poster or presentation as a formidable obstacle. Parent institutions may not allow study leave for preparing a manuscript for publication. The acid test of editorial peer review might be viewed as a distinct disincentive to publish. The net effect of these incentives and disincentives translates into a higher probability that research results will appear in the grey literature than in the published literature. This dynamic has likely had an adverse effect in preventing many research results from reaching a wider audience through publication. In spite of irregularities of index coverage by databases discussed above, the searcher still has a far greater likelihood of finding published rather than unpublished research results. Solutions include the possibility, afforded by the web, of mounting structured abstracts of presented papers or posters from annual meetings and publishing structured abstracts of research award winners and honourable mentions in newsletters (Wood, 2002).

Such grey literature may also correct the often-noted 'positive outcome bias' in the published literature (Moscati et al., 1994; Rosenthal, 1979). This has two dimensions: firstly, a study is more likely to be published if it produces dramatic results and, secondly, any results published tend to be more favourable than critical toward the described program. For example, a case study on the dramatic positive success of introducing a new technology to a specific information unit would fulfil both dimensions, thereby increasing the chances that editor and peer reviewers accept it for publication. It follows that a case study with negative results would have a lower likelihood of acceptance for publication.

Consider: 'When was the last time you read an article within the past ten years that described a library programme that failed?' When asked this question, only one participant in a recent continuing education course could respond positively, citing Pierce (2003). Indeed, with the exception of this one case and a series of research studies measuring the accuracy of librarians' answers to reference queries, a prolific area of inquiry between 1985 and 1997, it is nearly impossible to cite a research study without noteworthy positive results. This author submitted a randomized controlled trial of a communication study in which the results were neither positive nor dramatic. Even though many recognize the merits of this type of research design in reducing bias, the submission was rejected by two or three colleagues blinded to the identity of the author. One solution might be a new category of program evaluation research award which would describe a programmatic failure but then offer a detailed analysis of how similar mistakes could be avoided in the future. Case studies and program evaluations, two genres susceptible to positive outcome bias, could at the very least be required to include a 'lessons learnt' segment. Booth also notes the need to address the problems of positive outcome bias (Booth, 2002).

Literature external to the library domain

Many EBIP questions can be answered successfully by literature external to the library domain, even though practitioners often overlook this vast collection of disciplinary knowledge bases. By stripping away the library-specific elements of some EBIP questions we frequently recognize that identifiable literatures outside our own might produce high-quality answers. Consider the following questions based on those posed during a recent EBL class in Denver, Colorado:

- will confirmation of enrolment at time of registration and reminder notices two days before an informatics training class decrease the number of 'no shows'? Will a nominal fee decrease the number of 'no shows' for our training classes?
- is there a difference in results for the following methods of teaching library literature searching and online resources in terms of the amount of usage and effectiveness of searching: One-to-one training; class training?
- what types of user surveys yield the most useful information for library program planning?
- what kind of information can we give administrators to show the impact of library service?

By stripping away the library-specific elements of these questions we can restate these questions along with suggesting, in brackets, the subject domain wherein answers might be found:

- how does one increase attendance for training classes: by telephone confirmation or by a fee for non-attendance? (Education literature)

- which learning style works better and for whom: one-to-one training or classroom training? (Education literature)
- how can one write a survey that will yield honest and useful responses? (Social sciences or public policy analysis literatures)
- how can we demonstrate the impact of our service on the larger institution? (Management literature).

Although this chapter focuses upon the information practice knowledge base, we should remember to include the non-library literatures in our search for the best evidence to answer our EBIP questions. Obviously, some questions pertain to core activities such as the efficacy of specific library roles, e.g. training practitioners or students on database search skills, or on the effective identification and appraisal of information resources that require searching the library literature. Yet, searchers still might find relevant evidence to such core questions when searching other literatures without the library focus. At the very least, literatures outside the LIS field might suggest hypotheses we can test within it.

A search protocol for LIS practitioners

The busy practitioner searching for the answers to EBIP questions must be dextrous when choosing a search strategy. The logical starting point is LIS published literature. The grey literature, specifically the abstracts of papers or posters presented at professional meetings, might be the second tier of a search strategy. Finally, the vast literatures outside our profession might be a fruitful domain to continue a search for the needed evidence. This initial phase in finding the answers to EBIP questions can pose many challenges as has been clearly demonstrated above.

How good is the evidence base?

This next section addresses the additional challenge of appraising the validity and relevance of identified evidence from the library literature. A core characteristic of the EBIP movement has been the view that different types of evidence have different validity. Initially, the concept of a hierarchy of evidence developed slowly. The levels of evidence in Table 4.4 represent current thinking on discriminating between higher and lower quality evidence, depending upon the types of questions asked. The specifics have changed over recent years, but the underlying premise adheres to the principle that certain types of research design are better than others in reducing human or systematic bias. Some lower level research designs rely more heavily upon intuition which, it has been noted, 'can be wrong, particularly those of the less experienced' (Closs and Cheater, 1999). Of course, consistent with this observation is the corollary that within a particular research design the quality of the actual planning and implementation can vary dramatically. In a hypothetical (and highly unlikely) scenario of extremes, a well conducted descriptive survey might offer better evidence than a poorly conceived and executed cohort design in answering a prediction question.

Table 4.4 originally appeared in a previous publication (Eldredge, 2002b) so it is only briefly summarized here. The higher levels of EBIP evidence in Table 4.4 reflect the capacity of these types of research designs to minimize bias. Systematic reviews allow researchers to pose a clearly stated question and then search relevant evidence in the published or unpublished literature. Researchers then critically assess the available evidence according to strict predetermined criteria to synthesize all the considered evidence to make a recommendation. Meta-analyses resemble systematic reviews but they should not be confused with each other. A meta-analysis literally can pool compatible data from two research projects and create a larger body of data from which to draw conclusions. Some meta-analyses pool data from large numbers of compatible studies to make more certain inferences. In the area of using evidence to answer Exploration questions, however, the meta-analysis design will not work. Researchers attempting to synthesize the available qualitative evidence need to draw upon a variety of techniques described in the book *Summing Up* to create a systematic review for Exploration questions (Light and Pillemer, 1984).

Table 4.4   EBL levels of evidence, revised (Eldredge, 2002)

Prediction	Intervention	Exploration
Systematic review	Systematic review	Systematic review
Meta-analysis	Meta-analysis	Summing up*
Prospective cohort study	RCTs	Comparative study[+]
Retrospective cohort study	Prospective cohort study	Qualitative studies**
Survey	Retrospective cohort study	Survey
Case study	Survey	Case study
Expert opinion[++]	Case study	Expert opinion[++]
	Expert opinion[++]	

*   Please see the book *Summing up* (Light and Pillemer, 1984) for a comprehensive overview of creative ways to synthesize exploratory study data.

[+]   A comparative study in the exploration category involves two or more qualitative studies.

**   Qualitative studies include but are not limited to focus groups, ethnographic studies, naturalistic observations and historical analyses.

[++]   Expert opinion offered without rendering any supportive evidence.

This table assumes that 'positive outcome bias' has not occurred when assembling relevant evidence.

The highest-level single research designs vary according to the type of question posed in the EBIP process. Prediction questions rely upon cohort studies as the best research design for single studies. Prospective cohort studies, which collect data at the beginning of the study period, are considered to be more valid than retrospective cohort studies, which collect data on events that have already passed and therefore might have less complete and standardized datasets. Many usage studies in libraries and quite a few library education programs employ the cohort design (Eldredge, 2002b). Intervention questions rely upon randomized controlled trials (RCTs) as the best research design for single studies. RCTs identify two or more types of intervention. One 'intervention' typically consists of either no intervention or the standard intervention. For example, visitors to a library website might be randomized to a traditional online catalogue or an experimental form of the online catalogue. Those randomized to the traditional online catalogue would constitute the control group while those randomized into the experimental catalogue would be the intervention group (Eldredge, 2003). Exploration questions rely upon qualitative studies as the single best research design for single studies. Exploration questions probe into the reasons why people behave the way they do. They also seek to understand underlying processes. They are excellent designs for formulating hypotheses for testing with more quantitative research methods or for constructing theories.

Most research evidence from the LIS field occupies the lowest levels of evidence in Table 4.4. Dimitroff's analysis of health librarianship literature noted that 30% of this literature comprises actual research (Dimitroff, 1992). From this subset she determined that the more common research methods include descriptive (41%), observation (21%) and bibliometric (14%). This last category might be classified generally as descriptive surveys in Table 4.4. Other studies have concluded that the health librarianship literature consists of case studies, descriptive surveys, and some qualitative methods (Burdick et al., 1990; Haiqi, 1995a; Haiqi, 1995b; Haiqi, 1996; Mularski et al., 1991). This reflects the patterns generally encountered in the wider library literature (Atkins, 1988; Peritz, 1980–1981; Nour, 1985; Enger et al., 1989; Jarvelin and Vakkari, 1990; Buttlar, 1991; Crawford, 1999; Rochester and Vakkiri, 1998; Cheng, 1996; Nkereuwem, 1997; Olorunsola and Akinboro, 1998) with only minor variations across studies.

To this author's knowledge only three Cochrane-type systematic reviews in librarianship currently exist. (Editor's note: The designation 'Cochrane-type' has been inserted in recognition that there are many examples of reviews (and indeed meta-analyses) with varying degrees of systematicity in existence within librarianship (see Section 3). However, few fully adhere to the methods advocated by the Cochrane Collaboration. The qualifier 'in librarianship' is also important as, within the wider domains of informatics, and indeed consumer health information, systematic reviews are more common (again see Section 3). Two were published in the June 2003 special issue of *Health Information and Libraries Journal* (Brettle, 2003; Winning and Beverley, 2003). A third systematic review (Wagner and Byrd, 2003) was presented at the MLA Annual Meeting during May 2003. These three systematic reviews all address important questions facing the LIS profession. Saxton (1997) attempted to conduct a meta-analysis to evaluate general library reference services, but it was unsuccessful. Only 13 randomized controlled trials (RCTs) have been identified from fairly comprehensive Medline database searches and hand-searching of the core health librarianship literature (Eldredge, 2003). A similar study of cohort studies in health librarianship determined that, at the very least, 37 have been published with far more existing in unpublished form (Eldredge, 2002a). With the wide availability of computer technology, far more usage study cohort studies may have been conducted than this modest number might suggest. No one has conducted a similar inventory of qualitative studies to date. Consequently, the evidence base of high quality research for health librarianship is 'minuscule' (Eldredge, 2000). Despite their considerable extent, the medical and nursing evidence bases are still perceived as insufficient for answering many relevant questions for these professions (Closs and Cheater, 1999). Most professions are in the same boat, yet they have resolved not to be there for much longer. As other professions mobilize their resources to address these deficiencies, we too need to be proactive in correcting the deficiencies in our own knowledge base. If we are not careful, our evidence base might look like a backwater in the near future.

Fortunately, current trends suggest this situation will change within the next five years. With one international conference on EBL sponsored by the University of Sheffield during September 2001 and a second sponsored by the University of Alberta in Edmonton during June 2003, interest within the LIS profession certainly has taken hold. The MLA Research Section in the US, the Health Libraries Group in the UK, and clusters of librarians in Canada have been leading a wider, although scattered, international EBIP movement. An international collaboration calling itself the Evidence Based Librarianship Implementation Committee (EBLIC), convened by the MLA Research Section, has collected and published EBL questions important to the LIS profession generated by health sciences librarians around the world (EBLIC, 2001).

In conclusion, a strategy for rectifying this situation might thus be summarized as:

1 Identify the most important and answerable questions facing our profession.
2 Devote appropriate resources to answering these relevant questions.
3 Answer these questions with multiple identical studies at the highest individual study level of evidence as noted on Table 4.4.

4   Synthesize results with systematic reviews. If possible accompany these systematic reviews with meta-analyses for intervention or prediction questions, if the data makes such analyses possible and appropriate.

References

Alberani, V. and Pietrangeli, P. D. (1995) The Use of the Grey Literature in Information Science: production, circulation and use, *INSPEL*, **29**, 240–9.

Atkins, S. E. (1988) Subject Trends in Library and Information Science Research, 1975–1984, *Library Trends*, **36** (4), (Spring), 633–58.

Booth, A. (2002) On a Cautious Adoption of Innovative Projects, *Health Information and Libraries Journal*, **19** (4), 239–42.

Booth, A. (2003) Mirage or Reality?, *Health Information and Libraries Journal*, **19** (1), 56–8.

Brettle, A. (2003) Information Skills Training: a systematic review of the literature, *Health Information and Libraries Journal*, **20** (Suppl), (June), 3–9.

Burdick, A. J., Doms, C. A., Doty, C. C. and Kinzie, L. A. (1990) Research Activities Among Health Sciences Librarians: a survey, *Bulletin of the Medical Library Association*, **78** (4), 400–2.

Buttlar, L. (1991) Analyzing the Library Periodical Literature: content and authorship, *College & Research Libraries*, **52** (1), 38–53.

Cheng, H. (1996) A Bibliometric Study of Library and Information Research in China, *Asian Libraries*, **5** (2), 30–45.

Closs, S. J. and Cheater, F. M. (1999) Evidence for Nursing Practice: a clarification of the issues, *Journal of Advanced Nursing*, **30** (1), 10–17.

Crawford, G. A. (1999) The Research Literature of Academic Librarianship: a comparison of *College & Research Libraries* and *Journal of Academic Librarianship*, *College & Research Libraries*, **60** (3), 224–30.

Dimitroff, A. (1992) Research in Health Sciences Library and Information Science: a quantitative analysis, *Bulletin of the Medical Library Association*, **80** (4), 340–6.

Eldredge, J. D. (1998) The Vital Few Meet the Trivial Many: unexpected use patterns in a monographs collection, *Bulletin of the Medical Library Association*, **86** (4), 496–503.

Eldredge, J. (2000) Evidence-Based Librarianship: formulating EBL questions, *Bibliotheca Medica Canadiana*, **22** (2), 74–7.

Eldredge, J. (2002a) Cohort Studies in Health Sciences Librarianship, *Journal of the Medical Library Association*, **90** (4), 380–92, www.pubmedcentral.nih.gov/tocrender.fcgi?journal=93.

Eldredge J. (2002b) Evidence-Based Librarianship: levels of evidence, *Hypothesis*, **16** (3), (Fall), 10–14, http://gain.mercer.edu/mla/research/hypothesis.html.

Eldredge, J. D. (2003) Randomized Controlled Trial Design: unrecognized opportunities for health sciences librarianship, *Health Information and Libraries Journal*, **20** (Suppl 1), 34–44.

Enger, K. B., Quirk, G. and Stewart, J. A. (1989) Statistical Methods Used by Authors of Library and Information Science Journal Articles, *Library and Information Science Research*, **89** (11), 37–46.

Evidence-Based Librarianship Implementation Committee (2001) The Most Relevant and Answerable Research Questions Facing the Practice of Health Sciences Librarianship, *Hypothesis*, **15** (1), 9–17, http://gain.mercer.edu/mla/research/hypothesis.html.

Haiqi, Z. (1995a) A Bibliometric Study on Articles of Medical Librarianship, *Information Processing & Management*, **31** (4), 499–510.

Haiqi, Z. (1995b) Analysing the Research Articles Published in Three Periodicals of Medical Librarianship, *International Information & Library Review*, **27**, 237–48.

Haiqi, Z. (1996) Author Characteristics in Three Medical Library Periodicals, *Bulletin of the Medical Library Association*, **84** (3), 423–6.

Jarvelin, K. and Vakkari, P. (1990) Content Analysis of Research Articles in Library and Information Science, *Library & Information Science Research*, **12** (4), 395–421.

Light, R. J. and Pillemer, D. B. (1984) *Summing Up: the science of reviewing research*, Cambridge, MA, Harvard University Press.

Moscati, R., Jehle, D., Ellis, D., Fiorello, A. and Landi, M. (1994) Positive-outcome Bias: comparison of emergency medicine and general medicine literatures, *Academic Emergency Medicine*, **1** (3), (May/Jun), 267–71.

Mularski, C. A. and Bradigan, P. S. (1991) Academic Health Sciences Librarians' Publications Patterns, *Bulletin of the Medical Library Association*, **79** (2), (Apr), 168–77.

Nkereuwem, E. E. (1997) Accrediting Knowledge: the ranking of library and information science journals, *Asian Libraries*, **6** (1/2), 71–6.

Nour, M. M. (1985) A Quantitative Analysis of the Research Articles Published in the Core Library Journals of 1980, *Library & Information Science Research*, **7** (3), 261–73.

Olorunsola, R. and Akinboro, E. O. (1998) Bibliographic Analysis of Articles: a study of African Journal of Library, Archives and Information Science, 1991–1997, *African Journal of Library, Archive & Information Science*, **8** (2), 151–4.

Peritz, B. C. (1980–1981) The Methods of Library Science Research: some results from a bibliometric survey, *Library Research*, **2**, 251–68.

Pierce, J. B. (2003) A Tale of Two Levies, *American Libraries*, **34** (3), 40–2.

Rochester, M. and Vakkari, P. (1998) International LIS Research: a comparison of national trends, *IFLA Journal*, **24** (3), 166–75.

Rosenthal, R. (1979) The 'File Drawer Problem' and Tolerance for Null Results, *Psychological Bulletin*, **86** (3), 638–41.

Saxton, M. L. (1997) Reference Service Evaluation and Meta-Analysis: findings and methodological issues, *Library Quarterly*, **67** (3), 267–89.

Wagner, K. C. and Byrd, G. D. (2003) *Evaluating the Effectiveness of CML Programs: a systematic review of the literature*. Presented paper. MLA Annual Meeting May 2003.

Winning, M. A. and Beverley, C. A. (2003) Clinical Librarianship: a systematic review of the literature, *Health Information and Libraries Journal*, **20** (Suppl 1), 10–21.

Wood, B. (2002) Research Awards 2002: MLA papers and posters win commendations, *Hypothesis*, **16** (2), 1, 6–10, http://gain.mercer.edu/mla/research/hypothesis.html.

5

Why don't librarians use research?

Paul Genoni, Gaby Haddow and Ann Ritchie

Introduction

It is frequently asserted that librarians do not use research findings when making decisions related to their professional practice. It is claimed that their decisions are based on little more than instinct or colleagues' opinions, and that as a result their decision making may be ill-informed and high-risk. It is further claimed that this situation indicates a 'communication gap' between researchers and practitioners, and that this gap inhibits the maturation of librarianship, as many practitioners operate without an adequate understanding of the theoretical foundations to their practice.

This chapter examines the evidence related to the use of research by practitioners and the nature of the communication gap. In doing so it provides an overview of reasons advanced to explain why librarians do not use research data. It also explores the characteristics of the literature of librarianship, and the part played by education in preparing practitioners for the use of research-based evidence. Finally, it presents suggestions for improving the use of research by practitioners.

Scenario

The research

Considerable research has been conducted that compares and reviews information retrieval systems' features. Much of this research is conducted and published by researchers associated with the field of information science. Their aim is to identify systems' features that make information searching as easy and relevant to the searcher as possible. The findings of this research tend to be published in scholarly journals and is presented at research-oriented conferences.

The practice

The automated system of a medium size government library needs upgrading to incorporate new and improved features, such as Internet links and better searching capabilities. The librarian gains approval from the department to purchase a new system within a specified budget. Advertisements for automated systems in recent issues of the professional association's newsletter provide the contact details for local agents. However, before contacting the agents the librarian calls colleagues at other government libraries to ask for their opinions about systems to which they have upgraded in the last few years and posts a message to a discussion list requesting information about the relative merits of systems being used in other libraries. One of the responses is from a colleague who had heard from another source that system 'A' was 'clumsy' and that the support staff for system 'B' were difficult to contact. To ensure that the promised budget allocation is not lost to the library, the librarian moves quickly to reach a decision. Based on the opinions of colleagues and information from advertisements, the librarian selects three systems and arranges for the agents to visit the library and discuss and demonstrate their product. A final decision is made on the basis of the system's features as stated by the agents and from what is observable from the demonstration, peer recommendations, the budget available, and the skills of the salesperson.

The research-practice communication gap

How typical is the librarian portrayed in this scenario in their neglect of the research-based evidence? Librarianship is not alone in being concerned about a 'communication gap' between research and practice. The problem has been noted in a number of professional areas such as nursing (Camiah, 1997), information systems (Senn, 1998), and psychology (Latham, 2001). Professions that divide between 'practitioners' (inevitably the numerically larger proportion) and 'researchers' (frequently university-based) may find difficulty in sustaining a culture of practice that incorporates research evidence into its decision making. As Clayton (1992, 73) noted, however, even though a communication gap between research and practice 'is common to many professions other than our own [this] can hardly be of much comfort.'

Certainly, the existence of a communication gap between library and information researchers and practitioners has been reported on numerous occasions (Lynam et al., 1982; Lynch, 1984; Craghill and Wilson, 1987; McClure and Bishop, 1989; Robbins, 1990; Clayton, 1992; Rochester, 1999; Williamson, 1999;

Turner, 2002). It should be noted, however, that the evidence with regard to the reading habits of, and use of research by, librarians is fragmentary. Studies have typically been based on surveys featuring niche groups such as public library directors (Tjoumas, 1991), educators and school library media centre co-ordinators (Blake, 1991), and authors and editors (Floyd and Phillips, 1997); and/or have drawn their respondents from one country only. The latter includes surveys by Rochester (1995) and Haddow (2001) in Australia, Powell (2002) and Weaver (2002) in the United States, and Turner (2002) in New Zealand. Nevertheless, there is a need to understand the nature of the communication gap between researchers and practitioners in order to facilitate the transfer of research findings into professional practice.

What is 'research'?

A further issue that creates problems in interpreting the available research-based information is confusion surrounding the concept of 'research' literature. As Robbins (1990) has noted: '. . . few practitioners understand precisely what research means; they often confuse writing about information concerns with the scientific form of inquiry'. Few researchers who have investigated the issue have defined the concept of 'research' to survey participants. Potential misunderstanding as to what constitutes research literature therefore makes the interpretation of studies which investigate the research reading habits of librarians problematic – some survey respondents consider any published literature, irrespective of its origins or intentions, as being 'research'.

Given these problems, it is not surprising that available studies vary in their identification of the extent of the problem and its causes. The general tenor of their conclusions, however, was summarized by Turner (2002) after her recent examination of the gap between researchers and practitioners – that is, that 'the cross-fertilisation of ideas between these two communities appears to be rare in LIS, and a communication chasm indubitably exists'.

General barriers to the use of research literature

Some barriers to the use of research-based evidence are quite prosaic and hardly unique to librarianship. In Turner's (2002) survey the chief reason given for not consulting research was 'time constraints'. Generic issues raised by respondents included 'problems with physical availability' and 'problems with intellectual availability (e.g. poor bibliographic control of research findings)'.

Research material may also be difficult to access due to language barriers. Research results published only in English remain largely inaccessible to many practising librarians and, similarly, English-only speakers and readers will find a considerable proportion of the research produced by other language groups is inaccessible. Unlike some sciences that are supported by professional translation services, there is little evidence of use of such services by the library and information professions.

Another barrier preventing information professionals from gathering research evidence is the variety of disciplines within which relevant literature may be found. Booth (2002) notes that relevant research will be found not only in the literature of librarianship and allied information professions, but in literatures derived from education, management, marketing, computer science and business. To these might well be added psychology, systems analysis and mass communication. Indeed it is the fate of the information professions, frequently allied in practice as they are with other professional groups (e.g. law libraries, medical libraries, geoscience libraries), that evidence relating to the information needs of those allied professions will be found in the associated literature of such groups.

Notwithstanding the above, librarians have several inherent advantages when it comes to their potential to implement evidence-based practice. Their familiarity with literature searching and information retrieval, their access to collections of information and document supply services, and their familiarity with concepts of information 'quality', all suggest that they are better placed than other professions to identify and retrieve the best evidence their literature can provide. When looking for an explanation as to why this is not the case, it is therefore necessary to investigate the characteristics of library literature and the manner in which practitioners relate to it.

Characteristics of library literature

Much of the library literature is not research-based. Several commentators have noted difficulties in establishing a productive research culture for the profession (Dyer and Stern, 1990), such that the professional literature is dominated by anecdotal material and opinion pieces (Rochester, 1995; Haddow, 2001).

The amount of research-based publication is constrained by the lack of funding to support research projects. Professional associations and other agencies involved in librarianship have been criticized for their lack of support for research, with suggestions that they develop strategies aimed at coordinating and providing funding opportunities for collaborative research (Robbins, 1990; Clayton, 1992; Harvey, 2001). In common with other social sciences, research in librarianship tends to be carried out by individuals rather than teams. Coupled with the scarce funding, this leads to disparate research activities with fewer opportunities to share and compare research findings.

Others have noted that research is being done, but that the results are then not prepared for publication. In a recent editorial in the *Australian Library Journal* John

Levett noted the difficulty he had in soliciting research-based manuscripts from both academic researchers and practitioner-researchers, despite the 'relevant and often excellent work' being done (Levett, 2002). Levett suggested several reasons why completed research is not published. For practitioner-researchers these included the confidential nature of research carried out for particular institutions, and for academic researchers the exhausted state of PhD candidates by the time they submit their theses, and the excessive work demands being made of supervisors such that they have little time to assist students in preparing research for publication.

The quality of the research that *is* conducted and published has also been criticized (Fisher, 1999; Powell, 2002). Floyd and Phillips (1997) described as 'distressing' both the apparent lack of interest editors paid to testing the accuracy of research findings and their indifference to the qualifications of authors.

But neither the paucity of research-based material, nor indeed its quality, necessarily explains why that research which is available is not more widely consulted. For that, one needs to look towards issues related to perceptions of the nature or character of the research process, although even here the evidence – or at least the interpretation of it – is inconsistent.

A common observation made by practitioners is that the research literature lacks relevance. Several studies have identified the low level of practitioner interest in research literature, which they see as being esoteric and lacking applicability to the workplace (Ali, 1985b; McClure and Bishop, 1989; Turner, 2002). In reviewing previous literature on the topic, Clayton (1992) highlighted differences between the two groups, and noted: '. . . researchers' preferences for objective, verifiable data, while practitioners want experiential, problem-solving information; researchers' preferences for validity and reliability in research methods, while practitioners want projects to have pragmatic value and to be influential in a specific situation; and researchers' use of scientific and technical vocabulary, while practitioners expect standard professional jargon'.

Studies of reading habits support this assertion, with Tjoumas (1991) measuring the preference of public library directors for serials 'primarily oriented to practical information and applications'. More recently Turner (2002) has concluded that the 'perceived inadequacy of research to address practical workplace problems was a major reason for information professionals not consulting the research', and Weaver (2002) has noted the preference of US librarians for 'articles that pertain to their work life'.

Furthermore, there is also support for Clayton's assertion regarding the semantic impenetrability of at least some research writing, with Rochester (1996) concluding that 'most library and information science journals are not particularly readable, and abound with long words, convoluted sentences and abstruse jargon. This is especially so for research-oriented articles'.

Responses from library practitioners asked about their interest in research led Lynam, Slater and Walker to conclude that 'it would be fair to say that indifference ruled' (1982). In part this indifference might be explained by the lack of relevance to practice of the academy-based research that is published. If this were the sole issue, however, it could be expected that a practice-based research culture would emerge to satisfy the demand. Clearly, this has not occurred. Indeed, practitioners have received criticism for their part in the researcher-practitioner gap because of their proportionally low levels of published research when authorship of articles is examined for workplace affiliation (Olsgaard and Olsgaard, 1980; Swigger, 1985; Enger, Quirk et al., 1988; Mularski, 1991; Fisher, 1999). The issue, however, may not be a lack of workplace research, but rather that the workplace research that is conducted is not reported in the literature. Powell, Baker and Mika (2002) reported that over 40% ('higher than expected') of US practitioners surveyed engaged in research, but of these 74.1% did not publish their results and, after surveying practitioners' research activity in New Zealand, Finnie, Frame and Stewart (2000) noted a high level of activity but concluded that: 'research results are generally written up but not usually disseminated beyond the organization. Publication in professional journals is very rare'.

Practitioners' reported disregard for research because of its lack of practical utility is contradicted by opinion that points to the overwhelmingly applied nature of published research. Rochester (1995) identified that research papers in key Australian journals focused on practical problems rather than contributing to the longer term, theoretical development of the discipline. Robbins (1990) described practitioners' attitudes as a contributing factor to deficiencies in research, noting that their 'knowledge base is developed from previous practice, authoritative pronouncement, and intuition'. The practical orientation of library publishing, coupled with the narrow field of evidence gathering in the decision making process, are seen by other commentators as indicative of a profession which is still maturing. As noted by Saracevic et al. (1988): 'While there is nothing inherently wrong with common sense, professional art, and principles derived from experience or by reasoning, our knowledge and understanding and with them our practice would be on much more solid ground if they were confirmed or refuted, elaborated, cumulated, and taught on the basis of scientific evidence'.

'Culture gap' between researchers and practitioners

Practitioners complain that too much published research is overly theoretical and irrelevant to practice while researchers complain that too much of the published research is practice oriented or 'applied' and therefore unlikely to contribute to the development of a convincing theoretical base. Given this contention over the nature of the published research output, it seems likely that the communication gap between practitioners and researchers is grounded in the difference between what the two groups *actually do*. Although they share a common professional base, they are embedded in distinct and separate cultures with very different modes of communication.

Practitioners favour 'professional' journals delivering practical guidance and information aimed at supporting practitioners in their day-to-day work tasks, and researchers prefer a separate set of 'research' journals (Ali, 1985a). The former typically have a local or regional readership, while the latter are international. Even research which may have a strong local basis and interest for practitioners would probably be published not in a local 'professional' journal but in an international 'research' journal because of the higher prestige reward to the author (Clayton, 1992).

In comparing the reading habits between research producers and prospective consumers, Blake (1991) concluded that: 'Only in a very small number of instances do both respondent groups value the same professional journals. Direct communication links between library/information science faculty . . . and practising library/information professionals in this sub-field of the profession seem extremely tenuous' (1991, 137).

Improving links and the exchange of ideas between researchers, managers and policy makers was the focus of a recent report, which noted: 'the key to producing good research questions which meet decision makers' needs is to create and maintain high-quality, ongoing interactions between research and decision-maker partners' (Canadian Health Services Research Foundation, 2003).

Influence of library education

Frequently, poor practitioner use of research is attributed to the failure of educational institutions to provide graduates with a sound foundation in the skills required to undertake research, or indeed accurately to read and interpret research results (McClure and Bishop, 1989; Robbins, 1990; Clayton, 1992; Floyd and Phillips, 1997). However, evidence in this regard is again inconclusive. Stephenson (1990) investigated the reasons for the low levels of research conducted by practitioners by looking at the influence of learning research methods during library education as a means of explaining the extent of subsequent research activity. The study found that most graduates do complete a course in research methods, leaving unanswered the question as to why so little published research is produced by practitioners.

More recently, Powell, Baker and Mika's (2002) inquiry into the research-related reading habits of US librarians has again pointed to uncertainty as to whether education may be a determining factor. They found that: 'Approximately 15% of those who gave reasons for not reading research-based articles checked that they did not have the expertise in research methods' concluding that: 'surprisingly, the amount of (research) reading was not found to be significantly related to how well the respondent's master's degree program had prepared them to read and understand research-based publications'.

From the literature available it is clear that the specific research skills taught to library students vary widely. However, references made to a 'crowded curriculum' (Clayton, 1992), and the diversity of graduate students' previous research experience (Stephenson, 1990) suggest there are difficulties in providing research methods education that is both detailed enough to direct future research studies and broad enough to suit students' different needs.

Suggestions for narrowing the culture and communication gap

What, then is the real extent of the culture and communication gap between researchers and practitioners? An optimistic view may conclude that the gap is not as substantial as some commentators have concluded, and that it is simply an artificial divide promulgated by the habits that the two groups have developed of reading and writing for separate audiences in separate journals. After their substantial recent survey of research reading habits Powell, Baker and Mika (2002) reported that results were 'mixed', but that a 'substantial number of practitioners do engage in and care about research', and 'about half of the respondents reported that they do occasionally apply research results to their practice'.

A pessimistic assessment, however, would be that two distinct and separate cultures exist – that researchers carry out their work without regard for practical value, and that practitioners have a deep resistance to reading research, based on a perception that theory is unlikely to assist them with day-to-day decision making in their workplace. This is the view supported by the majority of the commentators on the subject.

How is this gap to be eliminated, or at least substantially reduced? Leaving aside issues related to both the quantity and quality of research, and focusing on the importance of bringing together the research and practice cultures to facilitate the research transfer process, thus making research relevant and accessible to practitioners, the following suggestions can be made:

Collaboration and ongoing communication between researchers and practitioners

These are critical to the process of designing and implementing practical research projects. The most effective way to achieve this may be for funding bodies, including professional associations, to develop research funding models that include collaboration as a prerequisite. This collaboration would provide a forum for developing a co-ordinated approach in which researchers and practitioners have a role in identifying and refining research questions, designing research projects that are relevant to practice and, finally, making decisions which will lead to implementation of the results.

Researchers need to find venues and a language to communicate effectively with practitioners. This may entail publishing summaries of research outcomes in journals and newsletters read by practitioners and written according to the needs and interests of that audience. Research reports might be supplemented by extending the practical and policy implications which research outcomes may have for practitioners (see for example Canadian Health Services Research Foundation, 2002).

Practitioners must increase their contribution to research literature. If researchers are correct in identifying that they (practitioners) are in fact productive researchers, then they should undertake to communicate the outcomes in their chosen journals. The writing-up of research needs to be recognized and rewarded by employers as a legitimate professional task.

Notwithstanding the uncertain evidence regarding *the role of education in research methods*, it does nonetheless seem necessary that graduates have at the very least an understanding of the concept of 'evidence-based practice' and can distinguish between research based evidence and anecdotal 'evidence' which is based on opinion or experience. Practitioners must be able to appreciate the value of good research and be critical readers of research literature.

Conclusion

This chapter has summarized evidence related to practitioners' use of research. It acknowledges that the research literature is ambivalent in some respects, but supports the majority view that research findings are under-utilized. It has suggested that the lack of use of research based evidence is indicative of not only a 'communication gap' between researchers and practitioners, but also a more general 'culture gap' which separates the two groups. Finally, some suggestions have been made as to how the communities of researchers and practitioners can be brought closer together in ways which would highlight the practical outcomes of the research process, and expose practitioners to the theoretical aspects of librarianship.

References

Ali, S. N. (1985a) Library and Information Science Literature: research results, *International Library Review*, **17**, 117–28.

Ali, S. N. (1985b) Library Science Research: some results of its dissemination and utilization, *Libri*, **35** (2), 151–62.

Blake, V. (1991) In the Eyes of the Beholder: perceptions of professional journals by library/information science educators and district school library media center coordinators, *Collection Management*, **14** (3/4), 101–48.

Booth, A. (2002) From EBM to EBL: two steps forward and one step back?, *Medical Reference Services Quarterly*, **21** (3), 51–64.

Camiah, S. (1997) Utilization of Nursing Research in Practice And Application Strategies to Raise Research Awareness Amongst Nurse Practitioners: a model for success, *Journal of Advanced Nursing*, **26**, 1193–202.

Canadian Health Services Research Foundation (2003) *If research is the answer, what is the question? Key steps to turn decision-maker issues into research questions*, www.chsrf.ca/docs/resource/research_e.pdf.

Canadian Health Services Research Foundation (2002) Communication Notes: Reader-Friendly Writing – 1:3:25, www.chsrf.ca/docs/resource/cn-1325_e.pdf.

Clayton, P. (1992) Bridging the Gap: research and practice in librarianship. In Clayton, P. and McCaskie, R. (eds), *Priorities for the future: proceedings of the First National Reference and Information Service Section Conference and the University, College and Research Libraries Section Workshop on Research*, Canberra, D. W. Thorpe, 73–6.

Craghill, D. and Wilson, T. D. (1987) *The impact of information research*, London, British Library.

Dyer, H. and Stern, R. (1990) Overcoming Barriers to Library and Information Science Research: a report of the first Advanced Research Institute held at the University of Illinois at Urbana-Champaign, *International Journal of Information and Library Research*, **2** (2), 129–34.

Enger, K. B. and Quirk, G. et al. (1988) Statistical Methods Used by Authors of Library and Information Science Journal Articles, *Library and Information Science Research*, **11**, 37–46.

Finnie, E., Frame, B. and Stewart, I. (2000) Research by New Zealand Library Practitioners, *New Zealand Libraries*, **49** (3), 85–7.

Fisher, W. (1999) When Write is Wrong: is all our professional literature on the same page?, *Library Collections, Acquisitions, and Technical Services*, **23** (1), 61–72.

Floyd, B. L. and Phillips, J. C. (1997) A Question of Quality: how authors and editors perceive library literature, *College & Research Libraries*, **58**, 81–93.

Haddow, G. C. (2001) The Diffusion of Information Retrieval Research Within Librarianship: a communication framework. (Unpublished PhD Thesis), University of Western Australia, Perth.

Harvey, R. (2001) Losing the Quality Battle in Australian Education for Librarianship, *Australian Library Journal*, **50** (1), 15–22.

Latham, G. P. (2001) The Reciprocal Transfer of Learning From Journals to Practice, *Applied Psychology: An International Review*, **50** (2), 201–11.

Levett, J. (2002) The Nature, Utility and Essential Unknowability of Research in our Disciplines: an editor's view, *Australian Library Journal*, **51** (2), 95–7.

Lynam, P., Slater, M. and Walker, R (1982) *Research and the Practitioner: dissemination of research results within the library-information profession*, London, Aslib.

Lynch, M. J. (1984) Research and Librarianship: an uneasy connection, *Library Trends*, **32** (4), 367–81.

McClure, C. R. and Bishop, A. (1989) The Status of Research in Library/Information Science: guarded optimism, *College & Research Libraries*, **50**, 127–43.

Mularski, C. A. (1991) Institutional Affiliations of Authors of Research Articles in Library and Information Science: update, *Journal of Education for Library and Information Science*, **13**, 179–86.

Olsgaard, J. N. and Olsgaard, J. K. (1980) Authorship in Five Library Periodicals, *College and Research Libraries*, **41**, 49–53.

Powell, R. R., Baker, L. M. and Mika, J. J. (2002) Library and Information Science Practitioners and Research, *Library & Information Science Research*, **24** (1), 49–72.

Robbins, J. B. (1990) Research in Information Service Practice, *Library & Information Science Research*, **12**, 127–8.

Rochester, M. (1995) Library and Information Science Research in Australia 1985–1994: a content analysis of research articles in *The Australian Library Journal* and *Australian Academic & Research Libraries*, *Australian Academic & Research Libraries*, **26** (3), 163–70.

Rochester, M. (1996) Professional Communication Through Journal Articles, *Australian Academic & Research Libraries*, **27** (3), 191–9.

Rochester, M. (1999) Value-adding in the Profession: promoting research, education and librarianship – a forum, *Education for Library and Information Services: Australia*, **16** (1), 47–9.

Saracevic, T. et al. (1988) A Study of Information Seeking and Retrieving. I. background and methodology, *Journal of the American Society for Information Science*, **39** (3), 161–76.

Senn, J. (1998) The Challenge of Relating IS Research to Practice, *Information Resources Management Journal*, **11** (1), 23–8.

Stephenson, M. S. (1990) Teaching Research Methods in Library and Information Studies Programs, *Journal of Education for Library and Information Science*, **31** (1), 49–66.

Swigger, K. (1985) Institutional Affiliations of Authors of Research Articles, *Journal of Education for Library and Information Science*, **26**, 105–9.

Tjoumas, R. (1991) Professional Journal Utilization by Public Library Directors, *The Serials Librarian*, **20** (2/3), 1–16.

Turner, K. (2002) Do Information Professionals Use Research Published in LIS Journals?, *68th IFLA Council and General Conference, August 18–24, 2002,* www.ifla.org/IV/ifla68/papers/009-118e.pdf (Accessed 7th January 2003).

Weaver, S. M. (2002) TheProfessional Reading Habits of American Librarians. *68th IFLA Council and General Conference, August 18–24, 2002,* www.ifla.org/IV/ifla68/papers/166-118e.pdf.

Williamson, K. (1999) The Role of Research in Practice: with reference to the assessment of the information and library needs of older people, *APLIS,* **12** (4), 145–53.

6

Formulating answerable questions

Andrew Booth

Introduction

The first stage of evidence-based practice, focusing or formulating your question (Richardson et al., 1995), is to convert a precise, yet possibly vaguely expressed, information need from practice into an answerable, focused, structured question (Rosenberg and Donald, 1995; Sackett and Rosenberg, 1995). This chapter describes general developments on question formulation in evidence-based practice and then places them within a context for evidence-based information practice. It will provide models for identifying the characteristics of an information need before proceeding to examples of questions generated by information practitioners. Questions generated by practitioners are compared with those answered by researchers, leading to a consideration of those research designs most useful in answering these questions.

✓	Define the problem
	Find evidence
	Appraise evidence
	Apply results of appraisal
	Evaluate change
	Redefine problem

Figure 6.1   The evidence-based practice process

Question formulation

You have had a particularly frustrating encounter at the enquiry desk. Although you have performed as best you can, and the reader has departed reasonably satisfied with your response, you cannot help thinking that you might have done things differently. From such nagging uncertainty comes a question: 'Am I doing the right things, and if so are they being done in the right way and at the right time?'.

Obviously such a question is not yet formulated. It needs to be defined in terms of its components. Does this uncertainty relate to all users or to a particular group of users? Is it a particular service, or aspect of a service, that is causing your disquiet? What are your options or alternatives? How would you know if you could have done things better?

Evidence-based healthcare has given formulating the question considerable attention (Ely et al., 2002; Ellis et al., 2000; Flemming, 1998; Booth 2000; Swinglehurst and Pierce, 2000). This includes classifying clinical questions into question types (Gorman and Helfand, 1997; Barrie and Ward, 1997; Ely et al., 1999; Ely et al., 2000), devising a structure or 'anatomy' for a 'focused' or answerable question (Richardson, 1998; Geddes, 1999) and discussing the characteristics of 'background' and 'foreground' questions (Richardson and Wilson, 1997). Effective question formulation leads to efficient searching for the needed evidence (Eldredge, 2000b; Snowball, 1997; Villanueva et al., 2001) and, conversely: 'Fuzzy questions tend to lead to fuzzy answers' (Oxman and Guyatt, 1988).

Additionally, as many initial questions lead to other questions, question formulation is iterative (Eldredge, 2000a). As Eldredge (2000a) comments: 'Questions drive the entire EBL process. EBL assigns highest priority to posed questions with greatest relevance to library practice. The wording and content of the questions will determine what kinds of research designs are needed to secure answers'.

A major factor in answering a question is prior knowledge on the topic. For example, if you are already aware of alternatives (e.g. electronic versus print journals) then you have a clear idea of the choices in front of you. However, if your question is not yet focused it may be phrased thus: 'What are the various ways that electronic current awareness services might be delivered?'. In this latter case you need to identify what your options are before starting to choose between them. Where your alternatives are apparent this is a *foreground question*, suggesting that you are at a point of decision-making. Where you have to acquire some background knowledge before exploring the different options available this is a *background question* (Richardson and Wilson, 1997). Foreground questions are usually answered from research studies published in the journal literature. Background questions may be answered from an up-to-date handbook such as the *Handbook of Special Librarianship* or from a state-of-the-art conventional literature review. Students, or those new to a profession, are more likely to ask background questions (Richardson and Wilson, 1997). Those who are more experienced in a profession are most likely to ask foreground questions unless encountering a completely unfamiliar situation or service.

A foreground question has several key components:

- A *population* – recipients or potential beneficiaries of a service or intervention
- An *intervention* – the service or planned action to be delivered to the population
- The *outcomes* – the ways in which the service or action can be measured to establish whether it has had a desired effect, and, optionally
- A *comparison* – an alternative service or action that may or may not achieve similar outcomes.

To illustrate: in pregnant mothers – (*Population*) is a touchscreen information service – (*Intervention*) more effective than printed information leaflets – (*Comparison*) in terms of knowledge of factors likely to cause prenatal harm – (*Outcomes*)?

This PIOC or PICO mnemonic is used by proponents of evidence-based practice to define an answerable question. (Occasionally the 'I' of Intervention is replaced by an 'E' for Exposure where the action is unintentional or unplanned. For example, '*increasing illiteracy*' (Exposure) among *school-leaving teenagers* (Population) measured in terms of *employability* (Outcome) compared with *literate schoolchildren* (Comparison) yields a similarly focused question. It is not necessary for all four elements to be present in your question. If you only have two elements, commonly a population and an intervention, then you probably have a background question, e.g. what are the benefits of *providing local history lectures* (Intervention) to an *inner city population* (Population)?

In a key article in *Hypothesis* Eldredge (2002) advances our understanding of three principal types of question in information practice:

Prediction questions

Prediction questions typically predict an outcome under certain circumstances. Frequently such questions are answered using a cohort study design. The cohort study design involves a defined population, an exposure to some phenomenon suspected of causing a change in the population, and observed outcomes. Prediction questions (and hence cohort studies) have examined information resources use, outreach, education, or public relations and marketing. Where several such cohort studies exist their results can be pooled in a meta-analysis, provided they have compatible data (e.g. similar outcomes).

Among prediction questions identified by Eldredge (2002) are:

- At what rate does the volume of published English language information resources in the health sciences grow per year?
- Does consumer health information have a positive impact on the prevention of disease in currently well patients?
- Which print journal subscriptions are best retained in a collection when an electronic version is available?
- What personality characteristics in librarians make them good or bad searchers?

Intervention questions

Intervention questions compare different actions with respect to achievement of an intended goal (or outcome). Does Intervention A demonstrably work better (efficacy) than Intervention B? Their value often lies in examining an alternative (or innovative) way of achieving a specified goal in contrast to a traditional way of achieving the same goal. Intervention B might well be what is considered 'standard practice'.

As an intervention is a planned or intended action, intervention questions might involve teaching, delivering a reference service or maintaining or weeding a collection. As with prediction questions, if the outcomes of two or more intervention studies are sufficiently similar (homogenous), and assuming the same type of intervention is being studied, results may be synthesized and pooled via systematic reviews or meta-analyses.

Eldredge (2002) again identifies intervention questions:

- Which web pages on a library website are most usable?
- Does weeding some classification ranges in a monographs collection result in higher usage than the unweeded but otherwise similar ranges?
- Does face-to-face contact versus electronic-only contact with a teaching faculty member by a library liaison librarian result in a more accurate perception of library services or resources?
- Are librarians or are library technicians more effective at answering reference questions or performing mediated literature searches?

Exploration questions

Exploration questions, as identified by Eldredge (2002) are broadly coterminous with Richardson's background questions and may be addressed by traditional overviews, systematic reviews or other forms of synthesis. Qualitative research, with its emphasis on investigating *why* things work rather than *whether* they work, provides the most appropriate paradigm for answering exploration questions. Typically, therefore, exploration questions begin 'with the word "why?" or imply a "why" inquiry' (Eldredge, 2002). They may be addressed through a plethora of research methods including focus groups, ethnographic studies, observation, interviewing, and historical analyses (Powell, 1999). Lacking the precision of a foreground question, exploration questions are characterized by 'open-endedness' when compared with prediction or intervention alternatives. Their usefulness in exploring the pivotal dimension of users' views, attitudes and values makes them particularly key to evidence-based information practice.

Eldredge (2002) identifies characteristic exploration questions as follows:

- Why do potential users, who are presently non-users, not use their library?
- Why do some people utilize reference services while others rarely or perhaps never utilize the same reference services, in spite of a recognized and shared need for information by all of these people?
- Why do some users prefer certain information resources over equally relevant information resources?
- Do librarians improve or worsen users' perceptions of information overload?

Of course, question formulation is not the prerogative of evidence-based practice. Other models of question formulation appear in the professional literature. For example, White (1998) devised a typology for content analysis of questions. Booth has worked with Wildridge and Bell (2002) to refine a variant on the PICO anatomy, with the mnemonic 'ECLIPSe' for questions regarding health policy and management:

- *Expectation* – what does the search requester want the information for?
- *Client Group*
- *Location*
- *Impact* – what is the change in the service, if any, which is being looked for? What would constitute success? How is this being measured?
- *Professionals*
- *Service* – for which service are you looking for information?

While the above models have the virtue of being firmly grounded in the context for which they were originally devised, it is our contention that a further, more generic variant on the PICO model, namely SPICE, may prove to be most intuitive to questions generated from information practice:

- *Setting*
- *Perspective*

- *Intervention*
- *Comparison*
- *Evaluation.*

In this case the population component is subdivided into the setting (or context of the service) and the perspective (e.g. user, manager, carer, information professional) which combine to moderate the impact of any intervention. So, from the perspective of an undergraduate student (PERSPECTIVE) in a university library (SETTING), is provision of a short term loan collection (INTERVENTION) more effective than a general collection (COMPARISON) in terms of the percentage availability of recommended texts (EVALUATION)?

Of course the actual model you use to articulate an information need is, to a certain extent, secondary. More important is that you use a systematic method to elicit an 'insight into the mental activities of participants engaged in problem solving or decision making' (White, 1998).

Question types

The Evidence Based Medicine Working Group (1992) devised a typology of question types to include diagnosis, ætiology, prognosis and therapy. A typology for evidence-based information practice, together with examples, might include the following:

- *Information needs* – What are users' preferences with regard to electronic journals, print journals or a hybrid model of provision?
- *Information behaviour* – Do students who use electronic library resources have better or worse outcomes (academic results, workload, use of time, user satisfaction, drop out rates) than those who use physical libraries?
- *Causation* – What conditions promote successful learning in a hospital setting?
- *Information delivery* – What are the implications of electronic journals and other resources for co-operative collection development and interlibrary lending?
- *Use studies* – Does desk-top access to databases and full-text affect library organization, personnel and work flow patterns in libraries?
- *Interventions to promote uptake and utilization of resources* – Do students who have been taught information skills perform better academically (as measured by exams and other assessment) than those who haven't? Are they more or less likely to continue to further study?
- *Information retrieval* – What are the relevant advantages of precision and recall when using an internet search engine?

- *Information presentation* – What is the optimal page width of a web page and how much of the page will a reader be likely to read before deciding whether or not it is useful to them?
- *Information impact* – Does consumer health information have a positive impact on prevention of disease?
- *Cost-effectiveness/cost-benefit* – Can we prove that qualified librarians are more effective than paraprofessional staff at answering reference questions and performing literature searches?
- *Service organization and management* – How can we identify and measure competencies required for library roles to ensure appropriate grading of new posts?

Practitioners' questions versus researchers' questions

Many of the above questions were identified when practitioners were asked: 'What are the most important research questions facing the profession?' (Eldredge, 2001). Questions generated by practitioners rarely match those addressed by researchers (Booth, 2001a). A comparison of funding priorities of commissioners of research with those of practitioners concluded: 'Why are practitioners' research priorities so much more concrete than those of the funding bodies?' (Farmer and Williams, 1999). This observation was subsequently echoed in a Delphi study on research priorities which recorded the practitioner's 'focus on answering practical questions' (Dwyer, 1999).

   Of course there are dangers in a practitioner-led approach; as librarians are poor at utilising and exploiting their own professional literature they may prioritize questions already answered. Enthusiasms for new technologies could result in more 'glamorous' questions rather than those that are more longstanding and fundamental to our practice. Finally, themes afforded a high profile through funding programmes or through completion of research may occupy a disproportionately significant place in their consciousness (Booth, 2001a).

Matching the research design to the question

Evidence-based healthcare has moved beyond energy-consuming arguments on the inherent superiority of any particular study design (Sackett and Wennberg, 1997): 'Our thesis is short: the *question* being asked determines the appropriate research architecture, strategy, and tactics to be used – not tradition, authority, experts, paradigms, or schools of thought'. Booth (2001b) illustrates this by examining three questions identified by the Medical Library Association and attempting to match them to an appropriate research design.

Conclusion

Formulating the question is fundamental to all evidence-based practice. Evidence-based information practice carries an inherent advantage in that question formulating and answering are key competencies for our profession. Our practice may thus be informed both by research within information science and by wider developments in evidence-based practice. Much remains to be done in constructing a comprehensive typology of question types and identifying priorities for primary research and secondary literature review. Once we have established the extent to which questions generated by information practitioners have already been addressed, the way will be set for tackling the outstanding issues that command our attention.

References

Barrie, A. R. and Ward, A. M. (1997) Questioning Behaviour in General Practice: a pragmatic study, *BMJ*, **315**, 1512–15.

Booth, A. (2001a) Research Column: turning research priorities into answerable questions, *Health Information and Libraries Journal*, **18** (2),130–2.

Booth, A. (2001b) Research Column: asking questions, knowing answers, *Health Information and Libraries Journal*, **18** (4), 238–40.

Booth, A. (2000) Formulating the Question. In Booth, A. and Walton, G. (eds), *Managing Knowledge in Health Services*, London, Library Association Publishing, 197–206.

Dwyer, M. A. (1999) Delphi Survey of Research Priorities and Identified Areas for Collaborative Research in Health Sector Library and Information Services UK, *Health Libraries Review*, **16** (3), 174–91.

Eldredge, J. D. (2000a) Evidence-Based Librarianship: an overview, *Bulletin of the Medical Library Association*, **88** (4), 289–302.

Eldredge, J. (2000b) Evidence-Based Librarianship: formulating EBL questions, *Bibliotheca Medica Canadiana*, **22** (2), 74–7.

Eldredge, J. (submitted on behalf of the Evidence-Based Librarianship Implementation Committee) (2001) The Most Relevant and Answerable Research Questions Facing the Practice of Health Sciences Librarianship, *Hypothesis*, **15** (1), 3–5, 9–17, http://168.17.205.219/mla/research/Hypo2001v.15%20no.1.pdf.

Eldredge, J. (2002) Evidence-Based Librarianship: levels of evidence, *Hypothesis*, **16** (3), 10–14.

Ellis, P., Green, M. and Kernan, W. (2000) An Evidence-based Medicine Curriculum for Medical Students: the art of asking focused clinical questions, *Academic Medicine*, **75** (5), 528.

Ely, J. W., Osheroff, J. A., Ebell, M. H., Bergus, G. R., Levy, B. T., Chambliss, M. L. and Evans, E. R. (1999) Analysis of Questions Asked by Family Doctors Regarding Patient Care, *BMJ*, **319** (7206), 358–61.

Ely, J. W., Osheroff, J. A., Gorman, P. N., Ebell, M. H., Chambliss, M. L., Pifer, E. A. and Stavri, P. Z. (2000) A Taxonomy of Generic Clinical Questions: classification study, *BMJ*, **321** (7258), 429–32.

Ely, J. W., Osheroff, J. A., Ebell, M. H., Chambliss, M. L., Vinson, D. C., Stevermer, J. J., Pifer, E. A. (2002) Obstacles to Answering Doctors' Questions About Patient Care with Evidence: qualitative study, *BMJ*, **324** (7339), 710.

Evidence Based Medicine Working Group (1992) Evidence Based Medicine: a new approach to teaching the practice of medicine, *JAMA*, **268** (17), 2420–5.

Farmer, J. and Williams, D. (1999) Are Research Priorities: a priority for research?, *Health Libraries Review*, **16** (1), 56–60.

Flemming, K. A. (1998) Asking Answerable Questions, *Evidence-Based Nursing*, **1** (2), 36–7.

Geddes, J. (1999) Asking Structured and Focused Clinical Questions: essential first steps of evidence-based practice, *Evidence Based Mental Health*, **2** (2), 35–6.

Gorman, P. N. and Helfand, M. (1995) Information Seeking in Primary Care: how physicians choose which clinical questions to pursue and which to leave unanswered, *Medical Decision Making*, **15** (2), 113–9.

Oxman, A. D. and Guyatt, G. H. (1988) Guidelines for Reading Literature Reviews, *Canadian Medical Association Journal*, **138** (8), 697–703.

Powell, R. R. (1999) Recent Trends in Research: a methodological essay, *Library and Information Science Research*, **21** (1), 91–119.

Richardson, W.S., Wilson, M.C., Nishikawa, J. and Hayward, R. S. (1995) The Well-built Clinical Question: a key to evidence based decisions, *ACP Journal Club*, **123** (3), A12–A13.

Richardson, W. S. and Wilson, M. C. (1997) On Questions, Background and Foreground, *Evidence Based Healthcare Newsletter*, **17**, 8–9.

Richardson, W. S. (1998) Ask and Ye Shall Retrieve, *Evidence Based Medicine*, **3**, 100–1.

Rosenberg, W. and Donald, A. (1995) Evidence Based Medicine: an approach to clinical problem solving, *British Medical Journal*, **310** (6987), 1122–6.

Sackett, D. L. and Wennberg, J. E. (1997) Choosing the Best Research Design for Each Question, *BMJ*, **315**, 1636.

Sackett, D. L. and Rosenberg, W. M. C. (1995) On the Need for Evidence Based Medicine, *Journal of Public Health Medicine*, **17** (3), 330–4.

Snowball, R. (1997) Using the Clinical Question to Teach Search Strategy: fostering transferable conceptual skills in user education by active learning, *Health Libraries Review*, **14** (3), 167–72.

Swinglehurst, D. A. and Pierce, M. (2000) Questioning in General Practice – a tool for change, *British Journal of General Practice*, **50** (458), 747–50.

Villanueva, E. V., Burrows, E. A., Fennessy, P. A., Rajendran, M. and Anderson, J. N. (2001) Improving Question Formulation for Use in Evidence Appraisal in a Tertiary Care Setting: a randomised controlled trial [ISRCTN66375463], *BMC Medical Informatics and Decision Making*, **1** (1), 4.

White, M. D. (1998) Questions in Reference Interviews, *Journal of Documentation*, **54** (4), 443–65.

Wildridge, V. and Bell, L. (2002) Brief Communication. How CLIP became ECLIPSE: a mnemonic to assist in searching for health policy/management information, *Health Information and Libraries Journal*, **19** (2), 113–15.

7

Identifying sources of evidence

Alison Winning

Introduction

Evidence-based information practice is no different from any other evidence-based speciality in requiring a thorough search of information resources relevant to the topic in question, in order to identify evidence and, subsequently, put it into practice. The evidence base can be identified through published and unpublished literature with the main sources taking the form of bibliographic databases and journals.

As a profession, librarians spend a large proportion of their time assisting users to identify appropriate information resources for their query. Subsequently they also devote a great deal of effort to training users in search methods and utilization of the resources to their greatest effect. How much time, and to what effect, do information professionals spend developing their skills in interrogating resources relevant to their own profession?

The multifaceted nature of librarianship and information science (LIS) means that the evidence base is contained in multiple and varied information resources. However, only a handful of papers address methods for accessing and interrogating the library literature (Crumley and Koufogoiannakis, 2002; Eldredge, 2000; McKibbon et al., 1999; Yerkey and Glogowski, 1990). It remains unclear which sources are most useful in this quest and what their relative advantages and disadvantages might be. This lack of clarity may compound the fact that information professionals are not enthusiastic consumers of LIS research (see Chapter 5) (Booth, 2000; Turner, 2002).

Scenario

You are a children's librarian within a public library service and have been seconded for two days a week to work on a project investigating the use of ICT in reader development. The library service wishes to develop an interactive web-based package to support the reading development of children. The package will also support writing and computer literacy skills. One of your first tasks is to complete the project initiation document.

Scenarios such as the one above will be familiar to many of you. As the librarian in the scenario you would perhaps want to consult the literature to identify similar initiatives to inform the development of your project and the writing of your document. To assist those of you seeking to develop an evidence-based approach to your practice this chapter identifies and presents a summary of information resources pertinent to evidence-based information practice.

	Define the problem
✓	Find evidence
	Appraise evidence
	Apply results of appraisal
	Evaluate change
	Redefine problem

Figure 7.1   The evidence-based practice process

The facets of librarianship

Figure 7.2 illustrates the wide-ranging subject specialisms in librarianship. Derived from a modified list of electronic journals available from the University of Wales at Aberystwyth (2002), it demonstrates the diffuse nature of the evidence base. The complexity of the matrix is further accentuated by the diverse skills and tasks listed in Figure 7.3.

This categorization, although not comprehensive, allows us to realize the breadth of LIS professional roles and hence the difficulties surrounding identification of the evidence base to support practice. As will be demonstrated later (Chapters 13–19) the many facets of the LIS role can be placed within a framework of six domains (Crumley and Koufogiannakis, 2002) as highlighted in Figure 7.4. These domains are designed to assist in focusing the question and managing the search for information.

Academic libraries	Public libraries
Children's librarianship	Rare book librarianship
Health libraries	Rural libraries
Law libraries	School libraries
Media librarianship	Solo librarians
Museums	Special libraries
National libraries	Subject librarianship

Figure 7.2   Subject specialisms

Acquisitions	Electronic information resources	Knowledge management
Archives	Electronic publishing	Learning technology
Bibliography	Health and safety	Legal issues
Business information	Hybrid library	Library finance
Cataloguing	Information and communications technology	Library and information staff
Classification and indexing	Information management	Library management
Collection management	Information policy	Library software and technology
Conservation and preservation	Information resources reviews	Management – general
Copyright	Information retrieval	Marketing
Current awareness	Information skills	Professional development
Distance learners	Information systems	Serials
Education	Interlending	Technical issues

Figure 7.3   Aspects of role

Reference/enquiries	Education
Collections	Management
Information access and retrieval	Marketing/promotion

Figure 7.4   Six domains of librarianship (Crumley and Koufogiannakis, 2002)

These six domains clearly require exploration outside the usual and traditional library databases (such as *Library and Information Science Abstracts* (*LISA*)). For example, relevant information may be retrieved from education and management oriented databases. Management and education literature may be of value even when not specifically focused on an LIS situation. Such skills are transferable and we may learn valuable lessons from management styles that can be implemented within an LIS setting. Searching certain subject-specific databases within these and other specialities, such as marketing and promotion, will yield useful related material that would otherwise be missed.

Scenarios and domains

Once you have targeted your question to a specific domain, it is important to iden-tify potential sources of information for that domain. Table 7.1 highlights possible resources you may wish to consult in relation to the six domains. Table 7.1 is adapt-ed from Crumley's previously published classification of library questions (Crumley and Koufogiannakis, 2002).

Table 7.1   Domain resources

Domain	Resource

• Reference/enquiries
• Collections
• Information access and retrieval
	• Traditional LIS databases:
	  Library and Information Science Abstracts (LISA)
	  Library Literature
	  Information Science and Technology Abstracts (ISTA)
	Plus:
	• Subject relevant databases, e.g. PsycInfo

• Education	• Traditional LIS databases:
	  Library and Information Science Abstracts (LISA)
	  Library Literature
	  Information Science and Technology Abstracts (ISTA)
	Plus:
	• Domain relevant database e.g. ERIC
	Plus:
	• Subject relevant databases e.g. BIOSIS

• Management	• Traditional LIS databases:
	  Library and Information Science Abstracts (LISA)
	  Library Literature
	  Information Science and Technology Abstracts (ISTA)
	Plus:
	• Domain relevant database e.g. Emerald
	Plus:
	• Subject relevant databases e.g. INSPEC

• Marketing/promotion	• Traditional LIS databases:
	  Library and Information Science Abstracts (LISA)
	  Library Literature
	  Information Science and Technology Abstracts (ISTA)
	Plus:
	• Domain relevant database e.g. Emerald
	Plus:
	• Subject relevant databases e.g. Web of Science

The children's library scenario outlined earlier in this chapter is primarily located within the education domain. A search of LIS databases may retrieve details of work performed in libraries around the use of ICT in the development of literacy skills. Investigation of ERIC or a similar education database may retrieve literature referring to the same issues within schools for teachers rather than librarians. This material is potentially of value. Of course, the children's library scenario would incorporate the other five domains of librarianship: marketing and promotion; information access and retrieval; management and collections, at various stages of the project.

Valuable literature may also exist in resources other than bibliographic databases. When planning a literature search you should therefore include the types of material shown in Figure 7.5 in your search protocol to complement your bibliographic database searches.

Electronic pre-print resources	Web resources
Electronic journals	Grey literature

Figure 7.5   Categories for inclusion in a search

Examples of these resources are given for the evidence-based practice scenarios in Table 7.2, and their content and use is explored in the following pages. The children's library scenario is represented in Table 7.2. To answer this question you would probably wish to search the LIS databases, in conjunction with a search of an education database, e.g. ERIC and also a subject-related database. In this case the Social Sciences Citation Index (SSCI) has been selected to reflect the scenario's interest in communication and educational development.

Table 7.2   Scenarios and potential information resources

Evidence-based practice question	Domain of librarianship	Potential resource
Are interactive web-based packages an effective way of developing reading, writing and computer-literacy skills in children?	Education	LISA Library Literature ISTA ERIC Soc Sci Index
Does the presence of a health information service within a public library meet the needs of the local community?	Collections	LISA Library Literature MEDLINE CINAHL AMED

(continued)

Table 7.2 (*continued*)

Evidence-based practice question	Domain of librarianship	Potential resource
What are the most effective methods for promoting library fee-based information services to geographically dispersed user groups?	Marketing	LISA Library Literature ISTA Emerald
Can a digital reference service provide as effective a service as a traditional reference service?	Reference	LISA Library Literature ISTA Emerald
How can change management methods assist in the smooth merger of two library services?	Management	LISA Library Literature ISTA Emerald

Access and ways of tackling access problems

A thorough, comprehensive search for published and unpublished literature to answer your evidence-based practice question requires that you utilize primary, secondary *and* tertiary information resources, as highlighted in Table 7.2. However, the resources you employ in your search for the evidence will ultimately be determined by your access to these resources. Database, journal and electronic journal subscriptions may be prohibitively expensive and this expense has to be justified by their potential value and likely volume of use. Hence LIS databases are commonly found in academic institutions or commercial organizations. As a profession we have poor levels of access to our own subject-specific databases.

By definition, a specialist library is likely to subscribe to subject-specific databases relevant to its users. A law library will have access to Lawtel but is unlikely to have access to subject databases of limited relevance to their users such as the *Cumulative Index to Nursing and Allied Health Literature (CINAHL)*. Professional organizations or societies frequently subscribe to databases relating to that profession or area of work. The Chartered Institute of Library and Information Professionals (CILIP), for example, offers its members a literature search service of LISA. It also provides visitors with access to other databases and a reference library.

Information resources

LIS databases

Librarianship and information science literature is harnessed by three main databases:

- *Library and Information Science Abstracts (LISA)*
- *Library Literature and Information Science Index*
- *Information Science and Technology Abstracts (ISTA).*

Library and Information Science Abstracts (LISA) www.csa.com/

LISA abstracts over 440 periodicals from more than 68 countries in more than 20 languages. *LISA* is updated every two weeks, contains literature from 1969 onwards, and held 242,000 records in December 2002. Major areas of coverage are shown in Figure 7.6.

Artificial intelligence	Information technology	Medical information
Book reviews	Internet technology	Online information retrieval
CD-ROMs	Knowledge management	Publishing and bookselling
Computer science applications	Librarianship	Records management
Information centres	Libraries and archives	Telecommunications
Information management	Library management	Technical services
Information science	Library technology	World wide web
Information storage	Library use and users	

Figure 7.6   LISA – major areas of coverage

Library Literature & Information Science Index www.hwwilson.com/

Library Literature & Information Science Index indexes articles and book reviews from more than 234 periodicals published in the US and elsewhere. Full-text coverage for selected periodicals is also included. Books, conference proceedings, theses, and pamphlets are also indexed (see Figure 7.7).

Automation	Information brokers
Cataloging	Internet software
Censorship	Library associations and conferences
Children's literature	Library and supplies
Circulation procedures	Personnel administration
Classification	Preservation of materials
Copyright legislation	Public relations
Education for librarianship	Publishing
Government	Websites

Figure 7.7   Library Literature & Information Science Index – major areas of coverage

Information Science & Technology Abstracts (ISTA) www.infotoday.com/ISTA/

ISTA, formerly *Information Science Abstracts*, contains literature concerning the science, management, and technology of information abstracted from books, journals, conference proceedings, reports, and patents (see Figure 7.8). ISTA is published nine times a year and contains over 135,000 records dating back to 1966.

abstracting and indexing	information management
classification	electronic publishing
online information retrieval	knowledge management

Figure 7.8   ISTA – major areas of coverage

Non LIS databases

MEDLINE www.nlm.nih.gov/databases/databases_medline.html

Primarily a biomedical database, MEDLINE also indexes the following major health librarianship journals: *Medical Reference Services Quarterly, Journal of the Medical Library Association* (previously *Bulletin of the Medical Library Association*), *Health Information and Libraries Journal* (previously *Health Libraries Review*).

You may wish to select relevant MeSH headings used to index LIS papers within MEDLINE from Figure 7.9 when performing a search.

Library Science	Information Science
Library Administration	Book Collecting
Library Associations	Chronology
Library Automation	Classification
Library Collection Development	Communication
Library Schools	Communications Media
Library Services	Computer Security
Library Surveys	Copying Processes
Library Technical Services	Data Collection
	Documentation
	Information Centers
Periodicals	Information Management
Databases, Bibliographic	Information Services
Bibliometrics	Information Storage and Retrieval
Education	Information Theory
Financial management	Library Science
Marketing	Medical Informatics

Figure 7.9   MeSH for LIS

CINAHL www.cinahl.com/

The Cumulative Index to Nursing and Allied Health Literature (CINAHL) database provides access to nursing and allied health literature, consumer health, biomedicine, and health sciences librarianship (see Figure 7.10). In total, more than 1200 journals are regularly indexed and there are more than 7000 records with full text. The database also provides access to books, dissertations, conference proceedings, standards of professional practice, educational software and audiovisual materials in nursing.

Health Sciences Librarians	Libraries
Librarians	Libraries, Academic
Clinical Librarianship	Libraries, Consumer Health
Librarianship	Libraries, Dental
Health Sciences Librarianship	Libraries, Electronic
Access to Information	Libraries, Health Sciences
Information Science	Libraries, Hospital
Censorship	Libraries, Medical School
Classification	Libraries, Mental Health
Communication	Libraries, Nursing
Communications Media	Libraries, Patient
Data Collection	Libraries, Pharmaceutical
Informatics	Libraries, Public
Information Centers	Libraries, School
Information Explosion	Libraries, Special
Information Management	Information Seeking Behavior
Information Needs	Information Retrieval
Information Services	Information Storage
Information Technology	Systems Development

Figure 7.10   NAHL subject headings for LIS

Emerald http://mustafa.emeraldinsight.com/

Emerald Management Reviews indexes 400 academic, trade and popular journals from 1988 onwards and contains over 150,000 articles. It was formerly known as ANBAR International Management Library. Subjects covered include: human resource management, quality, marketing, operations and finance, information management. Emerald also provides a service called *Emerald Abstracts*, a collection of abstracts from a range of journals hosted in four databases, one of which is *Current Awareness Abstracts*, this contains 23,000 abstracts from over 400 library and information management publications. Figure 7.11 shows Emerald LIS keywords.

Academic libraries	Information centres
Libraries	Databases
Information services	Librarians
Library services	

Figure 7.11   Emerald LIS keywords

EMBASE www.embase.com/

EMBASE contains around 9 million records from 1974 to present, with 450,000 citations and abstracts added annually. EMBASE harnesses current developments in biomedical and drug-related fields and contains a small body of librarianship and information science-related literature. Figure 7.12 shows EMBASE LIS keywords.

Information Centre	Library
Information Service	Library Science
Information Science	Librarian
Information Retrieval	Medical Informatics

Figure 7.12   *EMBASE LIS keywords*

ERIC (Educational Resources Information Centre) www.askeric.org/

ERIC was established in 1966 and contains more than 1 million abstracts of education-related documents and journal articles. Updated monthly, 91 entries in the thesaurus describe libraries and four entries describe information science. ERIC indexes around 30 relevant journals. Figure 7.13 shows ERIC LIS keywords.

Information Management	Library Education
Information Retrieval	Library Planning
Information Scientists	Library Research
Information Skills	Library Schools
Librarians; Libraries	Library Services

Figure 7.13   ERIC LIS keywords

INSPEC www.iee.org/Publish/INSPEC/

INSPEC primarily abstracts journals, conferences, books, reports, dissertations and articles on physics, electronics and computing from 1969 to the current day. Information science literature is also included. Figure 7.14 shows INSPEC LIS keywords.

Academic libraries	Information services
Digital libraries	Librarianship see Information science
Information science	Library automation
Libraries	Public libraries
Information retrieval	Research libraries
Information dissemination	School libraries see Academic libraries
Information centres	Special libraries
Information resource	

Figure 7.14   INSPEC LIS keywords

Electronic pre-print services

Electronic pre-print services provide a means to gain free access to the literature and thus resolve issues of availability. These services arose primarily from a science and technology base as a method of sharing knowledge quickly by removing the delay from submission to a journal, publication and then addition of the reference to a bibliographic database. A disadvantage however is that some pre-print services may not invoke an editorial or peer review process. Table 7.3 lists some electronic pre-print services.

Table 7.3   Electronic pre-print services

Service	Subject	URL
DoIS	Library and Information Science	http://dois.mimas.ac.uk/
BioMED Central	Biomedicine	www.biomedcentral.com/info/
PubMed Central	Life Sciences	www.pubmedcentral.nih.gov/

There is not yet a fully developed pre-print service within LIS. However steps are being taken to develop a service in the format of Documents in Information Science (DoIS). DoIS is a database of articles and conference proceedings published in electronic format in the area of library and information science. The database is compiled by volunteers in an effort to create a free bibliographic resource of scientific texts specializing in information science. DoIS is expanding continuously but when viewed in April 2003, 10,530 articles were available on the site, 7238 of which are downloadable.

Manchester Metropolitan University provides links to a range of pre-print services via the following URL: www.mmu.ac.uk/services/library/eresource/preprint.html.

Journals

Unfortunately none of the major LIS journals is available free in full text via the internet. Access options are limited and subscription is the only way to guarantee access to full text journals. Several research-oriented LIS journals are available in full text on the internet. The following sources of information (journal, web resource and grey literature) are extensive. The resources should be explored to reveal their full potential. Only an overview is provided within this chapter.

Index Morganagus
http://sunsite.berkeley.edu/%7Eemorgan/morganagus/index.html

Index Morganagus is a full text index of electronic journals produced by the Berkeley Digital Library SunSITE. A list of the journals indexed can be viewed on the site and simple searches can be performed. The list of journals indexed would not be regarded as mainstream and some titles are obscure. However it is a good resource from which to obtain full text copies of documents.

InformationR.net   http://informationr.net/

This site collates access to a wide variety of online full-text journals, filtering out sites that only provide the contents lists of journals and those that are not freely accessible. The *World List of Departments and Schools of Information Studies, Information Management, Information Systems, etc.* can be accessed here as can *Information Research: an international electronic journal.*

BUBL www.bubl.ac.uk

BUBL has a collection of links to current library and information science journals and newsletters accessible on the site at www.bubl.ac.uk/journals/

The journals are arranged by title and subject and are a mixture of internet journals and links to the tables of contents or abstracts of other journals. BUBL also indexes several subscription-based electronic journal providers providing a useful reference tool for access to relevant LIS journals.

Web resources

BUBL LINK www.bubl.ac.uk

BUBL LINK is a catalogue of selected internet resources covering a wide range of academic subject areas but is renowned as a subject gateway for library and information science. All items included within BUBL are selected, evaluated, catalogued and described. Relevant LIS subjects include those shown in Figure 7.15.

Librarians	Library management
Library and information science education	Library organizations
Library and information science news	Library resource sharing
Library and information science research	Library services
Library and information studies uk	Library suppliers
Library and information studies worldwide	Library systems
Library catalogues in england	Library technology
Library catalogues in ireland	Library user education
Library catalogues in london	Information management in business
Library catalogues in scotland	Information management in education
Library catalogues in wales	Information management in health
Library catalogues worldwide	Information management in libraries
Library history and culture	Information retrieval
Library information networks	Information society
Library internet use	Information technology

Figure 7.15 LIS subjects indexed within BUBL

BUBL primarily harnesses resources useful to the practising librarian; however it does contain several research-oriented resources. The Library and Information Science Research section of BUBL contains links to research institutions, free online journals and databases which may contain relevant LIS research literature. There is also a search facility within BUBL which conducts searches across all categories to reduce the browsing required.

The Researching Librarian www2.msstate.edu/~bea11/trl/

The Researching Librarian aims to support librarians of any specialism who may be exploring aspects of their practice through research, by providing links to the resources shown in Figure 7.16.

The Researching Librarian is US-based but does contain some international material. The site can be browsed or searched and is a valuable starting point for LIS professionals wishing to examine their practice.

Awareness	Journals	Tools
Databases	Proceedings	
Funding	Statistics	

Figure 7.16 Resources listed in *The Researching Librarian*

Infotrieve www.infotrieve.com/

Infotrieve is a research and delivery portal which aims to be a one-stop shop for such resources as Article Finder, Infotrieve's free-to-search proprietary bibliographic database containing over 22 million citations and over 10 million abstracts from more than 35,000 journals from fields such as medicine, biotechnology, science, engineering, and law. Infotrieve has an electronic journal collection from which articles can be ordered on a fee basis. A table of contents service is available as a current awareness tool. Medline, the biomedical database, can also be searched from this site using the Infotrieve interface.

Library Reference Center www.epnet.com/freeres.asp

Provided free by EBSCO, this database indexes and provides abstracts from over 30 important library trade magazines and journals, including *School Library Journal*, *American Libraries* and *THE Journal*. Literature contained within this database may not be harnessed by the larger bibliographic databases owing to the trade nature of many of the journals indexed within the Library Reference Center.

Internet Library for Librarians www.itcompany.com/inforetriever/index.html

Like BUBL, this site is primarily aimed at assisting librarians with the practical aspects of their roles rather than providing direct access to literature. However, the site does contain links to a wide range of LIS journals some of which are full text.

Grey literature

Within librarianship and information science the majority of the grey literature is produced by academic departments and government organizations. The following selection of resources is by no means comprehensive but may provide a solid starting point in the identification of grey literature when combined with LISA, BUBL and *The Researching Librarian*.

Non subscription sources

British Library Research and Innovation Centre Reports www.lic.gov.uk/publications/ricarchive/index.html

British Library Research and Innovation Centre Reports from 1997 to 1999 cover a whole host of librarianship issues and subject specialities. Titles include: *Promoting Reading to Adults in UK Public Libraries*; *Communicating Effectively in the Networked Library*; *Quality Management and Benchmarking in the Information Sector: results of recent research*. A brief abstract of the report is available on the site. Full-text reports can be ordered via the British Thesis Service at the British Library Document Supply Centre, Boston Spa (www.bl.uk/services/document.html).

Library and Information Commission (LIC)
www.lic.gov.uk/publications/researchreports/index.html

LIC Research Reports from 1999 and 2000 can be accessed via this URL. Abstracts and, in some cases, executive summaries are available from this page along with appropriate ordering processes. Titles include: *The Value and Impact of Homework Clubs in Public Libraries*; *The Really Effective College Library*; *Library Services for Visually Impaired People: a manual of best practice*.

Museums, Libraries and Archives Council
www.mla.gov.uk/information/research/00resrch.asp

Research reports published by The Museums, Libraries and Archives Council (then Resource) during 2001 and 2002 can be located at the above URL. Abstracts and summaries or full text are available for certain reports. Titles include: *Impact of School Library Services on Achievement and Learning*; *The Value and Impact of Virtual Outreach Services* and *Harmonising the Process of Procuring Library Management Systems: a feasibility study*.

ZETOC http://zetoc.mimas.ac.uk

ZETOC provides access to the British Library's Electronic *Table of Contents*. The database contains details of 20,000 current journals and 16,000 conference proceedings published per year. With around 20 million journal and conference records, the database covers a wide range of subjects including science, technology, medicine, engineering, business, law, finance and the humanities. Around 100,000 of the journals included are available for download. This service is free to JISC-funded further and higher education institutions in the UK and to the NHS.

Research institutions such as the Centre for Research in Library and Information Management (CERLIM) at Manchester Metropolitan University provide details of their research project publications on their relevant websites. Sites you may wish to visit when tracking down grey literature include:

- Centre for Research in Library and Information Management, Manchester Metropolitan University
  www.cerlim.ac.uk/pubs/publications.html
- Loughborough University, Department of Information Science
  www.lboro.ac.uk/departments/dils/research/disres.html

- University of Sheffield, Department of Information Studies
  www.shef.ac.uk/uni/academic/I-M/is/publications/index.html.

Individual conference websites are also valuable resources. You may wish to compile your own resource list, examples include:

- International Federation of Library Associations and Institutions (IFLA) provide access to their proceedings via the Internet, www.ifla.org
- CILIP, Umbrella, www.umbrella2003.org.uk/
- Online Information, www.imark.co.uk/ol03/

Subscription sources

SIGLE (System for Information on Grey Literature in Europe) www.kb.nl/infolev/eagle/frames.htm

SIGLE is a bibliographic database covering European grey literature in the fields of pure and applied natural sciences and technology, economics, social sciences, and humanities.

British National Bibliography for Report Literature www.bl.uk/services/bibliographic/natbib.html#bnbrl

References of reports, technical papers and dissertations produced by non-commercial publishers such as research institutions, private and public sector organizations, charities, and action groups which are new to the British Library and available for document supply are published in the British National Bibliography for Report Literature.

IRWI: Information Research Watch International www.csa.com

IRWI contains over 8500 records from more than 70 countries, providing references to new, ongoing and completed research in information and library science and related fields from around the world. The database gives access to information about current research prior to its appearance in the published literature, with details of researcher affiliation, research funding and funding bodies, duration, status of project and researcher contact information.

ProQuest Digital Dissertations wwwlib.umi.com/dissertations/

Digital Dissertations contains information about doctoral dissertations and masters theses from over 1000 North American and European universities and contains more than 1.6 million records. Pre-1980, the database contains citations only; post-1980, abstracts are included. *Dissertation Abstracts* is a subscription service although the most recent two years are freely available for searching.

Current awareness

Zetoc Alert http://zetoc.mimas.ac.uk/index.html

Zetoc Alert is a current awareness service which notifies you of the table of contents from particular journals you have identified, or allows you to receive details of articles which match a pre-defined search criterion such as an author's name or keywords from the title. Daily alerts are sent via e-mail as new data is added to the Zetoc database.

Conclusion

This chapter demonstrates the diverse nature of the library and information science profession and highlights its fragmented evidence base. Strategies for overcoming these challenges have been presented through utilization of the domains of librarianship and through the importance of compiling a search protocol or potential list of resources from the categories shown in Figure 7.17.

This chapter is not exhaustive, instead it is intended that you will build upon these synopses of selected resources to create a toolkit to support your own evidence-based information practice. Used in conjunction with later chapters exploring effective searching of LIS information resources, this chapter provides a rounded introduction to the location, access, structure and interrogation of the LIS evidence base.

Traditional LIS databases	Electronic journals
Domain-relevant databases	Web resources
Subject-specific databases	Grey literature
Electronic pre-print services	

Figure 7.17 Categories of material to be included in a search protocol

References

Booth, A. (2000) 'Librarian Heal Thyself': evidence based librarianship, useful, practicable, desirable? *Proceedings of the 8th International Congress on Medical Librarianship, July 2–5, London, UK*, www.icml.org/tuesday/themes/booth.htm.

Crumley, E. and Koufogiannakis D. (2002) Developing Evidence Based Librarianship: practical steps for implementation, *Health Information and Libraries Journal*, **19** (2), 61–70.

Eldredge, J. D. (2000) Evidence Based Librarianship: searching for the needed EBL evidence, *Medical Reference Services Quarterly*, **19** (3), 1–18.

McKibbon, A., Eddy, A. and Marks, S. (1999) *PDQ Evidence Based Practice and Principles*, Hamilton, BC, Decker Inc.

Turner, K. J. (2002) Do Information Professionals Use Research Published in LIS Journals? *Proceedings of 68th IFLA General Conference and Council 18–24 August*, Glasgow, Scotland, www.ifla.org/IV/ifla68/papers/009-118e.pdf.

University of Wales Aberystwyth Thomas Parry Library (2002) *Topic Listing of Electronic Journals in Librarianship and Information Science*, Aberystwyth, University of Wales, www.inf.aber.ac.uk/tpl/ejlib/topic.asp.

Yerkey, N. and Glogowski, M. (1990) Scatter of Library and Information Science Topics Among Bibliographic Databases, *Journal of the American Society for Information Science*, **41** (4), 245–53.

8

Searching the library and information science literature

Catherine Beverley

Introduction

Information professionals are specialists in conducting mediated literature searches (Eldredge, 2000). However, very few of us are skilled at retrieving literature that addresses questions in our own field. This is not a criticism, merely an observation of a profession whose foremost concern is to address the needs of its users.

This chapter provides practical advice on searching the library and information science (LIS) literature. It starts by considering the challenges faced when searching the LIS literature. This is followed by a consideration of how generic principles of information retrieval can be applied to the LIS electronic bibliographic databases. The chapter concludes by examining specific approaches to enhance your searching of the LIS literature.

	Define the problem
✓	Find evidence
	Appraise evidence
	Apply results of appraisal
	Evaluate change
	Redefine problem

Figure 8.1 The evidence-based practice process

Scenario

You are working in a small academic library and have recently received a letter from a subscription agent inviting you to transfer your journal subscriptions over from print to electronic. Instead of conducting yet another user survey, you decide it would be useful to undertake a literature review to inform your decision.

The challenges of searching the library and information science literature

Diffuse literature

Considering that the organization and retrieval of knowledge are fundamental to our professional practice, it is a cause of great concern that librarians do not possess a single source for accessing LIS literature (Atkins and Louw, 2000; Booth, 2000a). The databases that do exist are generally not as extensive or comprehensive as those available in other fields. Furthermore, the volume of literature in the field is growing at an exponential rate (Atkins and Louw, 2000). In order to conduct a comprehensive search, the range of sources we have to search is perhaps the widest of all professions. Chapter 7 introduced the major information sources, *Library and Information Science Abstracts* (*LISA*), being the best known within the library field. That chapter also signalled that questions to be addressed may necessitate searching databases in other disciplines. Examples include the computing literature which is partially covered by INSPEC, the management and marketing literature (e.g. *Emerald Reviews*), the education literature (e.g. Educational Resources Information Center (ERIC) and *British Education Index*), as well as various general social science databases (e.g. *Social Sciences Citation Index*, *ASSIA, British Humanities Index*). Additional resources may need to be searched; for example, MEDLINE, CINAHL and Health Management Information Consortium (HMIC) for health librarianship. In terms of our scenario concerning electronic journals, we would need to search as a minimum, LISA, INSPEC and Social Sciences Citation Index. From this brief overview, it is easy to see why some have argued that systematic literature searching of the LIS literature may be prohibitive for any one institution (Booth, 2000b).

This chapter focuses on electronic bibliographic databases. Other resources, such as general internet search engines and library catalogues (e.g. COPAC), are also important in the LIS field. Conference proceedings, magazine articles and self-published reports on the internet should not be overlooked (Atkins and Louw, 2000).

Multiple study designs

LIS research typically utilizes designs of limited applicability, such as the user survey (Booth, 1998). The most appropriate study design will vary according to the topic under investigation (Galliers, 1992; Booth, 2000a). For example, if you are interested in end-user searching compared with mediated searching, comparative studies, i.e. with at least one end-user group and one mediated group, are the most appropriate study design (Booth, 1998). The 'hierarchy of evidence' developed in the medical field, which places systematic reviews and randomized controlled trials (RCTs) at the top and expert opinion towards the bottom (Phillips et al., 1998), is likely to be of practical use only for effectiveness-type questions. Instead, a more 'forgiving' pragmatic 'design map' must be adopted, based on seeking the best available data rather than only the highest quality studies (Booth, 2000b). Atkins and Louw (2000) even suggest that several 'hierarchies of evidence' may need to be developed, to rank research and weight its results on the basis of study design (amongst other things). Returning to our electronic journals scenario, the most likely study designs employed would be user surveys and/or case reports. This has implications for searching: methodological search filters, commonly used by health librarians to retrieve literature of the highest quality (i.e. systematic reviews and RCTs) are largely redundant. In addition, very few LIS databases readily allow you to limit results either by publication or by study type.

Unhelpful abstracts

There is a marked difference between the structure of abstracts in the literature of the health sciences and in that of the information profession. Over recent years there has been an increasing drive to improve the quality of abstracts in healthcare (Haynes et al., 1990; Booth and O'Rourke, 1997). In contrast, the vast majority of LIS abstracts are unstructured and are poor at describing the study design and methodology (Booth, 1998). The implications of this are that it is difficult to index the records (see below) and the searcher has to 'second guess' the terms authors may have used. Attempts have been made to address this: in 2002, the Evidence Based Librarianship Implementation Committee Research Results Dissemination Task Force recommended that a structured abstract comprising, as a minimum, Objective, Methods, Results and Discussion, be required for all articles submitted to the major health library journals. It also required that a more detailed structured abstract be required for specific research designs such as effectiveness studies, reviews, qualitative studies, program descriptions, and case reports (Bayley et al., 2002).

Problematic indexing

As with many other databases the indexing on many LIS databases is problematic (Booth, 2000b). Although some, such as *LISA*, employ established thesauri, others, such as *Social Sciences Citation Index* (Web of Science), do not. This forces you to rely on free-text searching, yet the limitations of using this approach are well recognized and are documented later in this chapter. Even databases that use a thesaurus lack an entrenched and commonly agreed vocabulary of terms (Atkins and Louw, 2000). In *LISA*, for example, there is no thesaurus term for 'information needs analysis', even though this is among the most commonly undertaken type of study in information management.

Limited coverage of publication types

Many evidence-based disciplines seek to retrieve preferred publication types or study designs in order to address specific questions. This approach is commonly used to retain robust study types whilst excluding lower forms of evidence such as letters, editorials, etc. For example, therapy questions within medicine seek evidence in the form of clinical trials. Although the major electronic bibliographic databases allow searching of many fields (refer to Figure 8.2 for the search fields in *SilverPlatter LISA*), it is often not possible to restrict searches to specific publication types.

AB	Abstract	**LA**	**Language**
AN	**Accession Number**	PD	Project Duration *
AU	Author	**PY**	**Publication Year**
BDS	**Reed Business Information**	QL	Qualifications *
	Database Subset	RF	References *
BL	BLDSC Shelf Mark	RW	Research Workers *
CP	Copyright	SO	Source
CT	Contact Person *	TI	Title
CW	**Country of Research Work ***		
DE	Descriptors		
FS	Funding Source *	NB Highlighted fields are limit fields; fields
IS	ISSN	with an asterisk (*) are available in the
JNI	Journal Name Index	CRLIS database only

Figure 8.2   Search fields in *SilverPlatter LISA*

Applying generic search principles to library and information science databases

Although this chapter does not intend to describe generic search principles in detail because this topic is covered elsewhere (Lowe and Barrett, 1994; Greenhalgh, 1997;

Glanville et al., 1998; Falzon, 2000; Hunt et al., 2000), we shall briefly consider how you might apply these principles to the LIS databases.

Focusing the question

The importance of this has already been covered in Chapter 6. The SPICE framework is clearly of value for the large proportion of LIS questions that involve an intervention (e.g. current awareness service, catalogue, reference management software, interlibrary loans software, etc.). Figure 8.3 demonstrates how the SPICE framework can be applied to our electronic journals scenario. Even when the SPICE framework is not feasible, you will no doubt recognize the importance of breaking down your question into a series of concepts in order to facilitate database searching.

Setting/Perspective	Academic libraries
Intervention	Electronic journals
Comparison	Print journals
Evaluation	The views of users, the views of librarians, issues concerning accessibility, cost issues, etc.

Figure 8.3   Applying the SPICE framework to our electronic journals question

Free-text searching

In common with other databases, you can perform free-text searching in the LIS databases. This approach uses text words found in fields such as the title and abstract (Marshall, 1997). The drawbacks of this approach are well documented (e.g. Falzon, 2000), such as the problems associated with different spellings (e.g. organisation or organization) and different terminology (e.g. information professional, information manager, information specialist, librarian, knowledge manager, etc.). Fortunately, databases such as LISA (SilverPlatter) offer features such as truncation ('*') and wildcard ('?') symbols. Searching on librar*, for example, retrieves records containing the words, library, libraries, librarian, librarians, etc. For the electronic journals scenario, if you did not truncate 'e-journal', for example, you would fail to retrieve papers which contained the term 'e-journals'.

Thesaurus searching

In order to be comprehensive, a search should comprise a combination of free-text and thesaurus terms. Some, although not all, LIS databases provide a thesaurus. In LISA (SilverPlatter) the thesaurus allows you to select subject terms from a hierarchical vocabulary. Returning to the example of electronic journals provided in Figure 8.2, let us consider the issue of access. If you type in the word 'access' in the thesaurus in LISA (SilverPlatter) this results in an alphabetical list of terms, the most relevant of which is 'access to information' which is used for 'accessibility of information', 'availability of information' and 'freedom of information'. A number of related terms are also suggested, including 'access to materials', 'availability of documents', and 'universal availability of publications', all of which are worth searching in their own right. If, for example, you constructed a search strategy without using the thesaurus term 'electronic periodicals' in LISA, you would exclude a large number of relevant references which were about electronic journals, but which did not have the terms 'electronic journal', 'electronic journals', 'ejournal', 'ejournals', 'e-journal' or 'e-journals' in the title or abstract fields.

Operators

The standard Boolean operators (AND, OR and NOT) can be used in the major LIS databases; OR being used to combine terms within the same concept together (e.g. electronic journal* OR ejournal* OR e-journal*), AND to combine different concepts together (e.g. electronic journal* AND access*), and NOT to exclude irrelevant terms (e.g. NOT letter*). It is also possible to use proximity and adjacency operators in many databases. In LISA (SilverPlatter), for example, WITH can be used to retrieve records that contain two or more words within the same field, whereas NEAR retrieves records that contain those words within the same sentence. Finally, IN is used to search particular fields; for example, e-journal* IN TI will retrieve all records where the words e-journal or e-journals appear in the title of the record.

Limits

The most common way of limiting a search is by publication year (PY) and/or language (LA). Databases, such as LISA, enable you to restrict searches in this way via the use of limit fields. However, as noted earlier, the restriction to specific publication and/or study types has been shown to be more effective. INSPEC (SilverPlatter), for example, allows you to limit searches by record type (RT), while the *Citation Indexes* (*Web of Science*) offer the option of limiting to various document types, including 'article' and 'review'.

Specific approaches to searching the library and information science literature

The challenges of searching the literature and the difficulties in applying the generic search principles to databases in this field mean that additional approaches are required to searching the LIS literature. Searching is often more art than science

(Creighton University Health Sciences Library and Learning Resources Center, 2000). The techniques shown in Table 8.1 may assist you in searching the LIS literature. However, these are not exhaustive and approaches are not mutually exclusive; for a comprehensive search, multiple approaches will be required.

Table 8.1 The strengths and weaknesses of different search approaches

Approach	Strengths	Weaknesses
Traditional database searching	This is the most familiar approach to librarians. LIS databases have a range of tools available (e.g. truncation, thesauri, etc.) to assist in the search process.	There is a danger that the search may retrieve either too many or too few references. Not all LIS questions lend themselves to traditional database searching (e.g., it may be difficult to think of alternative terminology, etc.).
Use of search filters	Specific combinations of search terms filter out the lower quality evidence (e.g. editorials, letters, commentaries, etc.). This approach has been shown to be effective in other fields (e.g. the health sciences).	The right balance between specificity and sensitivity must be struck: relevant research studies must not be excluded, but the retriever does not want to trawl through a large set of search results. The lower quality evidence that is filtered out (e.g. editorials, letters, commentaries) may prove useful in providing background information to a topic area.
Citation pearl growing	Extremely useful approach if the searcher is experiencing difficulties identifying synonyms.	The technique requires the identification of an initial key reference. There is an underlying assumption that articles on the same topic are assigned the same descriptors; however, this is not always the case.
Snowball searching	Extremely useful approach if the searcher is experiencing difficulties identifying synonyms.	The technique requires the identification of an initial key reference. This approach may give rise to a biased set of references. It can often be difficult to determine the relevance of an article based on the bibliographic details alone.

(continued)

Table 8.1 (continued)

Approach	Strengths	Weaknesses
Other forms of citation searching	Citation searching can prove a useful starting point, particularly if the topic does not initially lend itself to traditional database searching.	This approach requires the identification of one or more key references. Citation searching may create a biased sample of references; e.g. authors are more likely to cite other authors that support their argument. Only a limited number of relevant journals are indexed on the Citation Indexes, and, therefore, citation searching may not be possible. The approach is not appropriate for very recent references. It is often difficult to know how many iterations of citation searches are necessary; usually, two iterations are sufficient.
Author searching	Author searching can prove a useful starting point, particularly if the topic does not initially lend itself to traditional database searching.	The chances of being able to conduct an author search are limited, particularly as there are very few prolific LIS researchers. Author searching will create a biased sample of references, all written by the same author.
Hand-searching	A manual page-by-page search of important journals minimizes the effects of lack of coverage or inconsistent indexing.	Handsearching is very time-consuming. This approach is really applicable only if a core set of journals can be identified.

Search styles

Many librarians, particularly in the health field, are familiar with selecting different search styles according to the topic under investigation. There are four major styles, all of which may be applied to searching the LIS literature (Harter and Peters, 1985; Hawkins and Wagers, 1990). These are detailed in Box 8.1. The 'building blocks' approach lends itself particularly well to the electronic journals scenario.

> ## Box 8.1   Search styles
>
> *Brief search*
> Two or more concepts are combined with a Boolean operator. For example:
>
> Term A (electronic journals) AND Term B (academic libraries).
>
> This style is generally used to retrieve a few relevant references on a topic area.
>
> *Building blocks*
> Concepts are searched separately and then combined using Boolean logic, i.e. the search is built up from lots of smaller searches. All the concepts in the search can be looked at individually before being combined. For example:
>
> Term Aa (electronic journal*) OR Term Ab (ejournal*) OR Term Ac (e-journal*) = X
> Term Ba (academic librar*) OR Term Bb (university librar*) OR Term Bc (college librar*) = Y
> Term Ca ('access to information') OR Term Cb ('availability of documents') OR Term Cc ('universal availability of publications') = Z
> X AND Y AND Z = final answer set.
>
> *Successive fractions*
> The search is refined by adding additional concepts after each individual search. It is generally used for searching broad topics that will result in a large number of records. The approach is particularly useful if you are unfamiliar with a particular topic:
>
> Term A (electronic journals) AND Term B (academic libraries) = X
> Term A (electronic journals) AND Term B (academic libraries) AND Term C (access) = Y (a subset of X).
>
> *Drop a concept*
> This style involves removing one or more concepts from the search strategy in response to the number and type of references retrieved:
>
> Term A (electronic journals) and Term B (academic libraries) and Term C (access) NOT Term D (letters).

Search filters

Search filters, (i.e. optimal permutations of search terms found in the titles, abstracts or the thesaurus indexing of references), have been shown in the health sciences to be effective at filtering out the highest quality evidence (Haynes et al., 1994, Paisley, 2000). Filters have been devised and tested to retrieve a range of study types, including practice guidelines, systematic reviews and RCTs. Various versions aim to maximize coverage (sensitivity), or precision (specificity). In each case you construct a search strategy according to the principles of the focused question, limit it according to year, language, etc. and finally combine the resultant set with the relevant filter. Filters in the LIS field are still in their infancy, mainly because the systematic review and RCT design are rare (Booth, 2000a) and because of the previously mentioned difficulty in limiting by publication or study design in the LIS databases. Nevertheless, specific combinations of terms may be used to retrieve the most relevant literature, similar to the approach adopted by McKibbon et al. (1999) in the health sciences. However, the filters illustrated below have not been tested for sensitivity and specificity and are presented as a guide only.

Research filter

A useful starting point is to consider how search results may be restricted to retrieve research studies, in preference to letters, editorials, commentaries, etc. The first step is to brainstorm as many 'research' terms as you can that may be found in either the title, abstract or thesaurus terms of relevant articles. Terms, such as research, researches, researched, researcher and researchers immediately spring to mind, but what about related terms, such as methodology, focus group, interview, survey, questionnaire, hypothesis, etc.? Evans (2002) has identified the principal terms for qualitative health research. Figure 8.4 lists some terms that may be appropriate for use in LISA (SilverPlatter). It is worth noting that the thesaurus term 'research' encompasses many narrower terms, including educational research, historical research, market research, research methods, research projects, research use, etc. It may be necessary to alter the filter for specificity, i.e. possibly restrict free-text terms to the title field only, in the light of references retrieved. Returning to the electronic journals example, the addition of this research filter resulted in just over 50 references, far more manageable than the previous 1,000 references! This final set of references includes numerous case reports of replacing print with e-journals in academic libraries across the world, examples of

#21	#1 or #2 or #3 or #4 or #5 or #6 or #7 or #8 or #9 or #10 or #11 or #12 or #13 or #14 or #15 or #16 or #17 or #18 or #19 or #20	#13	survey* in ti, ab
		#12	interview* in ti, ab
		#11	comparative* in ti, ab
		#10	comparison* in ti, ab
		#9	experiment* in ti, ab
#20	data analy* in ti, ab	#8	hypothes* in ti, ab
#19	ethnograph* in ti, ab	#7	methodolog* in ti, ab
#18	grounded theory in ti, ab	#6	research* in ti, ab
#17	qualitative* in ti, ab	#3	explode 'evaluation' in de
#16	quantitative* in ti, ab	#2	explode 'surveys' in de
#15	focus group* in ti, ab	#1	explode 'research' in de
#14	questionnaire* in ti, ab		

Figure 8.4 Proposed search filter *(SilverPlatter LISA)* for retrieving research studies in the LIS field

monitoring e-journal user behaviour using log files; as well as an example of an e-journals delivery service aimed at institutions in developing countries.

Other search filters

Figure 8.5 details four other search filters to be applied to the LIS literature: reviews, RCTs, information needs analyses and user studies.

Reviews filter			
#4	#1 or #2 or #3	#6	'user-demand' in de
#3	'literature-reviews' in de	#5	'needs-assessment' in de
#2	overview* in ti, ab	#4	'user-needs' in de
#1	review* in ti, ab	#3	'information-audits' in de
		#2	information* audit* in ti, ab
RCTs filter		#1	information* need* in ti, ab
#4	#1 or #2 or #3 or #4		
#3	RCT* in ti, ab	User studies filter	
#2	(random* near5 trial*) in ti, ab	#7	#1 or #2 or #3 or #4 or #5 or
#1	'clinical-trials' in de		#6
		#6	'user-satisfaction' in de
		#5	'user-feedback' in de
Information needs analyses filter		#4	'reader-surveys' in de
#6	#1 or #2 or #3 or #4 or #5 or	#3	user* stud* in ti, ab
	#6	#2	user* survey* in ti, ab
#7	'community-analysis' in de	#1	'user-surveys' in de

Figure 8.5   Other possible search filters *(SilverPlatter LISA)* appropriate for use in the LIS sector

Citation pearl growing

Citation pearl growing involves using a known highly relevant article (the pearl) to identify terms (both free-text and thesaurus) on which a search can subsequently be based. If no initial article is available, you can conduct a precise search, such as a title search, to identify a key reference. This procedure may be repeated several times until no further relevant terms are identified. This approach forms the basis of several Internet search engines, such as Excite, and is a useful start for many LIS questions.

Imagine you wanted to investigate what makes a good literature searcher. Unless this is your specific area of expertise, you are unlikely to know how to start searching on this topic. It certainly does not readily lend itself to the SPICE framework. Fortunately, you have identified an article by Ford et al. (2001) entitled, 'The role of individual differences in Internet searching: an empirical study' (this is examined in more detail in Special Topic F). Closer examination of the abstract and the indexing of this article suggests numerous other search terms such as literature searcher, internet searcher, information retriever, retrieval effectiveness, etc.

Snowball searching

This is a similar technique to citation pearl growing. However, this time you look at the references cited in a key article, then look at the references cited in those references and so on until no further relevant references are identified ('data saturation'). Although this is a very useful technique, you may end up examining a biased set of references, as authors are more likely to cite those authors (including themselves!) who support their arguments. It is also difficult to assess the relevance of a reference by its bibliographic details alone, i.e. without consulting an abstract.

Scanning the reference list of Ford et al. (2001) yields another article by Ford (1994) on cognitive styles and searching, as well as other references, including one which examines how internet experts search for information on the web (Hoelscher, 1998).

Other forms of citation searching

Other forms of citation searching, such as citation cluster and citation thread searching, can be conducted in the *Citation Indexes* (Web of Science). These techniques involve identifying those authors who have cited a particular reference since it was published. The main problem with this approach is that not all the relevant LIS journals are indexed on the *Citation Indexes* (Web of Science) and the technique does not work well for very recent references. Several authors (e.g. Pao, 1993; McCain, 1989) have highlighted the value of citation searching as a complementary strategy.

Author searching

Perhaps less useful than citation searching, but still a valid approach, is searching for specific named authors. This may also result in a biased sample of references, with references often being written by the same author, perhaps reflecting only one line of argument. Continuing with the same information retrieval example, the snowball search has already indicated that Nigel Ford is a key author in this field. A simple author search in LISA (SilverPlatter), ford-n* in AU, yields 49 references, approximately a quarter of which are potentially relevant.

Hand-searching

Hand-searching of key journals is appropriate for some LIS topics. This is particularly useful where journals are either inconsistently indexed, or not indexed at all, by databases previously searched. It can also prove useful in identifying a key reference upon which to base a citation search. However, hand-searching is time-consuming and should be used judiciously.

Conclusion

This chapter has suggested how to overcome the challenges associated with searching the LIS literature. In particular, it has demonstrated how generic principles of literature searching, such as focusing your question, free-text searching, thesaurus searching, Boolean and proximity operators, as well as limits, can be applied to the LIS databases. It has introduced several specific approaches to searching the LIS literature, including the use of search styles, methodological search filters and various search techniques, such as citation, author and handsearching. Figure 8.6 summarizes key points to remember when constructing a search strategy to answer a LIS question.

• Pre-plan your search	• Select the most appropriate search techniques for the sources that you have chosen (e.g. is it appropriate to use search filters?)
• Ensure that you are clear about the search parameters, such as whether you are aiming for sensitivity or specificity	
• Select the most appropriate sources to search	• Employ more than one search approach (e.g. citation searching as well as traditional database searching)
• Take into account the limitations of the LIS literature, such as problematic indexing	• Evaluate your search results and modify your search strategies accordingly
• Brainstorm alternative search terms	• Document the search process

Figure 8.6   Key points to remember when constructing a search strategy to answer a LIS question

References

Atkins, C. and Louw, G. (2000) Building Bridges: constructing a framework for evidence-based information systems, *Health Informatics Journal*, **6**, 121–6.

Bayley, E., Wallace, A. and Brice, A. (2002) Evidence Based Librarianship Implementation Committee Research Results Dissemination Task Force Recommendations, *Hypothesis*, **16** (1), 6–8.

Booth, A. (2000a) Research, *Health Libraries Review*, **17** (4), 232–5.

Booth, A. (2000b) 'Librarian Heal Thyself?': evidence based librarianship, useful, practicable, desirable? *Proceedings of the 8th International Congress on Medical Librarianship, July 2–5*, London, UK, www.icml.org/tuesday/themes/booth.htm.

Booth, A. (1998) Testing the Lore of Research, *Library Association Record*, **100** (2), 654.

Booth, A. and O'Rourke, A. J. (1997) The Value of Structured Abstracts in Information Retrieval in Medline, *Health Libraries Review*, **14** (3), 157–66.

Creighton University Health Sciences Library and Learning Resources Center (2000) *Search strategies and heuristics*, www.hsl.creighton.edu/hsl/Searching/SearchStrategies.html.

Eldredge, J. D. (2000) Evidence-based Librarianship: searching for the needed EBL evidence, *Medical References Services Quarterly*, **19** (3), 1–18.

Evans, D. (2002) Database Searches for Qualitative Research, *Journal of the Medical Library Association*, **90** (3), 290–3.

Falzon, L. (2000) Searching the Databases. In Booth, A. and Walton, G. (eds), *Managing Knowledge in Health Services*, London, Library Association Publishing, 222–36.

Ford, N., Miller, D. and Moss, N. (2001) The Role of Empirical Differences in Internet Searching: an empirical study, *Journal of the American Society for Information Science and Technology*, **52** (12), 1049–66.

Ford, N., Wood, F. and Walsh, C. (1994) Cognitive Styles and Searching, *Online and CDROM Review*, **18** (2), 79–86.

Galliers, R. D. (1992) *Information Systems Research: issues, methods and practical guidelines*, Oxford, Blackwell Scientific.

Glanville, J., Haines, M. and Auston, I. (1998) Finding Information on Clinical Effectiveness, *British Medical Journal*, **317**, 200–3.

Greenhalgh, T. (1997) How to Read a Paper: the Medline database, *British Medical Journal*, **315**, 180–3.

Harter, S. P. and Peters, A. R. (1985) Heuristics for Online Information Retrieval: a typology and preliminary listing, *Online Review*, **9**, 407–24.

Hawkins, D. T. and Wagers, R. (1990) *Online Bibliographic Search Strategy Development*, London, Taylor Graham Publishing.

Haynes, R. B., Mulrown, C. D., Huth, E. J., Altmans, D. G. and Gardner, M. J. (1990) More Informative Abstracts Revisited, *Annals of Internal Medicine*, **113**, 69–76.

Haynes, R. B., Wilczynski, N., McKibbon, K. A., Walker, C. J. and Sinclair, J. C. (1994) Developing Optimal Search Strategies in Detecting Clinically Sound Studies in MEDLINE, *Journal of the American Medical Informatics Association*, **1** (6), 447–58.

Hoelscher, C. (1998) *How Internet Experts Search for Information on the Web. Paper presented at the World Conference of the World Wide Web, Internet, and Intranet*, Orlando, Florida.

Hunt, D. L., Jaeschke, R. and McKibbon, K. A. (2000) Users' Guides to the Medical Literature: XXI. Using electronic health information resources in evidence-based practice, *Journal of the American Medical Association*, **283** (14), 900–4.

Lowe, H. J. and Barrett, G. O. (1994) Understanding and Using the Medical Subject Headings (MeSH) Vocabulary to Perform Literature Searches, *Journal of the American Medical Association*, **271**, 1103–8.

Marshall, J. (1997) *Online information retrieval, LIS2146: Definitions*, www.ils.unc.edu/classes/21462/defn.htm.

McCain, K. W. (1989) Descriptor and Citation Retrieval in the Medical Behavioral Sciences Literature Retrieval Overlaps and Novelty Distribution, *Journal of the American Society for Information Science*, **40** (2), 110–14.

McKibbon, A., Eddy, A. and Marks, S. (1999) *PDQ: Evidence-based principles and practice*, Hamilton, Ontario, BC, Decker, Inc.

Paisley, S. (2000) Filtering and Evaluating the Knowledge Base. In Booth, A. and Waltin, G. (eds), *Managing knowledge in health services*, London, Library Association Publishing, 251–67.

Pao, M. L. (1993) Persuing the Literature via Citation Links, *Computers & Biomedical Research*, **26** (2), 143–56.

Phillips, B., Ball, C., Sackett, D., Badenoch, D., Straus, S., Haynes, B. and Dawes, M. (1998) *Oxford Centre for Evidence-Based Medicine Levels of Evidence* (May 2001), http://minerva.minervation.com/cebm.

9

Appraising the evidence

Andrew Booth and Anne Brice

Introduction

This chapter outlines the principles of critical appraisal for different types of research study. It introduces generic schemes and discipline-specific checklists for use with information research. Outputs from the Critical Skills Training in Appraisal for Librarians (CriSTAL) programme are introduced and reviewed. Teaching scenarios from the CriSTAL programme are presented. Resources to assist in presenting and interpreting useful statistics are briefly identified.

	1 Define the problem
	2 Find evidence
✓	3 Appraise evidence
	4 Apply results of appraisal
	5 Evaluate change
	6 Redefine problem

Figure 9.1 The evidence-based practice process

What is critical appraisal?

'How do *you* decide whether an article is worth reading?'. Although many practitioners can identify the features of a good research article, these bear little resemblance to the factors that determine what we read. First in the list is *interest* – does the title or abstract address a current preoccupation or some burning professional concern? We devour descriptions of new and exciting technologies more eagerly than prosaic, but worthy, descriptions of enquiry desk or interlibrary loan procedures.

Next come *extrinsic factors*: Have *I* heard of the author? Is it published in a peer-reviewed journal? Does the article originate from a reputable institution? Although these factors bear some relation to the quality of an article they are not automatic indicators of research quality.

Finally come more rigorous *intrinsic factors* that relate to research design and aspects of methodology. These are the focus of 'critical appraisal', described by David Sackett, a founder of evidence-based medicine, as: 'To weigh up the evidence critically to assess its validity (closeness to the truth) and usefulness (clinical applicability)' (adapted from Sackett and Haynes, 1995, **1**, 4–5).

In other words, we put aside our prejudices regarding the source or nature of a research study and judge it entirely on its own merits. We thus take into account the three important factors of *validity*, *reliability* and *applicability* (Booth and Haines, 1998).

Validity 'refers to the extent to which the results of the research are likely to be free from bias' (Reynolds, 2000). In other words, is there some flaw in the way the research has been done that might 'explain away' its findings? Consider if you were to stand in your library with a clipboard, taking notes. How would users react? How would the staff respond? Their observed behaviour would probably differ, even if almost imperceptibly, from that when they are not observed. Similarly, if we conduct an experiment using a more rigorous design, such as a controlled trial, the study itself is likely to affect the environment within which it takes place. The question we ask is: 'How much have the methods used to obtain the results thrown into question the findings themselves?'

'Reliability' relates to the 'trustworthiness of results'. In other words, what is the likelihood that this study reports something that is reproducible as opposed to being a 'fluke' or chance result? The presence of such a result can be ascertained by statistical techniques that relate to the anticipated frequency of chance and the uncertainty surrounding a particular observation. It should be mentioned at this point that these statistical approaches do not relate to some 'absolute truth' but, rather, stem from arbitrary decisions on likelihood. Statisticians regard 5% (or 1 in 20) as a threshold for chance – if something occurs more frequently than this they consider it unlikely to have happened by chance.

'Applicability' relates to the extent to which the results are likely to impact on practice (See Chapter 10). It is often contrasted with 'statistical significance'. Practitioners are not concerned with whether you can *measure* a difference between the effect of two choices of action. Rather, they want to know whether the chosen action will *make* a difference to the users of the service. Is it worth doing? As Einstein reminds us: 'Not everything that can be counted counts, and not everything that counts can be counted' (Albert Einstein, 1879–1955).

It is the added dimension of 'applicability', relating research to practice, that makes critical appraisal different from, and more relevant than, 'critical reading' commonly encountered on an undergraduate course.

Critical appraisal in practice

Critical appraisal commonly starts with a problem or scenario. Having identified a likely source for the evidence (Chapter 7) and then searched the literature (Chapter 8) for a research study that addresses the problem, the next stage is to assess the quality of what we have found. Of course we may already have our own ideas on how to judge quality. However, it is usually more efficient to use a pre-existing checklist so that we do not overlook some important considerations. Multiple checklists exist – some originate from the pre-evidence-based era (Fowkes and Fulton, 1991), a series of User Guides was developed in support of evidence-based medicine, and others have appeared subsequently. Within the context of evidence-based information practice, contributions of note have come from our own unfunded Critical Skills Training in Appraisal for Librarians (CriSTAL) project) (Booth and Brice, 2003) and from the work of the Evidence Based Information Systems team in New Zealand (See Chapter 18).

The following scenario and corresponding article are used in the CriSTAL workshops:

Scenario – keeping a finger on the pulse

You have been invited to join a local implementation group looking at how to improve information services to those working in primary healthcare. The group is in agreement that there is a need to improve access to, and use of, information resources. However, there is considerable disagreement as to the best way of spending the available finances.

One of the medical staff on the team comes into the group's next meeting and places a sheaf of photocopies in the middle of the table. 'There you are,' she says triumphantly, 'this article from the Medical Journal of Australia (MJA) website is all the evidence we need'. You pick up a copy of the article in question: Jane M. Young and Jeanette E. Ward (Young and Ward, 1999), General practitioners' use of evidence databases, *MJA*, **170**, 56–8.

The group decides that, at the very least, it should consider the implications of this article at its meeting. Using the checklist provided, answer the following questions:

1   Would you consider this article to be suitable evidence to inform the group in making its decision?   YES   NO   DON'T KNOW
2   Should the local implementation group purchase the evidence databases for its primary healthcare teams?   YES   NO   DON'T KNOW
3   If your answer to question 2 is either 'NO' or 'DON'T KNOW' what other information would you need in order to make your decision?

Several features of the scenario are worth comment. The first question relates to *strength of evidence*. In other words, what is the validity and reliability of the article under consideration? Does it support a definite course of action? We should be able to agree whether this is a good or bad research study. Admittedly, different groups may choose to identify or give prominence to different features of the same study. However, particularly if a standard checklist is used, they should agree about its quality. The second question, however, addresses issues regarding *strength of recommendation*. What action will the group recommend based on the study? It is at this point that the values and preferences of the users enter the picture. You may make a different decision because of such considerations as available resources, the skill mix of staff, local policies and procedures and the wider political, social and cultural environment (See Chapter 10).

Finally, the scenario asks: 'If your answer to the previous question is either 'NO' or 'DON'T KNOW', what other information would you need in order to make your decision?'. This question encourages participants to consider other forms of evidence that might inform their decision. Local surveys or audits may help establish how the local library compares with that in the study. Are the users younger and more computer-literate? Are they more prosperous or better educated? Data on costs or technical specifications for equipment may have a bearing on the eventual decision. Alternatively you may look for additional literature to reinforce the findings of the study, to address a different but related question or to provide a different perspective on the same question.

Any decision seeks to optimize the balance between three perspectives:

- A *librarian* brings a professional perspective relating to whether or not the service works (the effectiveness of an intervention)
- A *manager* adds a consideration of whether the service is affordable (cost-effectiveness)
- The *user* perspective, finally and most importantly, will consider whether the service is acceptable and fair.

No research study is likely to address all three dimensions equally. Indeed, aspects such as user views may require other evidence, such as that from qualitative research.

Critical appraisal will not yield a single quantitative estimate for a context-laden and messy reality. However it can:

- reduce uncertainty
- allow you to focus on important issues
- help unravel complex problems
- harness group perspectives.

Increasingly, an information professional's role in supporting evidence-based practice requires familiarity with critical appraisal skills, resources and techniques (Landrivon and Ecochard, 1992; Dorsch et al., 1990; Scherrer and Dorsch, 1999). Involvement in critical appraisal has not been without controversy – not only do many other professional groups consider that librarians are ill-equipped to exploit research literature but even librarians themselves have concerns about adopting such a mantle.

The CRItical Skills Training in Appraisal for Librarians (CriSTAL) project aimed to establish whether it is practical for librarians to apply critical appraisal skills in their day-to-day practice (Booth and Brice, 2003). In doing so it sought to introduce a rudimentary knowledge of research design and to present necessary statistics in a way that is meaningful and non-threatening. The use of critical appraisal checklists for assessing the relevance and rigour of research findings is established in all disciplines that claim to pursue evidence-based practice and has led to development of guidelines for surveys, cohort studies, clinical trials and case-control studies (Crombie, 1996). Qualitative research, economic analyses and systematic reviews have also been targeted for a checklist approach. However, within the field of information practice two types of information literature were identified as particularly important and yet lacking an appropriate checklist: use studies and information needs analyses (Julien, 1996). (See Figure 9.2 in this chapter and Box 19.2 in Chapter 19.)

A. Is the study a close representation of the truth?
   1. Does the study address a clearly focused issue?
   2. Does the study position itself in the context of other studies?
   3. Is there a direct comparison that provides an additional frame of reference?
   4. Were those involved in collection of data also involved in delivering a service to the user group?
   5. Were the methods used in selecting the users appropriate and clearly described?
   6. Was the planned sample of users representative of all users (actual *and* eligible) who might be included in the study?

Figure 9.2   Twelve questions to help you make sense of a user study

(continued)

B. Are the results credible and repeatable?
   7. What was the response rate and how representative was it of the population under study?
   8. Are the results complete and have they been analysed in an easily interpretable way?
   9. Are any limitations in the methodology (that might have influenced results) identified and discussed?
C. Will the results help me in my own information practice
   10. Can the results be applied to your local population?
   11. What are the implications of the study for your practice?
   • in terms of current deployment of services?
   • in terms of cost?
   • in terms of the expectations or attitudes of your users?
   12. What additional information do you need to obtain locally to assist you in responding to the findings of this study

Figure 9.2   *(continued)*

The CriSTAL project utilized workshops modelled on the Critical Appraisal Skills Programme (CASP) format used to deliver appraisal training to health professionals. Participants were presented with the scenario from a library setting presented above, a research article and the corresponding checklist required to resolve the scenario.

Research design

Central to understanding critical appraisal is the so-called 'hierarchy of evidence' (Earl-Slater, 2001). This attempts to convey graphically the respective merits of different research designs according to their validity. It is important to note that such a hierarchy can be used only where you are considering the 'effectiveness' of interventions (i.e. whether a particular service or technology works). Issues around the acceptability of a service to users and other concerns of user preference are best addressed through qualitative research designs such as focus groups or Delphi processes. For this reason, other approaches, such as the concept of a 'signal-to-noise ratio' (Edwards et al., 1998), have received favour in some circles.

Eldredge (2002, 2003) has made two attempts at defining levels of evidence within librarianship. Within evidence-based healthcare a traditional hierarchy of evidence is given in Figure 9.3, and definitions of study types are given in Box 9.1 on page 112.

It is often effective to take librarians through such a hierarchy as a narrative whereby each successive design is seen to improve on its predecessor. In the absence of test-tube research and animal experiments(!) the entry point for a social science such as librarianship, is at the level of ideas, editorials and opinions.

In providing a literature searching training programme to users I might

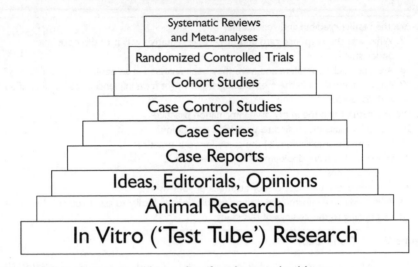

Figure 9.3   Conventional hierarchy of evidence in healthcare

ponder: 'I wonder if it would make a difference if I gave feedback to users on how good their searches are?'

In common with members of other pragmatic professions such as managers, social workers and teachers, my first recourse might be to ask a colleague for their *opinion*. While this might appear valid, my informant may be advancing an opinion without previous experience of the issue. My immediate concern would be, 'does an opinion advanced in theory hold up in actual practice?'

My next step might be to find a *case report* (or case study) where someone has actually tried this. Although this has the added virtue of being an actual occurrence I might have concerns about whether this is an isolated instance or whether it is likely to translate into practice (Fowkes and Fulton, 1991).

In accumulating a number of such cases we proceed to what is labelled a *'case series'*. This demonstrates the effect of an intervention in numerous different settings, some of which may even be exactly like my own. Nevertheless there may be considerable variation in the timing and duration of the intervention, the participants, the setting, and even the success factors or 'outcomes'. Published reports may differ in their definition of what exactly constitutes 'feedback'. We may be able to isolate a specific factor which may help to generate a hypothesis for further testing (Fowkes and Fulton, 1991).

The next stage would be to identify two broadly similar groups, one of 'successful searchers' and the other of 'unsuccessful searchers'. I would then ask all members of both groups whether they had received feedback on their searching. If one group had a higher proportion of those receiving feedback than the other then this would give an indication that such feedback does (or indeed does not) have an effect. At this stage matching cases (successful searchers) with controls (unsuccessful searchers) in a *case-control study* is purely indicative and cannot establish cause and effect (Schulz and Grimes, 2002). There could be other explanations (confounding factors), the recall or memory of our informants may be imperfect or their records may be incomplete. Such are the limitations of studies that look back (retrospective) to a previous intervention.

At this point I would want to carry out a prospective (forward-looking) study where the record-keeping is both consistent and complete. In such a study – a *cohort study* – I follow an opportunistic group of those who have feedback and another group of those who do not have feedback (Grimes and Schulz, 2002). I capture a significant amount of detail on both groups so that I could identify any differences that might otherwise explain a difference in search performance (Eldredge, 2002).

An advantage of the cohort study is that it does not require participating users or libraries to change what they would have been doing anyway. This strength is also a limitation in that it opens up the possibility that both groups differ at the beginning of the study and therefore all that we are measuring upon completion of the study is that original difference. For this reason we might randomize a population into one of two groups as part of a *randomized controlled trial* (RCT). This ensures that, except for the prospect of chance – for which we make a statistical allowance (conventionally at 1 in 20) – the two groups are similar at the beginning (Eldredge, 2003). We can thus assume with a certain degree of confidence that any measurable difference is caused by a difference between the effect of the intervention and its comparison. In fact this is exactly what was done in the following published study: Bradley, D.R., Rana, G. K., Martin, P. W. and Schumacher, R. E. (2002) Real-time, Evidence-based Medicine Instruction: RCT in a neonatal intensive care unit, *Journal of the Medical Library Association*, **90** (2), 194–201.

Once a specific question has been studied rigorously in several comparable studies we can synthesize these findings through a *meta-analysis* or *systematic review*. A systematic review tries to answer a clear question by finding and describing all published and, if possible, unpublished work on a topic. A systematic review therefore uses explicit methods to perform a thorough literature search and critical appraisal of individual studies and uses appropriate statistical techniques to combine these valid studies. If a finding is replicated across a number of studies in a range of settings we have increased confidence that this finding is directly attributable to the intervention.

A well conducted systematic review helps *practitioners* avoid being overwhelmed by the volume of literature. Review articles help us keep up-to-date, define the boundaries of what is known and what is not known and can help us avoid knowing less than has been proven. By critically examining primary studies, systematic reviews improve our understanding of inconsistencies within diverse pieces of research evidence. By quantitatively combining the results of several small studies, meta-analyses can create more precise, powerful, and convincing

---

Box 9.1   Definitions of research studies

Definitions:

Case report - a description of a particular service or event, often focusing on unusual aspects of the reported situation or adverse occurrences.

Case series - a description of more than one case.

Case-control study - An observational study in which the cases have the issue of interest (e.g. successful literature searching) but the controls do not.

Cohort study - An observational study of a particular group over a period of time.

Randomized controlled trial - An experimental study in which users are randomly allocated to one of two or more options, where some get the option of interest and others get another option (e.g. a standard service).

Systematic review - An approach that involves capturing and assessing the evidence by some systematic method, where all the components of the approach and the assessment are made explicit and documented.

Meta-analysis is a method of synthesizing the data from more than one study, in order to produce a summary statistic.

---

conclusions. *Researchers* use systematic reviews to summarize existing data, refine hypotheses and define future research agendas. Without systematic reviews, they may miss promising leads or embark on studies of questions that have been already answered.

Calls for systematic reviews within librarianship have been ongoing for over a decade. Trahan (1993) discussed the potential of meta-analysis for library and information science, concluding that meta-analysis can be an effective tool for library and information science research (for an example see Box 9.2). Booth (1998) reported on a feasibility study entitled 'Library LORE' (Literature Oriented Reviews of Effectiveness) which followed the review process recommended by the NHS Centre for Reviews and Dissemination. This required a systematic search of the literature, documentation of study characteristics and exploration of the practicalities of identifying and reviewing this literature. He concluded that it is possible to conduct a systematic review in an information setting with undoubted value to practitioners. Nevertheless, he observed that the potential of systematic reviews in librarianship is constrained by several factors:

- different methods used to address similar questions (technically known as 'heterogeneity')
- the poor quality of research designs
- deficiencies in indexing and abstracting that make identification and retrieval of candidate studies problematic.

More recently, Hjorland (2001) has questioned 'Why is meta analysis neglected by information scientists?'

Box 9.2 Published example of a meta-analysis (abridged)

Telemedicine versus face to face patient care: effects on professional practice and health care outcomes (Cochrane Review)

Background: Telemedicine is the use of telecommunications technology for medical diagnosis and patient care. From its beginnings telemedicine has been used in a variety of healthcare fields, although widespread interest among healthcare providers has only now become apparent . . .

Objectives: To assess the effects of telemedicine as an alternative to face-to-face patient care.

Search strategy: We searched the Effective Practice and Organisation of Care Group's specialised register, The Cochrane Library, MEDLINE (1966 to August 1999), EMBASE (to 1996), CINAHL (to August 1999), Inspec (to August 1996), Healthstar (1983 to 1996), OCLC, Sigle (to 1999), Assia, SCI (1981 to 1997), SSCI (1981 to 1997), DHSS-Data.

We hand-searched the *Journal of Telemedicine and Telecare* (1995-1999), *Telemedicine Journal* (1995–1999) and reference lists of articles. We also hand searched conference proceedings and contacted experts . . .

Selection criteria: Randomized trials, controlled before-and-after studies and interrupted time series comparing telemedicine with face-to-face patient care. The participants were qualified health professionals and patients receiving care through telemedicine.

Data collection and analysis: Two reviewers independently assessed trial quality and extracted data.

Main results: Seven trials involving more than 800 people were included . . . The studies appeared to be well conducted, although patient numbers were small in all but one. Although none of the studies showed any detrimental effects from the interventions, neither did they show unequivocal benefits and the findings did not constitute evidence of the safety of telemedicine. None of the studies included formal economic analysis . . .

Reviewers' conclusions: Establishing systems for patient care using telecommunications technologies is feasible, but there is little evidence of clinical benefits. The studies provide variable and inconclusive results for other outcomes such as psychological measures, and no analysable data about the cost effectiveness of telemedicine systems. The review demonstrates the need for further research and the fact that it is feasible to carry out randomized trials of telemedicine applications . . .

Citation: Currell, R., Urquhart, C., Wainwright, P. and Lewis, R. Telemedicine versus Face to Face Patient Care: effects on professional practice and health care outcomes (Cochrane Review). In: *The Cochrane Library*, Issue 2, 2002, Oxford, Update Software.

Facilitating critical appraisal

Healthcare librarians have a long history of involvement in facilitating critical appraisal activities. Increasingly they apply this expertise to examining the evidence base for their own professional practice. This may be in the form of a regular professional journal club (Doney and Stanton, 2003; Grant, 2003, Koufogiannakis, Dorgan and Crumley, 2003) or an ad hoc continuing professional development event. In either case the stages required to facilitate such an opportunity are as in Figure 9.4.

Stage 1	Identifying a topic area
Stage 2	Finding a relevant article
Stage 3	Devising a scenario
Stage 4	Choosing a checklist
Stage 5	Deciding on a workshop format

Figure 9.4   Stages of facilitating critical appraisal

The effectiveness of critical appraisal has been established by findings from
CASP evaluations of their general appraisal programmes (Burls, 1997) and a recent
systematic review of critical appraisal research studies (Hyde et al., 2000).

Interpreting statistics

Participants at critical appraisal sessions view prior knowledge of statistical techniques as a major impediment to appraising a paper. Library and information
studies graduates do not generally receive a comprehensive grounding in statistical techniques and their interpretation. Difficulties encountered tend to be of
three types:

1   the actual terminology used
2   the specialist nature of the tests and techniques employed
3   the actual measures used.

Suggested solutions involve use of tools, worksheets and glossaries of terminology to enable participants to get the most from learning possibilities in the
workshop. Box 9.3 provides a brief list of statistics resources drawn from the library
literature or from the wider field of evidence-based practice.

Box 9.3   Resources for understanding statistics

Library statistical texts

Hafner, A. W. (1997) *Descriptive Statistical Techniques for Librarians*, 2nd edn, Chicago,
American Library Association.

Hernon, P. (1994) *Statistics: a component of the research process*, rev. edn, Norwood, NJ, Ablex.

Hernon, P. (1994) Determination of Sample Size and Selection of the Sample: concepts, general sources and software, *College and Research Libraries*, **55** (2), 171–9.

Janes, J. (2001) Categorical Relationships: chi-square, *Library Hi Tech News*, **19** (3), 296–8.

Janes, J. (2001) Causality, *Library Hi Tech News*, **19** (2), 191–3.

Janes, J. (2001) The logic of Inference, *Library Hi Tech News*, **19** (1), 96–8.

Janes, J. (1999) Descriptive Statistics: where they sit and how they fall, *Library Hi Tech News*,
17 (4), 402–8.

Janes, J. (2002) Comparing the Means of Two Groups – the *t*-test, *Library Hi Tech News*, **20**
(4), 469–71.

(continued)

Box 9.3 *(continued)*

Osif, B. A. and Harwood, R. (2001) Statistics for Librarians, *Library Administration and Management*, **15** (1), (Winter), 50–5.

Osborn, C. E. (2000) *Statistical Applications for Health Information Management*, Gaithersburg, MD, Aspen Publishers.

Evidence-based practice statistical texts

Ajetunmobi, O. (2002) Chapter 1 – Basic Stats. In *Making Sense of Critical Appraisal*, London, Arnold, 1–57.

Banerjee, A. (2003) *Medical statistics: Made Clear: an introduction to basic concepts*, London, Royal Society of Medicine Press.

Greenhalgh T. (2001) Chapter 5 – Statistics for the non-statistician. In *How to Read a Paper: the basics of evidence based medicine*, 2nd edn, London, BMJ Books, 76–93.

Pereira-Maxwell, F. (1998) *A–Z of Medical Statistics: a companion for critical appraisal*, London, Arnold.

Critical appraisal tools and products

Critical appraisal takes time and specialist skills. Not all librarians can aspire to practising the full process of critical appraisal for all research studies they encounter. Indeed, advocates of evidence-based practice have refined their vision to acknowledge this (Guyatt et al., 2000). Instead they encourage the production of such products of appraisal as critically appraised topics (CATS) so that practitioners benefit from appraisals of others (Sauve et al., 1995; Wyer, 1997). A CAT from an information context (facetiously labelled a 'CAT-Log') is given in Box 9.4.

Box 9.4   CAT-Log

Touch screen no better than leaflets in improving understanding of prenatal tests.

Question: In women booking antenatal care (population) is a touch screen system alongside a leaflet (intervention) more effective in terms of uptake, understanding, satisfaction with information and levels of anxiety (outcomes) than a leaflet alone (comparison)?

Design: Randomized controlled trial; intervention group (touch screen and leaflet), control group (leaflet only)

Setting: Antenatal clinic in university teaching hospital

Subjects: 875 women booking antenatal care

Outcome measures: Informed decision making on prenatal testing as measured by uptake and understanding of five tests, satisfaction with information received and anxiety levels as measured by the Spielberger state-trait anxiety inventory (STAI).

Results: The only significant difference in uptake was that more women in the touch screen group underwent detailed anomaly scanning ($p=0.0014$). Both groups showed significant improvements in knowledge over baseline (16 weeks gestation) by time of second questionnaire (20 weeks' gestation). Both groups reported high levels of satisfaction with the leaflet,

(continued)

Box 9.4 (*continued*)

with over 95% of the touch screen group also reporting that they would recommend the touch screen to other pregnant women. Compared with the baseline questionnaire, anxiety had declined significantly in the touch screen group mainly amongst 'first-time' pregnancies. **Commentary**: A major problem with any experimental information-based intervention is the high level of dropouts during the course of the study with the likelihood of this increasing with each successive round of questionnaires. This is clearly seen in the flowchart of progress of participants through the trial. So, of 1477 invited to participate, 280 declined and a further 147 were ineligible. Of the 1050 actually randomized a further 175 dropped out without filling in the baseline questionnaire. So nearly 41% of potential subjects had dropped out even before the first measurements were taken. This attrition continued, with a further 104 dropping out at the time of the second questionnaire and 37 dropping out at the third and final questionnaire. Clearly there must be concerns about the applicability (or indeed practicability) of such an intervention in practice. Another major limitation is that 47% of participants had received higher education, making the study population unrepresentative of the population at large. The authors' own statement is significant 'Like all new technologies, these devices should be subject to rigorous evaluation' (Graham et al., 2000) whilst, in the accompanying commentary Jeremy Wyatt concludes 'with limited evidence of benefit for these expensive tools over well designed leaflets they seem to fit best into the National Institute for Clinical Excellence (NICE) category C: for NHS use only in the context of rigorous research studies' (Wyatt, 2000).

References

Graham, W. et al. (2000) Randomised Controlled Trial Comparing Effectiveness of Touch Screen System with Leaflet for Providing Women with Information on Prenatal Tests, *BMJ*, **320**, 155–9.

Wyatt, J. (2000) Commentary. Evaluating Electronic Consumer Health Material, *BMJ*, **320**, 159–60.

Conclusion

It is not sufficient to improve the depth of critical appraisal skills in the profession. An associated challenge is to investigate better ways of getting appraised and synthesized research reports to the profession in more readily accessible formats (see Chapter 12). The success of critical appraisal as a foundation for evidence-based librarianship depends on the production of rigorous and useable research studies. As a CRISTAL participant observed: 'the frustrating thing is the gap between the ideal of how library research/writing should be and how most of it actually is . . . '.

References

Booth, A. (1998) Testing the Lore of Research, *Library Association Record*, **100** (12), 654.

Booth, A. and Brice, A. (2003) Clear-cut?: facilitating health librarians to use information research in practice, *Health Information and Libraries Journal*, **20**, (Suppl 1), 45–52.

Booth, A. and Haines, M. (1998) Room for a Review?, *Library Association Record*, **100** (8), 411–12.

Bradley, D. R., Rana, G. K., Martin, P. W. and Schumacher, R. E. (2002) Real-time Evidence-based Medicine Instruction: RCT in a neonatal intensive care unit, *Journal of the Medical Library Association*, **90** (2), 194–201.

Burls, A. J. E. (1997) *An Evaluation of the Impact of Half-day Workshops Teaching Critical Appraisal Skills*, Oxford, Institute of Health Sciences.

Crombie, I. K. (1996) *The Pocket Guide to Critical Appraisal*, London, BMJ Publishing Group.

Doney, L. and Stanton, W. (2003) Facilitating Evidence-based Librarianship: a UK experience, *Health Information and Libraries Journal*, **20** (Suppl 1), 76–8.

Dorsch, J. L., Frasca, M. A., Wilson, M. L. and Tomsic, M. L. (1990) A Multidisciplinary Approach to Information and Critical Appraisal Instruction, *Bulletin of the Medical Library Association*, **78**, 38–44.

Earl-Slater, A. (2001) Critical Appraisal of Clinical Trials: critical appraisal and hierarchies of the evidence, *Journal of Clinical Governance*, **6**, 59–63.

Edwards, A. G. K, Russell, I. T. and Stott, N. C. H (1998) Signal Versus Noise in the Evidence Base for Medicine: an alternative to hierarchies of evidence, *Family Practice*, **15** (4), 319–22.

Eldredge, J. D. (2002) Cohort Studies in Health Sciences Librarianship, *Journal of the Medical Library Association*, **90** (4), 380–92.

Eldredge, J. D. (2003) The Randomized Controlled Trial Design: unrecognized opportunities for health sciences librarianship, *Health Information and Libraries Journal*, **20** (Suppl 1), 34–44.

Fowkes, F. G. R. and Fulton, P. M. (1991) Critical Appraisal of Published Research: introductory guidelines, *BMJ*, **302**, 1136–40.

Graham, W. et al. (2000) Randomised Controlled Trial Comparing Effectiveness of Touch Screen System with Leaflet for Providing Women with Information on Prenatal Tests, *BMJ*, **320**, 155–9.

Grant, M. J. (2003) Journal Clubs for Continued Professional Development, *Health Information and Libraries Journal*, **20** (Suppl 1), 72–3.

Grimes, D. A and Schulz, K. F. (2002) Cohort Studies: marching towards outcomes, *Lancet*, **359** (9303), 341–5.

Guyatt, G. H., Meade, M. O., Jaeschke, R. Z., Cook, D. J. and Haynes, R. B (2000) Practitioners of Evidence Based Care, *BMJ*, **320**, 954–5.

Hjorland, B. (2001) Why is Meta Analysis Neglected by Information Scientists?, *Journal of the American Society for Information Science and Technology*, **52** (13), 1193–4.

Hyde, C., Parkes, J., Deeks, J. and Milne, R. (2000) *Systematic Review of Effectiveness of Teaching Critical Appraisal*, Oxford, ICRF/NHS Centre for Statistics in Medicine.

Julien, H. (1996) A Content Analysis of the Recent Information Needs and Uses of Literature, *Library and Information Science Research*, **18**, 53–65.

Koufogiannakis, D., Dorgan, M. and Crumley, E. (2003) Facilitating Evidence Based Librarianship: a Canadian experience, *Health Information and Libraries Journal*, **20** (Suppl 1), 76–8.

Landrivon, G. and Ecochard, R. (1992) Principles of the Critical Appraisal of Medical Literature, *Health Information and Libraries*, **3**, 29–34.

Reynolds, S. (2000) In Reynolds, S. and Trinder, E., *Evidence-based Practice: a critical appraisal*, Oxford, Blackwell Science.

Sackett, D. L. and Haynes, R. B. (1995) On the Need for Evidence-based Medicine [EBM Notebook], *Evidence-Based Medicine*, **1**, 5–6.

Sauve, S., Lee, H. N., Meade, M. O., Lang, J. D., Farkouh, M., Cook, D. J. and Sackett, D. L. (1995) The Critically Appraised Topic: a practical approach to learning critical appraisal, *Annals of the Royal Society of Physicians and Surgeons of Canada*, **28**, 396–8.

Scherrer, C. S. and Dorsch, J. L. (1999) The Evolving Role of the Librarian in Evidence-based Medicine, *Bulletin of the Medical Library Association*, **87**, 322–8.

Schulz, K. F. and Grimes, D. A. (2002) Case-control Studies: research in reverse, *Lancet*, **359** (9304), 431–4.

Trahan, E. (1993) Applying Meta-analysis to Library and Information Science Research, *Library Quarterly*, **63** (1), 73–91.

Wyer, P. C. (1997) The Critically Appraised Topic: closing the evidence-transfer gap, *Annals of Emergency Medicine*, **30**, 639–40.

Young, J. M. and Ward, J. E. (1999) General Practitioners' Use of Evidence Databases, *Medical Journal of Australia*, **170**, 56–8.

10

Applying evidence to your everyday practice

Denise Koufogiannakis and Ellen Crumley

Introduction

This chapter examines how to determine whether research is applicable in your situation, including the questions you can ask to help you decide whether or not to use research you have found. Several variables affect the applicability of results. These can be broken down into questions to help guide you through your decision making process. Following this, a scenario is developed, using examples to illustrate the levels of applicability.

	Define the problem
	Find evidence
	Appraise evidence
✓	Apply results of appraisal
	Evaluate change
	Redefine problem

Figure 10.1   The evidence-based practice process

Scenario

You are a health librarian working within an academic institution. Your role involves teaching evidence-based searching to clinicians. You wonder whether you can use pre-existing search strategies to filter the literature or whether you need to create new ones. You have tended to use your own saved searches to filter results for quality but these are burdensome to maintain and share with others. You wonder if, instead, you should direct clinicians to use the filters you have discovered on PubMed (www.ncbi.nlm.nih.gov/entrez/query/static/clinical.html).

As manager of reference services within your library, you are concerned that existing services might not be meeting the needs of your users. You would like local data to support new service initiatives, based upon user expectations. Developing your own research project seems daunting, so you search the library literature to determine whether anyone else has done something similar that you could adapt.

You have also been invited to participate in a new library issues group forming on campus. You wonder whether you could afford the one hour per month that participation in this group would require.

Determining applicability

You have conducted a literature search, found some relevant articles and evaluated them for validity. What can be done with this new-found knowledge? Even if you have the best available evidence how useful is it if it does not translate well to your population or situation? How much work are you willing to do to translate evidence into a useful tool?

The evidence you find can be applicable at different levels. At the most basic, the findings may yield an improved understanding of your question. You may not find an answer, but what you read will enhance your comprehension of the issues and enable you better to understand and manage your own situation. In other cases, the best evidence to help answer your question may be purely indicative and you may not feel comfortable adapting it to your situation. In this case, you may need local research to validate what you have found. If you are very lucky, you will find a highly valid study that easily applies to your situation. This is the ideal and a reason for doing your search and evaluation in the first place; if you find something directly relevant, using that evidence will make your life much easier!

Applicability can be thought of in terms of whether a study is generalizable or relevant to your situation. Although such a judgement may appear self-apparent, what explicit criteria might be used when applying the results from a research study to your own environment? In view of different degrees of applicability it is beneficial to have a frame of reference when making such a determination. Otherwise, you may miss the real reason why you are trying to change or implement a particular service or programme.

In medicine, the *Users' Guides to the Medical Literature* series places a great emphasis on applicability when critically appraising research (Dans et al., 1998, 545–9). In healthcare, applicability is measured against the patient being treated. If a particular treatment is not directly applicable to that patient, then the evidence will not apply in that situation. However the emphasis cannot be directed solely at ruling out evidence: 'ask whether there is some compelling reason why the results should not be applied to the patient' (Evidence-Based Medicine Working Group, 2002). The data should be strong enough to warrant that the evidence *not* be applied in that specific case.

Ultimately, the most important question is: 'Is the research I am considering applicable to my situation?' While becoming familiar with a body of research is important, if that research is not appropriate to your user group or environment, then it is not really useful and it may need to be augmented to inform your decision. How do you know if findings are directly applicable or not? Variables that affect the applicability of results for librarianship include the following:

Variables

User group – how does the user group in the study compare to your group of users? You will need to consider issues such as demographic factors; the type of organization in which the study took place (i.e.: academic library versus public); the size of the institution; the age of the participants, etc.

Ask yourself:
- Is the user group similar in nature to mine?
- Did the research measure outcomes that are important to my situation and my users?
- Does the age of the user group impact on my decision?
- Will my users be better off as a result of this new product or service?
- Does this service or product fit with the values, needs and preferences of my user group?

Timeliness – is this research recent enough to fit with your present situation and your users' needs? Technological literature is especially important to review since changes are often quick, pronounced and rapidly adopted with little research to support their utility. When exploring collection decisions regarding e-journals or consortial deals, material older than five years is probably not directly relevant, other than for background information.

Ask yourself:
- Has the situation changed since this evidence was gathered?
- Is there a potentially newer technical solution that I should also explore?

Cost – is implementing an intervention feasible in your work environment? Will there be enough financial support to carry through what is necessary to achieve a similar result? Without a solid backing, it may not be realistic to jump in and adopt the best evidence immediately. You may need to build your case and add local validation in order to gain support.

Ask yourself:
- Are the potential benefits worth the cost/realistic in my situation?
- How big an impact is the result likely to have and is it worth the cost to achieve this effect?
- Does the result have any negative side effects for my users that may be costly in the long run?
- Are there other, less costly things that can be done instead, or prior to implementation, to control costs?

Politics – will the concept be accepted and will it make enough of an impact within the environment in which you work? Or, will it create adversity with regard to your role? Who are (or should be) the major stakeholders? For instance, clinical librarianship has recently gained momentum against the backdrop of evidence-based healthcare (EBHC). Where EBHC is integrated into an institution, the concept and role of clinical librarians is more likely to be accepted than in an environment where these principles are not actively practised or supported.

Ask yourself:
- Is there support for this initiative within my institution and whom do I need to partner or target to garner support?
- What will be the positive and negative effects of this initiative in my environment?
- Will my employer/users embrace this different way of doing things?

Severity – how critical is implementation of this intervention? If your group has a problem that requires immediate change, you may be more willing to attempt potential solutions even if the demonstrated benefits in a research study are only marginal. Sometimes a demonstration of immediate action is enough to appease others until a better solution can be found.

Ask yourself:

- What is the level of severity of the issue?
- Will implementation of the intervention make a difference with the problem at hand? If so, how much of a difference and is it worth the effort?
- Are there other remedies for this situation?
- Are the potential consequences so severe that any solution will only work in the short term?

Asking these questions will help you weigh the relevance of specific research articles. The more often your answers favour the research, the more confident you can be in implementing the evidence. These questions will also help you determine the extent to which you will apply a particular study:

- whether it is directly applicable
- whether it needs to be locally validated
- whether it simply improves your understanding.

Evidence that is directly applicable

The librarian in our opening scenario presents a good example of finding and incorporating evidence that is directly applicable. The evidence-based medicine (EBM) movement has seen many librarians developing search strategies, known as quality filters, to help clinicians be more precise in their searches rather than sift through a large number of articles.

The Clinical Queries feature in PubMed is based upon a study published in the *Journal of the American Medical Informatics Association* (Haynes et al., 1994, 447–58). This research examined which search terms retrieve higher quality studies in the areas of etiology, prognosis, diagnosis, and treatment/prevention. Today, librarians and healthcare professionals searching for high quality articles on a topic in PubMed turn to these clinical queries to increase the precision of the search. No further local validation needs to be done, although many librarians have developed their own variations of search filters.

Because the research leading to Clinical Queries was done on an entire database, it is easily applied to many different populations. Librarians can look at the research and decide that it is useful for retrieving quick, quality information from PubMed for the healthcare professionals with whom they work. Applying these filters makes their job easier and more efficient. Even though the searches are no longer as sensitive and precise (current research is updating them), they can certainly be used as a quick method for obtaining some relevant articles. We are certain there is not a compelling reason to avoid using this evidence in our daily practice. Our librarian can save time by recommending the use of the pre-existing quality filters in PubMed.

Evidence that needs to be locally validated

Some research may provide a good sense of the issues and help with decision making. However, if you are to feel confident that the results are true for your user population you may find it useful to replicate it within your own environment. Through a literature search, the librarian in our scenario discovered the LibQUAL+ survey, 'a research and development effort that is measuring users' perceptions of library service quality across institutions via a Web-based survey' (Askew Waller and Hipps, 2002). The survey found areas where library services were both meeting and falling below user expectation. The LibQUAL+ tool encourages individual libraries to implement the survey tool for their own users while allowing them to benchmark their own results against a group of institutions. Askew Waller and Hipps note: 'Many of the participating libraries already knew that these changes were necessary; the survey confirmed those beliefs and provided evidence to justify targeted funding increases. Several libraries used additional data-gathering methods – such as focus groups and local surveys – to supplement their LibQUAL+TM results or investigate them in more detail'.

When librarians locally validate existing evidence, they are building the evidence base. For large projects, such as the LibQUAL+ survey, more participating institutions means a stronger collective result to which individual results can be compared. As Cook points out: 'A cohort of best practices across all the dimensions that define library quality may emerge, facilitating the efforts of administrators to tailor available resources to the institutional mission. Trends across the dimensions can be identified at the national level, placing local results in an important context for librarians and campus administrators alike' (Cook et al., 2001).

Looking at the broad picture, while also taking into account local needs, is important – especially when dealing with research about user expectations of our facilities, collections and services. Emphasizing the 'localness' on these issues is important, but does not always require work to be done from scratch, as the LibQUAL+ project demonstrates. The librarian in our scenario can apply the LibQUAL+ survey instrument in her own situation and gather local data based on user initiatives. She can place her local findings within the larger contexts of other participating institutions further to support her initiatives.

Evidence that improves understanding

The most common way that librarians apply evidence is through an improved understanding of the issues. Keeping up with the research literature allows you to see the bigger picture. Research also helps enhance your understanding of possible ways to do things as well as suggesting why you might choose to implement change. If a question arises in your day-to-day practice (e.g. how might something work better or how might users be better served?), using research will help to improve your understanding of concerns surrounding those questions. You may not be ready to implement research directly or even to validate the research locally, but you will have a better sense of what can be implemented, and which evidence is valid and best applied to your situation. As Williamson (1999) points out: 'For all research, the theoretical or conceptual framework is important and the literature review plays an important part in its formulation. Theory is important because it informs the research process and helps to direct it. When an investigator is aware of the theoretical implications of a study, usually more pertinent and potentially significant research questions are likely to be asked.' While the librarian in the third scenario must decide whether she has the time to attend the library issues group, it is worth her trying as it will likely bring worthwhile returns for a small investment of time.

At the University of Alberta, health sciences librarians have facilitated the exchange of information and ideas with the formation of a monthly librarian discussion group (Koufogiannakis et al., 2003). Discussions include professional issues and topics that have arisen in the literature or are currently of interest. A professional group enables individual members to confront issues and think about how they apply in their own situation. Librarians leave the discussion invigorated and may seek further evidence to work through their questions. The support of colleagues with whom they can discuss issues and potential solutions is key to facilitating change for group members.

Librarians can also add to their knowledge base by examining specific sections of a research paper. This can include reviewing the sections of research that provide an overview of the literature. Doing so will broaden your understanding of a topic while the references may lead to more relevant articles with even more bearing on your own questions. The 'Methods' section of papers may yield a methodology that is readily transferable to your own context, even if the research itself addresses a different population or a different question. Likewise, the data-collection instruments used in a published research article may be adapted either completely or in part for use in your own setting. By finding out what is applicable to you, you can use that information to strengthen your knowledge.

Conclusion

The evidence base for librarianship has something to offer each librarian when trying to find an answer to a question. While finding evidence that is directly applicable may be difficult, given such a scattered body of research evidence, this will improve as our evidence base grows. When using research to help with a question, look for high quality studies, but do not be too quick to dismiss everything as irrelevant. Try to take what does apply from the research and use it to resolve the problem at hand. Remember that there are different degrees of applicability and that you can turn to published research as a starting point. Ask yourself if what you have found is useful for your own situation, and to what degree it may be applied. Directly use what you can, adapt components of other research to aid in your own process, or use the existing research to come to a better understanding of the issues you may face. Enacting such a process and asking yourself questions of applicability will allow you to practise librarianship in an evidence-based manner.

References

Askew Waller, C. and Hipps, K. (2002) Using LibQUAL+TM and Developing a Culture of Assessment in Libraries, *ARL*, **221**, 10–11.

Cook, C. et al. (2001) The Search for New Measures: The ARL LibQUAL+ Project – A Preliminary Report, *portal: Libraries and the Academy*, **1.1**, 103–12.

Dans, A. L. et al. (1998) Users' Guides to the Medical Literature: XIV. How to decide on the applicability of clinical trial results to your patient, Evidence-Based Medicine Working Group, *JAMA*, 279.7, 545–9.

Evidence-Based Medicine Working Group (2002) In Guyatt, G. and Rennie, D. (eds), *Users' Guides to the Medical Literature: a manual for evidence-based clinical practice*, Chicago, IL, AMA Press.

Haynes, R. B. et al. (1994) Developing Optimal Search Strategies for Detecting Clinically Sound Studies in MEDLINE, *Journal of the American Medical Informatics Association*, **1** (6), 447–58.

Koufogiannakis, D., Dorgan, M. and Crumley, E. (2003) Facilitating Evidence Based Librarianship: a Canadian experience, *Health Information and Libraries Journal*, **20** (Suppl 1), 76–8.

Williamson, K. (1999) The Role of Research in Professional Practice: with reference to the assessment of the information and library needs of older people, *Australasian Public Libraries and Information Services*, **12** (4), 145–53.

11

Evaluating your performance

Andrew Booth

Introduction

The final stage of evidence-based practice is evaluating your own performance (Figure 11.1). This has two aspects: firstly, on a technical level:

- How have you performed with regard to the stages of evidence-based practice?
- Did I ask a specific focused question?
- Did I find efficiently the best evidence to answer my question?
- Did I evaluate the evidence reliably according to validity and usefulness?
- Did I apply the results of the research appropriately to a specific user or group of users?

Evaluating your performance in this context helps you become a better *evidence-based* practitioner.

Secondly and more importantly, has the service that you introduced or modified as a result of undertaking the evidence-based process actually made the anticipated difference? Evaluating your performance in this context helps you become a better evidence-based practitioner. As Todd (2002) identifies: 'evidence-based practice thus has two important dimensions. First, it focuses on the conscientious, explicit and carefully chosen use of current best research evidence in making decisions about the performance of the day-by-day role. Second, evidence-based practice is where day-by-day professional work is directed towards demonstrating the tangible impact and outcomes of sound decision making and implementation of organizational goals and objectives'.

Evaluation will consider both direction and degree; did the intervention have the *planned effect* (as opposed to the opposite effect) and did the effect have the *expected magnitude*? It may also lead you to redefine the original problem (Figure 11.1).

	Define the problem
	Find evidence
	Appraise evidence
	Apply results of appraisal
✓	Evaluate change
✓	Redefine problem

Figure 11.1　The evidence-based practice process

Because change strategies involve organizational and individual factors, differences between what you anticipate and what actually happens can have various causes:

- differences between the political, cultural or economic environment in the published study and that in which you are operating (applicability differences)
- differences between the technologies employed in the published study and those available to you locally (intervention differences)
- differences between the morale, motivation and commitment of staff in the published study compared with those locally (motivational differences).

For example, early experiences of clinical librarianship in the UK failed to demonstrate the benefits shown by more recent endeavours. As mentioned in Chapter 10, one possible explanation is the increasingly supportive culture of evidence-based healthcare and clinical accountability, placing clinical librarianship central to the organizational agenda. Another factor may be easier access to better information products. Information professionals are also now better at exploiting these.

Individual, service and organization level evaluation

If you as an evidence-based information practitioner are to demonstrate the success, or otherwise, of an intervention you must identify adequate mechanisms for evaluation. These might operate at three levels (Sacchanand, 2000):

- Individual performance – how can I assess the value of my own contribution?
- Group or project performance – how can we assess the contribution of our work group or the resources at the disposal of our project?
- Organizational level – how can we assess the contribution of our organization, particularly in comparison with similar organizations?

Scenario – The enquiry service

Ms Go-ahead has recently restructured the enquiry service along more evidence-based principles within the independent charitable foundation for which she works. In evaluating her performance she considers three aspects:

1 To what extent has this achievement contributed to my own development as an information professional and service manager? Indeed, what have I learnt about my own personal strengths and weaknesses?
2 To what extent has this development contributed to the improved functioning of the enquiry service team?
3 To what extent has this change improved the capacity of my organization to fulfil its objectives? How has this changed the performance of my own organization in comparison to similar development charities?

Having identified the key components in evaluating performance, Ms Go-ahead can now start identifying how best to measure performance within these areas.

Structure, process and outcome

You should be aware that evaluation often includes three elements identified by Donabedian (1980), namely structure, process and outcome. *Structure* relates to the physical assets that enable a service to be provided and how they are configured (e.g. people, buildings and equipment). *Process* relates to how things are done within a service. *Outcome*, the most elusive of the three, is the effect that a service has on its users and the population from which they are drawn. It is important to be able to isolate the effect of each of these on a service.

Suppose you have observed that large queues are backing up at the issue desk. You try to identify the reason for this unwelcome phenomenon. Is it a shortage of staff or issuing terminals on the enquiry desk (*Structure*)? Is the procedure for issuing books unnecessarily complex and might it be streamlined (*Process*)? Upon closer investigation you discover that staff on the issue desk are so friendly that users spend a disproportionate length of time engaged in conversation! What is more, as they treat everyone equally there are few complaints, with people actually welcoming the unwarranted delay (*Outcome*)! Rather than embark upon an expensive programme of purchase of new terminals or an extensive period of retraining, you work with your team on ways to preserve beneficial interaction with your users at points other than the issue desk.

Individual

Reflective practitioners

Like many librarians, you may work in comparative isolation where opportunities for formal, external professional development and evaluation are comparatively rare (Bryant, 1995). This need not mean that you cannot evaluate your own performance. The concept of 'the reflective practitioner' was coined by Donald Schon to provide a model for individual, self-directed, experience-based professional learning and development (Schon, 1991). In a fast-changing society where change cannot be predicted, it is a real asset for you, as an information professional, to demonstrate that you possess the abilities to analyse critically, to make informed judgements and to direct actions. Schon (1991) claims that reflection is essential if you are to survive in a world where both theory and practice are subject to continual change.

According to Schon (1983) opportunities for reflection fall into two types:

- *Reflection-on-action* involves you in thinking about and reviewing an area of practice after the event. You can self-critique, think through options for further development and evaluate your current understanding of relevant issues.
- *Reflection-in-action* is more dynamic, as you reflect during the event rather than after it. This enables you to examine your decisions and thereby 'surface' the knowledge that has evolved within your practice.

Reflective practice requires that you learn from your practical professional experience. According to Schon (1983), you can engage at one of two levels; either at a superficial, problem-solving level according to tradition or under pressure of work, or at a deeper level involving more meaningful and difficult inquiry. As a busy and practical professional you are likely to find yourself aiming somewhere between these two extremes. You may feel that you have very little time to engage in reflective practice. However, reflection need not be intrusive, time-consuming or overly complex. It can be as simple, or as complicated, as you want it to be.

Sharing your observations with either a group or a mentor (see below) may help you to overcome perceived barriers to reflection. If others in the group have experienced similar situations you may be able to draw lessons from this commonality of experience. Even if this is not the case you can be reassured that organizational policies and procedures embody such a wide range of acceptable practice that information professionals with different levels of knowledge and experience can still demonstrate their own competence.

Portfolios

One mechanism for reflective practice is the portfolio. Typically, your portfolio will chart two aspects of your development, the *personal* and the *professional*. As we have seen, both the personal experience of the individual practitioner and the accumulated body of professional knowledge codified as explicit knowledge are central to evidence-based practice.

Diaries

If maintaining a portfolio appears overly self-conscious then you might wish to use a less formal approach. Librarians involved in projects have found it useful to maintain a regularly updated diary (Goodall, 1994). Others have found it helpful to record ongoing experiences in a laboratory-type benchbook. In either case it is important that you do not merely catalogue your activities and 'to do' lists. Instead you should try to record the learning points, key decisions and choices, and uncertainties encountered in daily practice (Heath, 1998). You might focus on 'critical incidents', illustrated by individual case histories. You can subsequently analyse such incidents (Hunt, 1993), either personally or by discussing them with your colleagues or a mentor, thereby creating a positive learning environment (Marland and McSherry, 1997).

Mentors

Mentoring is a popular response to the challenge to develop an analytical approach to personal and professional practice and to receive professional support when working in isolation (Nankivell and Shoolbred, 1997). Clutterbuck (1991) identifies mentoring as a powerful tool for developing individual capacity within an organization. It may assist you in overcoming difficulties, adapting to new circumstances or reaching major career and life goals. Ritchie and Genoni (2002) describe how, for new graduates: 'mentoring introduces the protégés to and reinforces their understanding of the various standards of practice, conduct and participation which are underpinned by a set of professional values, and constitute acceptable norms within a profession'.

Mentoring may help you both as an individual (in self-learning) and as a member of a group or service (in team management). Within the context of evidence-based practice, the advantages of mentoring are apparent. It can help your organization to realign itself in new directions suggested as you acquire new evidence. It may give you the confidence to implement new practices as you pursue continuous quality improvement. Of course, such mentoring will only be successful if you work within an organization that is itself a professional learning community (McCann and Radford, 1993).

Group

Action learning

At a group level, reflective practice is frequently embodied in action learning or action research (Todd, 2002). These approaches are designed to solve practical problems in a workplace setting. The connection with evidence-based practice is apparent: action research projects, which are characteristically local, small-scale, and collaboratively planned and implemented, are ideally suited to demonstrating evidence-based practice. Action research can be described as a family of systematic, investigative approaches which pursue action (or change) and research (or understanding) at the same time (Todd, 2002).

Individuals or stakeholders, as a group, collaborate, discuss the problem, identify the context, review possible solutions, choose a methodology, implement the solution, and decide the criteria to be used to evaluate success. As a process, action research is not only collaborative, self-reflective, and critical: it is also documented at all stages of the cycle, including assessment and evaluation (Todd, 2002). If such a group is practitioner-initiated and driven (Greenwood and Levin, 1998) solutions should reflect an awareness of the surrounding context, any constraints in time or expense and the values of the host institution (Stringer, 1996).

Of course, the fact that you and your colleagues can identify workplace problems and appropriately diagnose their causes and context does not make you an evidence-based practitioner. Action learning sets can be 'islandized', generating solutions only from among the group members. However, where a group specifically examines the published evidence to enhance its knowledge base, develop new skills and attitudes, and initiate evidence-based approaches to everyday workplace situations, then the potential to 'inject' evidence will be much more apparent. As the new practitioner-led evidence base evolves, you will increasingly discover opportunities to demonstrate reflective practice and to realize the rewards of participating in innovative evidence-based practice.

Service

Recent years have seen much interest in service quality as a yardstick for evaluating service performance. Some common approaches to service quality are characterized in Box 11.1. Issues around measurement of service quality are not themselves unequivocal; Hernon and Nitecki (2001) have demonstrated that service quality indeed has its own research agenda. Ironically – indeed depressingly – even such comparatively established techniques as library accreditation, a form of organizational audit, employ standards that are not necessarily evidence-based. This mirrors the contrariwise evolution of quality assurance, where audit, outlining *what to count*, precedes evidence-based practice, which identifies *what really counts* (Booth, 2002)!

Box 11.1 Methods for evaluating service quality

Quality assurance is a collective term for 'activities and systems for monitoring and improving quality. QA involves monitoring and evaluating quality, but also includes other activities to prevent poor quality and ensure high quality' (Ovretvriet, 1998).

Audit is specifically 'setting standards or protocols, comparing practice with standards and changing practice if necessary. Audits are usually carried out internally for self-review and improvement'. 'Peer audit can use already existing standards or practitioners can develop their own' (Ovretvriet, 1998).

Organizational audit is 'an external inspection of aspects of a service, in comparison to established standards, and a review of an organization's arrangements to control and assure the quality of its products or services. Audits use criteria (or 'standards') against which auditors judge elements of a service's planning, organization, systems and performance' (Ovretvriet, 1998).

Performance measures have received heightened interest in recent years with an increasing service orientation to public services (Urquhart, 1997). They give 'direct measures of aspects of performance such as efficiency' (Ovretvriet, 1998). Bertot (2001) considers a number of performance measures that librarians might find useful in determining overall quality criteria. He suggests a framework so that librarians can select statistics and performance measures that relate to service quality.

Performance indicators are less direct than performance measures as they act like 'flags' to alert a manager's attention and encourage further examination (Ovretvriet, 1998). There is resistance in the library community to the use of so-called 'hard' performance indicators. Indeed, Usherwood and Linley (1999) argue that public library services cannot be examined by statistics alone, and describe indicators that use both soft and hard data. Performance measures for the electronic library are reviewed by Brophy (1999) while Hewlett (1999) reviews performance indicators in NHS libraries.

Benchmarking is a specific use of performance indicators. A local audit is conducted and data compared with published data from elsewhere. Such comparisons run the risk of being inappropriate and are often accused of being stripped of, or even devoid of, meaningful context.

Organization

Organizational learning

The growth in popularity of the 'learning organization' parallels the exponential rise in evidence-based practice. Definitions of learning organizations suggest an important relationship with work-based practice (Griego et al., 2000). Information units should not merely facilitate evidence-based practice opportunities for other employees but should also stimulate all information professionals to practise evidence-based practice in pursuit of the organization's objectives.

Implementation and evaluation

Implementation brings together evidence (research evidence, professional experience and user preferences), context (culture, leadership and measurement) and facilitation (characteristics, role and style). Most successful implementation occurs when the evidence is scientifically robust ('high' evidence); the context is receptive to change, with sympathetic cultures; there are appropriate monitoring and feedback systems and strong leadership ('high' context); and when there is appropriate facilitation of change using the skills of external and internal facilitators ('high' facilitation). To maximize the uptake of evidence into practice, the evidence, context and facilitation should be located towards the 'high' end of each continuum (Kitson et al., 1998).

Once research has established that some intervention can achieve desired outcomes, the next challenge is to demonstrate that such changes have actually been achieved (Cullen, 1998). Evaluation must be planned at the beginning of change to assure that it is measuring what is important. Evaluation methods must be rigorous and yet practicable. A successful implementation project will not only achieve its original objectives (outcome) but will also positively contribute to the knowledge and satisfaction of staff involved in bringing it to fruition (process). Herein lies an ambiguity of evidence-based practice – is success measured in the completion of the evidence-based practice process, or is it truly present only if the outcomes themselves are positive?

Towards a culture of evidence-based practice

As implied above, reflective thinking, empowerment and innovation are major determinants of a culture of evidence-based practice. You and colleagues involved in delivering a service could reflect, either individually or within a group learning process, on your professional growth and your ability to identify, interpret and use research studies. Step 5 of the evidence-based practice process, evaluating your performance as a practitioner of EBP, includes the presence (or indeed absence) of evidence-based decisions in your day-to-day professional activity (outcome measures). It also includes your demonstration of evidence-based skills (process measures) where the outcome is equivocal or as yet indeterminate. In short, you can ask yourself about your ability to:

- ask answerable questions
- find the best external evidence
- critically appraise the evidence and evaluate it for its validity and potential usefulness
- integrate critical appraisal of the best available external evidence from systematic research with individual expertise in personal daily practice.

Evaluation of your performance completes the 'pathway' of practising evidence-based practice (Straus, 1998). You can evaluate your progress through each stage of asking answerable questions (were they?), searching for the best evidence (did I find good evidence quickly?), performing critical appraisal (did I do so effectively and efficiently?), and integrating the evidence with your expertise and your users' unique features (did I find an acceptable strategy?). Self-evaluation allows you to revisit earlier steps that need further improvement.

Conclusion

The presence of an empowering environment will be reflected in your participation in developing evidence-based policies and procedures or even in producing systematic reviews, guidelines or individual critically appraised topics. While innovation is not necessarily a marker of evidence-based practice – hence the need to evaluate new technologies – it should be possible to demonstrate achievement in terms of innovative practices, presentations, publications and changes in practice.

It is ironic that many techniques advocated in this chapter are most readily associated with the progress of a new professional. The nomination of a mentor, regular periods of reflective practice, the maintenance of a portfolio, perhaps even supported by a carefully kept diary of professional activity – all these figure prominently early in our professional careers. Nevertheless, as we have demonstrated, evaluation is essential to evidence-based practice. The evidence-based information practitioner will consider the above as a toolbox to stand them in good stead at whatever stage they may be in their professional career.

References

Bertot, J. (2001) Measuring Service Quality in the Networked Environment: Approaches and considerations, *Library Trends*, **49** (4), 758–75.

Booth, A. (2002) Mirage or Reality, *Health Information and Libraries Journal*, **19**, 56–8.

Brophy, P. (1999) Performance Measures for the Electronic Library, *SCONUL Newsletter*, **16**, 3–5.

Bryant, S. L. (1995) *Personal Professional Development and the Solo Librarian*, London, Library Association Publishing.

Clutterbuck, D. (1991) *Everyone Needs a Mentor. Fostering talent at work*, London, Institute of Personnel Management.

Cullen, R. (1998) Does Performance Measurement Improve Organisational Effectiveness? In *Proceedings of the Second Northumbria International Conference on Performance Measurement in Libraries and Information Services*, Newcastle-upon-Tyne, Information North, 3–20.

Donabedian, A. (1980) *Explorations in Quality Assessment and Monitoring. The definition of quality and approaches to its assessment*, Ann Arbor, MI, Health Administration Press.

Goodall, D. (1994) Use of Diaries in Library and Information Research, *Library and Information Research News*, **18** (59), 17–21.

Greenwood, D. and Levin, M. (1998) *Introduction to Action Research: Social research for social change*, Thousand Oaks, CA, Sage.

Griego, O. V., Geroy, G. D. and Wright, P. C. (2000) Predictors of Learning Organizations: a human resource development practitioner's perspective, *The Learning Organization*, **7** (1), 5–12.

Heath, H. (1998) Keeping a Reflective Practice Diary: a practical guide, *Nurse Education Today*, **18** (7), 592–8.

Hernon, P. and Nitecki, D. (2001) Service Quality: a concept not fully explored, *Library Trends*, **49** (4), (Spring), 687–708.

Hewlett, J. (1999) Performance Indicators in NHS libraries, *Health Libraries Review*, **15** (4), 245–53.

Hunt, S. A. (1993) Moving Forward by Looking Back . . . Using a Reflective Diary, *Journal of Clinical Nursing*, **2** (3), 126–7.

Kitson, A., Harvey, G. and McCormack, B. (1998) Enabling the Implementation of Evidence-based Practice: a conceptual framework, *Quality in Health Care*, **7**, 149–58.

Marland, G. and McSherry, W. (1997) The Reflective Diary: an aid to practice-based learning, *Nursing Standard*, **12** (13–15), 49–52.

McCann, I. and Radford, R. (1993) Mentoring for Teachers: the collaborative approach, In Cadwell, B.J. and Carter, E. M. (eds), *The Return of the Mentor: strategies for workplace learning*, Washington, DC, Falmer Press, 25–41.

Nankivell, C. and Shoolbred, M. (1997) Mentoring in Library and Information Services: a literature review and report on recent research, *New Review of Academic Librarianship*, **3**, 91–144.

Ovretveit, J. (1998) *Evaluating Health Interventions*, Buckingham, Open University Press.

Ritchie, A. and Genoni, P. (2002) Group Mentoring and Professionalism: a programme evaluation, *Library Management*, 23 (1/2), 68–78.

Sacchanand, C. (2000) *Workplace Learning for Information Professionals in a Changing Information Environment*, 66th IFLA Council and General Conference Jerusalem, Israel, 13–18 August.

Schon, D. A. (1983) *How Professionals Think in Action*, New York, Basic Books.

Schon, D. (1991) *The Reflective Practitioner: how professionals think in action*, Avebury, Ashgate Publishing Ltd.

Straus, S. E. and Sackett, D. L. (1998) Bringing Evidence to the Clinic, *Archives of Dermatology*, 134 (12), 1519–20.

Stringer, E. (1996) *Action Research: a handbook for practitioners*, Thousand Oaks, CA, Sage.

Todd, R. (2002) Evidence Based Practice II: getting into the action, *Scan*, 21 (2), 2002, 34–41.

Urquhart, C. (1997) Performance Measurement in Library and Information Services: health advice from the Value and EVINCE studies, *Library and Information Briefings*, no. 71.

Usherwood, B. and Linley, R. (1999) New Library – New Measure: A social audit of public libraries, *IFLA Journal*, 25 (2), 90–6.

12

Disseminating the lessons of evidence-based practice

Ellen Crumley and Denise Koufogiannakis

Introduction

Dissemination of research results is vital to the progress of the profession as well as helping to improve practice. It involves not only making your research available, but also ensuring that it is accessible to others and presented in a manner that is easy to understand. In addition, it is important to use a variety of techniques for delivering information in order to provide evidence (or to conduct research where no data are available) for what we do as librarians and to help others understand how we define our role.

In this chapter, we explore the evidence for dissemination and the different methods by which research and knowledge can be circulated. We also provide an overview of how distribution is used by librarians and investigate innovative ways to make your research known. Two types of disseminators, those who conduct research and those who use research findings in their practice, are examined throughout the chapter.

Scenario

As a special librarian, you work with a business research group consisting of a statistician, a research assistant and an MBA. Your role includes conducting environmental scans, facilitating access to online resources and performing comprehensive literature searches. You are also being asked to order documents for employees and other time-consuming tasks which could be done by other staff. You report to the vice president of the organization, who understands little about your role, yet she speaks on your behalf at board meetings. Since you see your boss infrequently, you prepare carefully for your meetings. You wish to communicate your needs and wants better, using evidence. You also want to find effective ways to get vital information to your supervisor. As a solo librarian, you also worry that you are isolated from other librarians and want to find ways to keep up with issues of relevance to your profession while at the same time gaining the support of your colleagues.

Effective dissemination

Dissemination continues to be a hot topic in recent literature. In order to be effective, research needs to be user-friendly, that is, understandable by those to whom we report, as well as to our colleagues. Many libraries are run by non-librarians and many librarians report to a person in another discipline who may not clearly understand their role and function within the organization. Thus, it is in our best interests to ensure not only that our research is disseminated to non-librarians but also that it can be interpreted by them. Both what is being disseminated and the method of distribution should have a clear purpose as well as being easy to follow. Something as basic as good leadership ability or visibly changing your practice, based upon research, can be useful. It is also valuable if you adopt 'approaches that increase staff members' knowledge and skills' (Corrigan et al., 2001) in order to stimulate professional development and encourage others to incorporate new practices or strategies in your workplace.

In order to be effective disseminators, librarians need to have the skills to interpret and utilize research done by others, even if they are not conducting research themselves. If we are familiar with research, it is more likely that we will seek to utilize it in our daily work. That is: 'When we do apply research results to practice, we can tell each other about it' (Humphreys, 1996).

It is only 'through the evaluation and summarizing of research studies that the knowledge base is continuously built' (Williams, 1997). Librarians can become: 'Leaders who use transformational skills [and] encourage team members to view their work from more elevated perspectives and to develop innovative ways to deal with work-related problems' (Corrigan et al., 2001). For instance, putting research in context or 'translating' it for others at a regular meeting will ensure that it is associated with common activities. Our research librarian communicates with her boss at meetings where she can demonstrate her expertise by corroborating her opinion with research.

Methods of dissemination

Numerous methods can be used to communicate research in your environment. Robbins discusses three types of dissemination: 'one way, two way and audience based' (1992), but there are many other options to consider. While publishing and conferences are typically thought of as the most effective ways to distribute information, several other dissemination options are available to librarians. We can easily adopt or adapt discussion groups or call meetings to meet some of our needs. Perhaps online journal clubs or e-mail discussion groups such as list-servs can be used to help with problems. Table 12.1 provides an overview of how the most common distribution techniques are used in librarianship and, in the following discussion, we provide examples of how they can easily be incorporated into your daily routine.

Table 12.1   Methods currently being used to share research findings

Category	Dissemination methods
Education/professional development	Workshop, continuing education, conference, training, journal club, discussion group
Management/policy	Organizational policy/guideline, meeting
Publication	Publishing/writing, internet, electronic vs. print
Personal communication	Word of mouth, focus group, leadership, reading, sharing articles, e-mail, list-serv, networking, mentoring

Education/professional development

Each year, librarians have many opportunities to share their research and meet colleagues through workshops and conferences. Many participate in one or many professional development opportunities, where, for example, they can learn about new technologies or different approaches to reference work. For librarians currently working on a research project, a contributed paper presentation at a conference is often a good first choice to present the findings. Peers will ask questions and give constructive feedback, which can be used before publishing the results.

Two methods of dissemination that are newer to librarianship are journal clubs and discussion groups. Health librarians at the University of Alberta meet monthly to exchange views about topics of interest (Koufogiannakis et al., 2003). A journal club is a good way to meet other librarians and discuss recent research articles that pertain to your practice. Getting together with colleagues to communicate issues enables you to share knowledge as well as generate enthusiasm and ideas for the improvement of practice through research. The librarian in our scenario may want to explore starting a journal club or discussion group. By meeting other librarians who are in a similar situation, she will feel less isolated and can discuss professional issues to keep her on top of what is happening in her field. This is also the ideal group within which she can find support and discuss potential solutions to the issues she faces at work.

Management/policy

Research can be incorporated into workplace policy and the management team in several ways. For instance, administrators may have the opportunity to modify or effect change of organizational policy/procedures based upon new research. Front-line librarians can influence their supervisors/administrators by providing research-based evidence (or revealing a lack of evidence) when presenting an idea that can be further advanced by their administrator. This avenue enables results to be disseminated formally throughout the organization. Our research librarian may need to present evidence during meetings to support her value as a librarian. Examples of other projects that have had a positive impact elsewhere, or research that can be used to support her position, may equip her to demonstrate her unique knowledge to attendees.

Since most librarians attend numerous meetings, introducing research to support new ideas or to change an established practice can be beneficial. Attendees will learn from, and perhaps be inspired by, the example set by the librarian presenting the evidence. Using research results to support a perspective will raise the bar for a professional approach to decision making, and others will soon follow this example. Creating institutional best practice guidelines is a way to pass on valuable information to both managers and co-workers within a climate of evidence-based practice. However, we need to be mindful that these can be time-consuming and will require time for updating. Defining her role more clearly by using the Special Libraries Association's *Competencies for Special Librarians of the 21st Century*, helped our research librarian demonstrate how her expertise can be used most effectively in her organization. It also helped her negotiate much-needed changes to her role.

Publication

Although most professions have traditionally published in a paper format, publication is not restricted to print materials. It can also incorporate grey literature such as websites. In some cases, presenting at a conference can have a greater and more immediate effect on an audience than going through the formal publication process. With the advent of online journals such as *BioMed Central*, publication time has been shortened to weeks instead of months and results are available shortly after projects are completed. However, it is important to weigh up the benefits and weaknesses of electronic versus print publication and decide which method of publishing will achieve the most benefit for you.

Publication in indexed journals widens your dissemination realm and increases the chance that someone will find your article when it is needed. Many disciplines have an accessible database or core collection of information (e.g. PEDRO for physiotherapy and ERIC for education). Librarianship requires similar attention if the results of our research are to be made available via a single source, accessible by domain (e.g. reference, education, etc.) when searching (Crumley and Koufogiannakis, 2002).

Many librarians conduct research, but the reality is that many of us also have an unpublished study or two waiting to be written up. In our forthcoming study exploring librarian research, we looked at 220 international library and information science journals, of which 111 are peer-reviewed/refereed and publish research (Koufogiannakis et al., 2003). Thus, there are numerous high-quality journals to which librarians can submit their research. While publishing is the most noticeable method of dissemination, its effectiveness and uptake of results by librarians requires further study.

Personal communication

Librarians are great communicators and the many methods available to us include word of mouth, mentoring, reading and sharing articles with colleagues. We also have extensive contact with others through list-servs and e-mail. Many of us work in teams and have many opportunities to share research in discussions with librarian and non-librarian colleagues. We also actively seek feedback from our users and can be leaders in modelling practice based upon research (or in demonstrating that more research needs to be done if we are to make such a claim). We can learn from the example of a group of nurses who used a consultative process with interested members in making decisions about dissemination as a team (Corrigan, 2001).

Disseminating the findings of research can be as easy as keeping up in your areas of interest by subscribing to current awareness services and passing on research articles to colleagues via e-mail. Not only will your colleagues be pleased to receive an article that is of interest to them, but you may also start a discussion at coffee that day about that very topic. In every small action, you are demonstrating that research is an important and integrated part of your work environment.

It would be useful for the librarian from our case scenario to join a professional association and talk with other librarians in similar positions to find out how their role has been defined. She can set up a e-mail current awareness service to inform her colleagues regularly about recent research, and she can disseminate librarian research, particularly if it relates to aspects of her job that are important to the group. In addition, she can work with her colleagues in the discussion group to create an e-mail network to share librarian research by monitoring journals and subject areas of interest.

Conclusion

Not only is dissemination important, but it can be done effectively in a variety of ways. Sometimes it will take institutional or systematic change to implement a practice change. However, by adopting an attitude that research is important, and incorporating it into everyday decisions, your leadership in this area will influence those around you. If you are interested, explore those areas where research information is lacking and slowly enhance those areas by conducting a study or two. By disseminating research via education, management, publication or personal communication strategies, your example may soon become the norm. Using a combination of these methods will enable gradual change of attitude within an organization and a more formal recognition of the importance of research in its development.

References

Corrigan, P. W. et al. (2001) Strategies for Disseminating Evidence-based Practices to Staff who Treat People with Serious Mental Illness, *Psychiatric Service*, **52** (12), (December), 1598–606.

Crumley, E. and Koufogiannakis, D. (2002) Developing Evidence-based Librarianship: practical steps for implementation, *Health Information and Libraries Journal*, **19** (4), 61–70.

Humphreys, B. L. (1996) Libraries and Collaborative Research: toward a better scientific base for information practice, [editorial], *Bulletin of the Medical Library Association*, **84** (3), (July), 433–6.

Koufogiannakis, D., Crumley, E. and Slater, L. (2003) *A Content and Citation Analysis of Librarianship Research, Canadian Health Libraries Association Conference*, Edmonton, Alberta, May 31–June 3.

Robbins, J. B. (1992) Affecting Librarianship in Action: the dissemination and communication of research findings. In *Applying Research to Practice*, Urbana, IL, University of Illinois at Urbana–Champaign Graduate School of Library and Information Science, 78–88.

Special Libraries Association, www.sla.org/content/SLA/professional/meaning/comp.cfm.

Williams, K. S., Crichton, N. J. and Roe, B. (1997) Disseminating Research Evidence: a controlled trial in continence care, *Journal of Advanced Nursing*, **25** (4), 691–8.

13

Six domains of evidence-based information practice

Andrew Booth and Anne Brice

In a pivotal address at the 2001 first Evidence Based Librarianship Conference in Sheffield, UK, Crumley and Koufogiannakis (2002) proposed that the discipline of evidence-based information practice could be organized within the following six domains, based upon the major areas dealt with in daily practice for librarians:

- Reference/enquiries – providing services and access to information that meets the needs of library users
- Education – finding teaching methods and strategies to educate users about library resources and how to improve their research skills
- Collections – building a high-quality collection of print and electronic materials that is useful, cost-effective and meets user needs
- Management – managing people and resources within an organization
- Information access and retrieval – creating better systems and methods for information retrieval and access
- Marketing/promotion – promoting the profession, the library and its services to both users and non-users.

They went on to observe the usefulness of this approach as a contribution to the evidence-based practice process: 'As with EBHC, matching librarianship questions with one of the above domains can help librarians decide where to search and the appropriate search terms they should use to answer that type of question. This also allows librarians to focus upon what they are *really* asking, rather than permitting the question to snowball in many different directions'.

Structure of 'domain chapters'

We have decided to use this structure to present a brief overview of the main types of study, with illustrative examples, in each domain. Although this prototypic taxonomy is by no means perfect – staff development probably merits a category in its own right and the evidence base for knowledge management will imminently command its own category – like the originators themselves we believe it to be a useful parallel to the evidence-based healthcare paradigm.

Each principal chapter in Part 3 follows a similar pattern – after a brief introduction and consideration of the definition of the domain it proceeds to look at the most relevant sources of evidence and the general quantity and quality of research. It then examines principal examples of evidence-based practice designs such as systematic reviews and randomized controlled trials before considering designs with special importance to that domain. A consideration of domain-specific concerns regarding Critically Appraising the Evidence and Applying the Evidence, leads naturally to identification of future research priorities. Some of the chapters are followed by one or more exemplar chapters containing Special Topics illustrating the evidence base within that domain.

Relative importance of each domain

In a posting to an Evidence-based Librarianship course run in early May 2003, Ellen Crumley, co-originator of the 'six domains', shared the following findings from an (as yet) unpublished study *A Content and Citation Analysis of Librarianship Research*, presented at the Second Evidence Based Librarianship Conference in Edmonton, Alberta (www.ualberta.ca/~pryan/programweb.pdf).

The domain with the *most* evidence and that with the *highest quality* evidence, based on one year's published output from the LIS literature, was Information Access & Retrieval. More detailed findings are provided in Figures 13.1 and 13.2.

1	Information access and retrieval	4	Management
2	Collections	5	Education
3	Reference/enquiries	6	Marketing/promotion

Figure 13.1 Ranking of domains from highest to lowest in terms of *quantity* of evidence

1	Information access and retrieval	4	Education
2	Collections	5	Management
3	Reference/enquiries	6	Marketing/promotion

Figure 13.2 Ranking of domains from highest to lowest in terms of *quality* of evidence

Ellen Crumley, in a posting to the FOLIO Evidence Based Librarianship Course of June 2003, considers that the domains which should be prioritized for future research are Management and Marketing/Promotion, citing the numerous staffing issues likely to be faced as the library workforce is 'lost' and there are problems filling top management positions. Threats to funding, particularly with the perception that everything is 'free on the internet', require that we re-examine our priorities in management and marketing/promotion.

About the special topics

At such an early stage in the development and dissemination of evidence-based information practice the editors believe it important to model potential evidence-based products. We therefore invited the authors of the Special Topics, who have had a close association with the development of evidence-based healthcare, to apply one of four models of evidence product to a predetermined topic inhabiting one of the six domains. The four models are as follows:

1   *The Guideline*: patterned on the model developed by the Scottish Intercollegiate Guidelines Network, this typically addresses a broad topic of library practice or policy and synthesizes the evidence. The emphasis is on practical guidance so where high-quality evidence is absent some interim judgement, based on lower-grade evidence, is advanced.

2   *The Evidence Digest*: based on a model developed by the King's Fund and then modified by one of this book's editors (Andrew Booth) at the School of Health and Related Research, University of Sheffield, these brief summaries of evidence have gained popularity in the *Journal of Clinical Effectiveness* and, latterly, the *Journal of Clinical Excellence*. Their main function is to serve as a 'launch pad' or 'starting point' to the evidence on a particular focused question of current interest.

3   *The Evidence Briefing*: mirroring the briefing format pioneered by the National electronic Library for Health (NeLH) Specialist Library for Health Management, and latterly adopted by the Social Care Institute for Excellence (SCIE), these briefings tend to provide a concise overview to evidence and good practice resources. Again developed by Andrew Booth at the University of Sheffield, their principal aim is to make readers aware of the issues surrounding the evidence base for a particular, usually broad, topic.

4   *The Critically Appraised Topic*: this examines evidence from one recent journal article and appraises it for reliability, validity and applicability. A commentary on implications for practice is included. The 'bottom-line' is provided in an indicative title.

Contributors were able to select the type of evidence-based product they considered most appropriate to the topic under consideration. Although basic guidance was given on the four formats, they were able to employ flexibility in their approaches. For example, the Vancouver style of referencing used by Robert Kiley (pages 159–163) and Maria J. Grant (pages 251–256) is much better suited to evidence summaries and tables so this could be employed in preference to the Harvard style used elsewhere within the book.

14

Examining the evidence base for reference services and enquiry work

Andrew Booth

Introduction

This chapter briefly defines the essentials of reference services and enquiry work before identifying questions that users or funders of such a service might seek to answer. From here the chapter considers sources that might yield answers to such questions before making a brief assessment of relevant studies that have already examined this area, assessing them for quantity and quality.

The chapter concludes with a description of priorities for future research. This chapter is followed by a special topic illustrating what research evidence tells us about current awareness services.

What is evidence-based reference/enquiry work?

The first domain identified by Crumley and Koufogiannakis (2002) is *Reference/enquiries* by which they mean 'providing services and access to information that meets the needs of library users'. Reference services fall into three distinct types:

- *information service* – providing answers to enquirers' questions
- *instructional service* – teaching people to find information on their own
- *guidance* – advising and assisting users to identify and select appropriate materials on particular topics.

Instructional service potentially overlaps with the education domain (Chapter 15). However, a workable distinction is to consider that an instructional service offers task-specific instruction to achieve a specific information need whereas the educational domain covers more general non task-specific activities as required for skills transfer or lifelong learning. The complexity increases further with technological developments whereby a straightforward bibliographic enquiry might be resolved as document delivery. Technology has further complicated things as 'subject portals' are developed to support reference work.

Asking the question

On first appearance this domain appears to lie completely within the evidence base of the library literature. However, is the reference interview truly unique to librarianship? The consultation in medical practice is a well researched interaction between a service provider and a service user. Similarities between the reference interview and the consultation reveal intriguing areas for investigation. The literature concerning the problem or 'heartsink' patient has parallels in that of the difficult user (Blessinger, 2002; Fescemeyer, 2002). Interestingly, the movement towards evidence-based patient choice (EBPC) has stimulated research interest in the consultation. In a qualitative study Ford et al. (2003) conducted semi-structured interviews with key informants to identify the elements and skills required for a successful EBPC consultation. Six themes emerged from the data:

- the research evidence/information itself
- the doctor–patient relationship
- patient perspectives
- decision-making processes
- time issues
- establishing the patient's problem.

Such analyses provide a useful framework for investigation of the reference interview. Similarly, a related study on barriers to the EBPC consultation (Ford et al., 2002) provides useful illumination of the 'barriers' literature surrounding the reference interview.

Questions identified by Eldredge (2001) that fall within this domain include (Box 14.1):

Box 14.1 Questions from the reference/enquiry work domain

- Do student employees at service desks (circulation, information, reference, etc.) provide effective and efficient service when compared to the time needed to hire, train, and supervise them?
- How can we best measure if library staff members provide accurate information at service desks? (For example, do they accurately explain library policies and accurately answer factual reference questions?)
- Is it most efficient to have a combined circulation/photocopying service desk or separate desks and staff for each function?
- Can we prove that librarians are more effective at answering reference questions and running literature searches than library technicians?
- How do you measure the effectiveness of reference services (not just via e-mail)?

Finding the evidence

Main sources for evidence relating to reference and enquiry work are the library literature databases (See Chapter 7). However, the wider subject discipline of human interaction and communication, within which this profession-specific domain is located, also includes research studies from the psychology (PsycInfo), computer science (INSPEC) and other behavioural and social sciences (e.g. ASSIA and *Social Science Citation Index*). It will be helpful to phrase our search questions in broader terms, at least initially. For example, issues relating to perceived unhelpfulness of enquiry staff might be addressed by the more generic 'barriers' literature.

The evidence base

Although there are isolated instances of higher quality studies such as meta-analyses and randomized controlled trials, this domain is mainly populated by other types of research study.

Table 14.1   Research methods of importance within reference/enquiry work domain

Research methods of particular importance within this domain
Cohort studies
Qualitative research
Surveys and questionnaires

Meta-analysis

Evaluation of reference services was an early application for meta-analysis. Saxton (1997) looked at the consistency of findings from reference studies across multiple studies investigating whether they could be combined to obtain a more accurate estimate of strength of association. This research illustrates the value of meta-analysis within a library context.

Randomized controlled trials

Eldredge (2003) identifies one randomized controlled trial within enquiry and reference services. Eight healthcare teams were randomly selected; four teams serving as an intervention group and four teams serving as a control group. (Marshall and Neufeld, 1981). The interventions were clinical librarians providing information services for healthcare professionals, patients, and patients' families. The study found increased meeting of information needs in the intervention group. This was the first reported randomized controlled trial in librarianship.

Cohort studies

Cohort studies are much more common within this domain, with individuals who present to a service or enquiry point constituting a naturally-occurring cohort. Large numbers are achievable by amalgamating data across several similar sites. For example, 208 physicians in Rochester, New York were studied with regard to information provided by fifteen hospital libraries (Marshall, 1992). Similarly, a random sample of 442 physicians in rural and urban Texas were studied for the effect of distance from the library on their behaviour. Unsurprisingly, physicians near the library were more likely to use library resources and to be able to search MEDLINE (Bowden et al., 1994). Probably the defining study on the impact of reference services within the health domain is a cohort study where in-patients in Detroit hospitals were the subject of MEDLINE searches run by hospital librarians. By analysing searches against patient records it was revealed that those patients who had been the subject of MEDLINE searches necessitated reduced lengths of stay and lower costs (Klein et al., 1994). Other cohort studies identified by Eldredge (2002) include Urquhart and Hepworth (1995), Curtis et al (1997), Feldman and Bowden (2001) and Kars and Olson (2001). A less common study of patient information examined the personality types of women diagnosed with multiple sclerosis (Baker, 1994)

Su, Shiao-Feng and Lancaster (1995) compared two expert systems against what an experienced reference librarian would have done. Sixty library students were divided into those with no reference experience and those with some experience. No student group performed as well as experienced reference librarians.

Booth et al. (2000) examined the effect of structuring a search request form on the pre-search reference interview. In this multicentre before-and-after study involving six different libraries, 195 minimally structured forms collected over four months were compared with data from 185 EBM-structured forms collected over a subsequent four-month period following a brief training intervention (Phase 2).

Qualitative research

Durrance and Fisher (2003) argue that reference research has been particularly informed by qualitative research studies. Viewed organizationally, the reference desk is merely a service point and, like any other, may be explored by such techniques as focus groups. Massey-Burzio (1998) uses this methodology to examine user perceptions of the reference desk.

Other research methods

Interaction between users and human intermediaries in the information search situation is receiving renewed interest because it is believed that such patterns of interaction may be replicated in a user's interaction with an electronic catalogue. Many studies have been conducted, predominantly in academic libraries and examining bibliographic databases. Belkin, Brooks and Daniels (1987) categorized the elements of user-intermediary interaction through *discourse analysis* of mediated database searches.

In public libraries, an often-quoted study by Lynch (1977) applied *content analysis* to 300 unobtrusively recorded reference interviews to categorize librarians' questions. Dewdney (1992) used a similar technique to study the effect of training on librarians' question behaviour. Pejtersen (1986) used recorded interactions between librarians and users to develop a classification scheme for fiction, adapted to users' search strategies, and, subsequently to design a catalogue interface based on this classification.

Nordlie (1996) captured interactions at the reference and information desk of a medium-sized Norwegian public library. Interactions were audiotaped and supplemented with unobtrusive *observation* to record verbal and non-verbal communication. Librarians carried recording equipment to record interactions away from the reference desk. Issues with this study included the fact that the data was not a true random sample, as types of users and types of questions vary over the year. To establish, however, that it was representative, if not random, a control was used. The sample was compared with user questions collected during a week at a different time of the year. Themes and types of questions matched recorded data while the age and sex distribution of users in the sample approximated to that for registered borrowers.

Where interactions are primarily technology-mediated, other techniques, such as transaction log analysis, may be used (Peters, 1989; Hunter, 1991; Peters,

1993) (See Chapter 18). More recently, attention has focused on internet-based reference services. A symposium on the web-based reference interview, (*Internet Reference Services Quarterly*, **7** (3), 1–41, 2002), addresses this issue. Taher (2002a) examines whether the web-based reference interview saves the time of the interviewee. The same author (Taher 2002b) examines state-of-the-art publications in the area of real-time reference interview. Qayyum (2002) considers the effect of such services on the nature of queries posed by library patrons, and Bowman (2002) discusses the use of the library home page as a reference tool and its importance in the online reference interview process.

Due mainly to ease of administration, questionnaire studies are common within this domain. Mondschein (1990) examines SDI (selective dissemination of information) use and analyses data through descriptive statistics and multiple regression analysis. An economic study (contingent valuation survey technique) has been used to estimate the value that users attach to reference desk service in an academic library (Harless and Allen, 1999).

Critically appraising the evidence

The big issue in appraising research studies from this domain involves arguments regarding applicability and generalizability. With so many moderating factors that may impact on the success, or otherwise, of an enquiry service or even of an individual enquiry, it is difficult to analyse the specific contribution of any factor. With respect to the utilization of checklists this domain does not seem to require tailored checklists to appraise key studies. Checklists already exist for systematic reviews, randomized controlled trials, surveys and qualitative studies (Ajetunmobi, 2002).

Acting on the evidence

The evidence available within this domain may be generally of low quality but, at least in terms of implementation, reference and enquiry work has several inherent advantages. The knowledge required to deliver such services may be more easily codified in terms of procedures, policies and guidelines. While there will always be the 'exception to the rule' these could be analysed within a framework of 'variance analysis' whereby deviations from procedure are examined closely. Within the context of evidence-based practice it is important to acknowledge that variances can be positive or negative. Positive variances occur when the reference interaction is more successful or effective than outlined in procedures or policies. Negative variances reflect poorer performance than expected. For example a reference service may not be particularly geared to answering a certain type of enquiry. A member of staff might identify a useful resource on the internet that had previously been overlooked. Noting this positive variance would result in the incorporation of this resource in a future revision of this procedure. Such codification of procedures suggests the potential for the use of guidelines, protocols and algorithms.

Guidelines, protocols and algorithms

Practice guidelines may be defined as 'systematically developed statements to inform both librarian and user decisions in specific . . . circumstances' (adapted from Field and Lohr, 1992). *Algorithms* are a specific form of written guideline that break strategies down into their component steps and thus 'require observations to be made, decisions to be considered and actions to be taken' (Hadorn et al., 1992). Algorithms help people decide what to do next. They are guidelines represented schematically, typically in a decision-tree or flowchart format. Finally *protocols* are written statements which define the management of broad user problems or issues. As such they are written at a broader level than guidelines and may contain information that is wider than procedural knowledge. To this degree they may resemble policies, rather than procedures, although not all procedures embody evidence-based considerations. To illustrate, you may have a guideline on answering statistical enquiries. This might be accompanied by an algorithm that takes you through the principal sources in a preferred order in a recommended way of tackling that enquiry. The overarching protocol might embody broader principles such as keeping the user informed of progress, the need for clear documentation of sources and the requirement to supply definitions for all statistics retrieved.

In 2001 a Task Force of the Medical Library Association's Evidence Based Librarianship Implementation Committee (Booth et al., 2001) produced the following Recommendation/Position Statement on practice guidelines (Box 14.2).

Although examples of guidelines and protocols are rare, the potential is there. Hernon and Metoyerduran (1992) used focus group interviewing to examine the views of librarians about the literature of library and information science. They identified commonalities of practice that could be addressed in a 'good practice guideline'. For example, when conducting literature searches for the preparation of conference papers and manuscripts, librarians tend to search the literature selectively for timely articles. Interestingly, in the context of these chapters on the EBIP domains, some librarians value the literature of subject disciplines more than that of library and information science.

Box 14.2   MLA statement on practice guidelines

It is recommended that the Medical Library Association take the following steps to develop practice guidelines:

1   Research and develop . . . best available evidence practice guidelines.
2   . . . Gain good understanding of how and/or why topics are selected for guideline development.
3   Develop list of priority tasks, procedures, processes, and/or services . . . which merit the need for guidelines, and the reasons why. Topics should be practitioner- and not literature-driven.
4   Based on known models, apply best approach(es) to formulating a complete library guideline, i.e.:
5   Establish a process for periodic review and updating of established guideline(s) based on new evidence.
6   Research the desirability/need to integrate the practice guideline initiative with other MLA initiatives, e.g. benchmarking.

Submitted by the Task Force members: Andrew Booth, Molly Harris, Jessie McGowan, and Suzetta Burrows, August 2, 2001.

Future research

In the report the *LIS Research Landscape* (McNichol and Nankivell, 2003) electronic information services were the most mentioned domain for research priorities. Questions to be addressed included the impact of digital resources on information-seeking behaviour and the use and non-use of electronic information services. However such priorities have a downside: 'recent changes in focus in the LIS domain, for example greater focus on electronic information sources, meant that less attention was being paid to some of the classic traditional areas of library research such as classification and reference work'.

Janes and Hill (2002) propose a larger-scale investigation of librarians' experiences with changes resulting from introduction of digital reference services, suggesting areas for future research and questions to be answered.

More qualitative work is needed to compare the reference interview with other models of professional user interaction. This might lead to development of enquiry protocols or guidelines – as a tool for induction and continuing professional development.

References

Ajetunmobi, O. (2002) *Making Sense of Critical Appraisal*, London, Arnold.

Baker, L.M. (1994) Monitors and Blunters: patient health information seeking from a different perspective, *Bibliotheca Medica Canadiana*, **16** (2), 60–3.

Belkin, N. J., Brooks, H. M. and Daniels, P. J. (1987) Knowledge Elicitation using Discourse Analysis, *International Journal of Man–Machine Studies*, **27**, 127–44.

Blessinger, K. D. (2002) Problem Patrons: all shapes and sizes, *Reference Librarian*, **75/76**, 3–10.

Booth, A., O'Rourke, A. J. and Ford, N. J. (2000) Structuring the Pre-search Reference Interview: a useful technique for handling clinical questions, *Bulletin of the Medical Library Association*, **88** (3), 239–45.

Booth, A., Harris, M., McGowan, J. and Burrows, S. (2001) Submitted on behalf of the Evidence-Based Librarianship Implementation Committee Task Force on Practice Guidelines Recommendation/Position Statement, *Hypothesis*, **15** (2), 7.

Bowden, V. M., Kromer, M. E. and Tobia, R. C. (1994) Assessment of Physicians' Information Needs in Five Texas Counties, *Bulletin of the Medical Library Association*, **82** (2), 189–96.

Bowman, V. (2002) The Virtual Librarian and the Electronic Reference Interview, *Internet Reference Services Quarterly*, **7** (3), 3–14.

Crumley, E. and Koufogiannakis, D. (2002) Developing Evidence-based Librarianship: practical steps for implementation, *Health Information and Libraries Journal*, **19** (4), 61–70.

Curtis, K. L, Weller, A. C. and Hurd, J. M. (1997) Information-seeking Behavior of Health Sciences Faculty: the impact of new information technologies, *Bulletin of the Medical Library Association*, **85** (4), 402–10.

Dewdney, P. (1992) Recording the Reference Interview: a field experiment. In Glazier, J. D. and Powell, R. R. (eds), *Qualitative research in information management*, Englewood, Co., Libraries Unlimited, 122–50.

Durrance, J. C. and Fisher, K. E. (2003) Determining How Libraries and Librarians Help, *Library Trends*, **51** (4), 305–34.

Eldredge, J. (submitted on behalf of the Evidence-Based Librarianship Implementation Committee) (2001) The Most Relevant and Answerable Research Questions Facing the Practice of Health Sciences Librarianship, *Hypothesis*, **15** (1), 9–17, http://gain.mercer.edu/mla/research/hypothesis.html.

Eldredge, J. (2002) Cohort Studies in Health Sciences Librarianship, *Journal of the Medical Library Association*, **90** (4), 380–92.

Eldredge, J. D. (2003) The Randomized Controlled Trial Design: unrecognized opportunities for health sciences librarianship, *Health Information and Libraries Journal*, **20** (Suppl 1), 34–44.

Feldman, J. D. and Bowden, V. M. (2001) Library Use Survey of Texas Health Science Center – San Antonio Faculty: comparison of 1996 and 2000. Poster presented at MLA 2001, 101st Annual Meeting of the Medical Library Association, Orlando, FL, 25–30 May.

Fescemyer, K. (2002) Healing After the Unpleasant Outburst: recovering from incidents with angry library users, *Reference Librarian*, **75/76**, 235–44.

Field, M. J. and Lohr, K. N. (1992) *Guidelines for Clinical Practice: from development to use*, Washington, DC, National Academy Press.

Ford, S. et al. (2002) Barriers to the Evidence-based Patient Choice (EBPC) Consultation, *Patient Education and Counseling*, **47** (2), 179–85.

Ford, S. et al. (2003) What are the Ingredients for a Successful Evidence-based Patient Choice Consultation?: a qualitative study, *Social Science and Medicine*, **56** (3), 589–602

Hadorn, D. C., McCormick, K. and Diokno, A. (1992) An Annotated Algorithm Approach to Clinical Guideline Development, *JAMA*, **267**, 3311–4.

Harless, D. and Allen, F. (1999) Using the Contingent Valuation Method to Measure Patron Benefits of Reference Desk Service in an Academic Library, *College & Research Libraries*, **60** (1), 56–69.

Hernon, P. and Metoyerduran, C. (1992) Literature Reviews and Inaccurate Referencing – an Exploratory Study of Academic Librarians, *College & Research Libraries*, **53** (6), 499–512

Hunter, R. N. (1991) Successes and Failures of Patrons Searching the Online Catalog at a Large Academic Library: a transaction log analysis, *RQ*, **30**, 395–402.

Janes, J. and Hill, C. (2002) Finger on the Pulse, *Reference and User Services Quarterly*, **42** (1), 54–65.

Kars, M. and Olson, S. (2001) A Retrospective Study of PubMed Training and Loansome Doc Registration Improving Access to the Medical Literature, *Journal of Hospital Librarianship*, **1** (2),67–72.

Klein, M. S, Ross, F. V., Adams, D. L. and Gilbert, C. M. (1994) Effect of Online Literature Searching on Length of Stay and Patient Care Costs, *Academic Medicine*, **69** (6), 489–95.

Lynch, M. J. (1977) *Reference Interviews in Public Libraries*, PhD Dissertation, Rutgers, The State University of New Jersey (unpublished).

McNichol, S. and Nankivell, C. (2003) *The LIS Research Landscape: a review and prognosis*, Birmingham, Centre for Information Research, University of Central England.

Marshall, J. G and Neufeld, V. R (1981) A Randomized Trial of Librarian Educational Participation in Clinical Settings, *Journal of Medical Education*, **56** (5), 409–16.

Marshall, J. G. (1992) The Impact of the Hospital Library on Clinical Decision Making: the Rochester Study, *Bulletin of the Medical Library Association*, **80** (2), 169–78.

Massey-Burzio, V. (1998) From the Other Side of the Reference Desk: focus group study, *Journal of Academic Librarianship*, **24** (3), 208–15.

Mondschein, L. G. (1990) SDI Use and Productivity in the Corporate Research Environment, *Special Libraries*, **81** (4), 265–79.

Nordlie, R. (1996) Unmediated and Mediated Information Searching in the Public Library, *ASIS 1996 Annual Conference Proceedings*, www.asis.org/annual-96/ ElectronicProceedings/nordlie.html.

Pejtersen, M. A. (1986) Design and Test of a Database for Fiction Based on an Analysis of Children's Search Behavior. In Ingwersen, P. et al. (eds), *Information Technology and Information Use: toward a unified view of information technology*, London, Taylor Graham, 125–45.

Peters, T. A. (1989) When Smart People Fail: an analysis of the transaction log of an online public access catalog, *Journal of Academic Librarianship*, **15** (5), 267–73.

Peters, T. A. (1993) The History and Development of Transaction Log Analysis, *Library Hi-Tech News*, **11** (2), 41–66.

Qayyum, M. A. (2002) Internet Reference Services and the Reference Desk: does the nature of a user's query really change?, *Internet Reference Services Quarterly*, **7** (3), 15–22.

Saxton, M. L. (1997) Reference Service Evaluation and Meta Analysis: findings and methodological issues, *Library Quarterly*, **67** (3), 267–89.

Su, Shiao-Feng and Lancaster, F. W. (1995) Evaluation of Expert Systems in Reference Applications, *RQ*, **35** (2), 219–28.

Taher, M. (2002a) The Reference Interview Through Asynchronous E-Mail and Synchronous Interactive Reference: does it save the time of the interviewee?, *Internet Reference Services Quarterly*, **7** (3), 23–34.

Taher, M. (2002b) Real-time (Synchronous Interactive) Reference Interview: a select bibliography, *Internet Reference Services Quarterly*, **7** (3), 35–41.

Urquhart, C. and Hepworth, J. (1995) The Value of Information Supplied to Clinicians by Health Libraries: devising an outcomes-based assessment of the contribution of libraries to clinical decision-making, *Health Libraries Review*, **12** (3), 201–13.

Special topic (A)
Provision of a current awareness service for research staff (Guideline)

Robert Kiley

Scenario

As a recently appointed librarian at an academic institution you are asked to investigate the potential for a current awareness service (CAS) for research staff. Conscious of the need to provide an effective service – balancing cost with the needs of the researchers – you look at evidence to answer the question: 'In a library serving the research community (Population) what are the optimal criteria for implementing a current awareness service (Intervention) from the perspective of the users and management (Outcomes)?'

This guideline is aimed at academic, special and health librarians.

Introduction

All researchers need to be aware of the latest peer-reviewed research. For health professionals, 'among the many challenges physicians face, keeping our personal fund of medical knowledge up-to-date is one of the most difficult'.[1] General physicians wishing to keep up-to-date need to read 19 articles a day, 365 days a year.[2]

To manage this problem – and ensure researchers are alerted to new research – librarians offer current awareness services. This guideline examines evidence for providing an effective service.

Trends in current awareness services

Current awareness services appeared in three distinct phases:

Phase 1: analogue services

The need for CAS to keep researchers abreast of developments in their field was recognized as early as 1978.[3] At this time, CAS were typically limited to photo-copying, distributing tables of contents and producing accession lists, bulletins, displays and newspaper clippings.[4]

Phase 2: databases and diskette services

By the 1990s, CAS were more sophisticated (but more expensive), with the development of electronic commercial services, such as *Current Contents on Diskette* and the British Library's *CASIAS* product. Online database vendors (OVID, Dialog, etc.) introduced SDI services that allowed librarians to define (and store) various search profiles. These could be run when the database was updated and new 'hits' mailed to the researcher. Literature from this period typically compares one alerting service with another. Bandemer and Tannery[5] compare four different alerting services, whilst Davies et al.[6] attempt a more comprehensive sur-vey of over 25 different services.

Phase 3: the web and end-user empowerment

With the advent of the web, CAS have evolved yet further. Fourie[4] identifies eight distinct *types* of service, ranging from traditional tables of contents and database alerting services, through to filtered news services (e.g. MyYahoo and NewsAlert) and web-based agents that 'learn' researchers' interests and subsequently alert them to new resources.

Web-based services combine two elements – identifying new resources, and full-text article supply – into one seamless activity. The web also allows researchers to define their own search profiles without intervention from information pro-fessionals.

Criteria from the user's perspective

CAS should deliver 'the right information, to the right user at the right time, in the right format, covering the right sources'.[4] Bandemer and Tannery[5] identify three key requirements of an effective CAS:

- ease of use
- coverage
- currency.

Ease of use includes the ability to mark records (for export, printing, e-mailing etc.), combine searches and save search profiles. Coverage is also important, as is currency. The facility to import results into a personal database (e.g. Reference Manager) is a further useful feature.[7]

Immediate access to full text is also considered a high priority. As de Stricker[8] states: 'users have become accustomed to full text as current awareness, as opposed to the traditional two-step process of reviewing citations and ordering document copies'. Rowley[9] found that 96% of engineering faculty users who received a table of contents service considered full text links 'important' or 'very important'. Researchers expect everything to be free at the point of use.[10]

Finally, researchers expect to be alerted to all relevant information – but do not want to be overwhelmed: 'unfortunately, current-awareness subscriptions often end up overwhelming users'.[8]

To meet the needs of researchers, CAS must be easy to use and up-to-date, with as exhaustive coverage as possible. Results should be delivered directly to the desktop and users must be able to link directly to full text for any item of interest. Access to all relevant information must be free at the point of use (Evidence Level: 4).

Criteria from the management perspective

Many managers may feel that delivering such an effective CAS is an almost hopeless task. Notwithstanding developments in technology, budgetary concerns must be considered. Research from the Association of Research Libraries shows that between 1986 and 1999 the cost of journal subscriptions increased by 207% – far higher than inflation and increases in library budgets – whilst numbers of subscribed titles fell by 6%.[11]

Library managers should consider the cost benefit of developing an in-house service or using a commercial one – the 'most critical decision' facing the librarian.[12] Palmer[13] shows the staff cost of electronic alerting services is *less* than that associated with a paper-based CAS. Librarians increasingly turn to current awareness services/individual article supply (CASIAS) as an 'alternative to local access to journals they have cancelled'.[12] Fernandez[14] describes how a user survey was used to justify cancellation of *Current Contents on Diskette*.

CAS search results can be used to measure the relevance of a journal collection. In one such study, over 90% of articles identified by CAS were available in the local library.[15] Conversely, this type of study can be used to identify new subscriptions and to quantify the impact of previous cancelled titles.

Library managers must ensure services are cost-effective in meeting user needs. Research shows that the cost of providing electronic alerting services is less than that associated with more traditional paper-based services. Such services can be effective in providing access to journal titles that have been cancelled and helping librarians develop an effective collection development policy (Evidence Level: 4).

Priorities for further research

Of approximately 300 articles on current awareness on the LISA database most describe various CAS or compare competing products. Though this is useful, further research is needed:

- What do researchers actually need from a CAS? Most user surveys[10, 12, 14] predate widespread use of the internet. Should librarians simply provide lists of bibliographic citations with full-text links to users, who already have desktop access to virtually unlimited information? Should they add value, perhaps by providing a digest summary compiled from websites, e-print servers, press releases, circulars, discussion lists etc?
- What impact has the development of e-print servers had on traditional CAS? For example, what is the time delay between a paper published on the physics e-print server (http://lib-www.lanl.gov/) and its being indexed in INSPEC? Meeting the needs of researchers – who want up-to-date information – requires an increasing number of diverse tools. Research on the costs of providing exhaustive searching is also required.
- Do subscription-based CAS offer value for money? For example, with numerous *free* alerting services (Infotrieve, Ingenta etc.) is there a need to subscribe to services like ZETOC, or Information Quest?
- Are librarian-mediated CAS still required or should current awareness be left to the end-user?
- Finally, is there evidence on the effectiveness of CAS – do researchers who have access to CAS produce more or better (high-impact) research?

References

1   Laine, C. and Weinberg, D. S. (1990) How can Physicians keep up-to-date?, *Annual Review of Medicine*, **50**, 99–110.
2   Davidoff, F., Haynes, R. B., Sackett, D. L. and Smith, R. (1995) Evidence-based Medicine: a new journal to help doctors identify the information they need, *BMJ*, **310**, 1085–6.
3   Williams, M. E. (1978) Online Retrieval – Today and Tomorrow, *Online Review*, **2** (4), 353–66
4   Fourie, I. (1999) Empowering Users – Current Awareness on the Internet, *The Electronic Library*, **17** (6), 379–88.

5   Bandemer, J. and Tannery, N. H. (1998) A Comparison of Four Current Awareness Services, *Medical Reference Services Quarterly*, **17** (2), 29–37.

6   Davies, M., Boyle, F. and Osborne, S. (1998) CAS-IAS Services: where are we now?, *The Electronic Library*, **16** (1), 37–48.

7   Cox, J. and Hanson, T. (1992) Setting up an Electronic Current Awareness Service, *Online*, **16** (4), 36–43.

8   Stricker, de U. (2002) Keep Me Posted . . . but not too much. Challenges and opportunities from STM current awareness providers, *Searcher*, **10** (1), 52–9, www.findarticles.com/cf_0/m0DPC/1_10/81596542/print.jhtml.

9   Rowley, J. (1994) Revolutions in Current Awareness Services, *Journal of Librarianship and Information Science*, **26** (1), 7–14.

10 Brunskill, K. (1997) Measuring Researchers' Preferences for CASIAS, *The New Review of Information Networking*, 93–102.

11 Association of Research Libraries. *Research Library Trends: ARL Statistics 2000–2001*, www.istl.org/istl/02-winter/article3.html.

12 Brunskill, K. (1997) The Issues Surrounding the Provision of CASIAS Services in Libraries, *Interlending and Document Supply*, **25** (2), 57–63.

13 Palmer, T. (1999) Current Awareness Services, *Bibliotheca Medica Canadiana*, **21** (2), 303–4.

14 Fernandez, L. (2002) User Perceptions of Current Awareness Services: a faculty survey, *Issues in Science and Technology Librarianship*, **33** (Winter), www.istl.org/istl/02-winter/article3.html.

15 Youngen, G. K. (1999) Using Current Awareness Search Results to Measure a Journal Collection's Relevancy, *Library Collections, Acquisitions and Technical Services*, **23** (2), 141–8.

15

The contribution of evidence-based practice to educational activities

Anne Brice and Cindy Carlson

Introduction

This chapter examines issues relating to evaluation of educational interventions. It considers the types of questions that might be framed from an educational perspective, the sources that might supply answers to such questions, and the quality of the evidence base. Whether evidence from education research is put into practice, and barriers to acting on the evidence are also considered. Key studies from within the domain are used to illustrate issues and methods. Educational approaches within an information setting encompass everything from user education to staff development and training. A subsequent special topic examines the evidence base for the training of users in information skills.

What is evidence-based education?

What do we mean by evidence-based education, and what kinds of research might those involved in teaching and learning do? Much existing published research centres on education policy, and very little is actually evidence-based. In addition, much research has been carried out in the context of primary and secondary education, where much of the controversy and public interest lies. In fact, even here Davies et al. (2000) suggest that the evidence base is weak and that 'there is often not a culture of teachers using research to inform their everyday school practice'. In this chapter we focus on research undertaken with regard to adult and lifelong learning. However we should acknowledge, albeit in passing, the considerable work that exists looking at evidence-based practice in relation to the contribution of the school librarian (Todd, 2001; Todd, 2002a; Todd, 2002b; Todd, 2003).

Evidence-based education is '(t)he integration of professional wisdom with the best empirical evidence in making decisions about how to deliver instruction'. The authors of this definition argue that professional wisdom is important for helping to adapt empirical evidence to local situations, and that randomized control trials are the best way to establish empirical evidence.

Fierce debate surrounds the relevance and appropriateness of research methodologies for educational interventions. Some see the gold standard of evidence in this context as multiple replications of small scale, randomized controlled trials of feasible interventions in real-life settings (Fitz-Gibbon, Tymms and Coe, 2000) while others strongly challenge this view (Morrison 2001; Hammersley 2001). To date, the evidence base for adult learning has been developed foremost in continuing medical education (Davis et al., 1999), medical education (Wolf, Shea and Albanese 2001) and health promotion (Perkins, Simnett, and Wright 1999). It is unsurprising that interest in evidence for health-related education should be so dominant, given the wide-ranging impact of the evidence-based medicine movement, with its emphasis on continuing professional development and lifelong learning, and interest in the relationship between learning and behaviour change. The influence of the EBM paradigm is perhaps seen most clearly in 'best evidence medical education' programs that prepare residents, for example, to teach medical students (Morrison and Hafler, 2000; Hart and Harden, 2000).

Important catalysts have been the development of the Campbell Collaboration (Wolf, Shea and Albanese, 2001), previously described in Chapter 2, and the Cochrane Collaboration Effective Practice and Organisation of Care Group (EPOC, 2003), both of whom provide a comprehensive list of topics and priorities for systematic reviews for evidence of effectiveness in education.

A health warning is appropriate here with regard to an over-reliance on traditional ideas of what constitutes 'evidence' and the application of knowledge based learning. As indicated above, many authors in the education research field indicate some problems with the focus on evidence-based education. Schon (1991), in particular, points to the importance of the 'artistic, intuitive processes' that professionals 'bring to situations of uncertainty, instability, uniqueness and value conflict. He argues that professional knowledge and the application of formulaic approaches are not enough in dealing with real-life problems, and that all professionals need to develop skills in 'reflection-in-action' as well as being able to cope with the unexpected.

Asking the question

Approaches to gathering evidence for what works in health promotion have emphasized that data collection methods depend entirely on the research question that is being asked (Webb 1999). When exploring what evidence is available on specific topics in education, Oakley (2002) found large discrepancies in how systematic literature searches into available evidence had actually been conducted in two different areas of health promotion. In both cases, different systematic reviews for each topic area were compared, and found to be widely divergent in terms of the studies reviewed. Oakley's team, upon systematically searching for studies on smoking prevention programmes for young people, found 70 studies altogether, whereas the two systematic reviews they looked at had together only identified 27, and only three of those were common to both studies. The implications of these discrepancies for interpretation are clear.

Greenhalgh et al. (2003) in researching the effectiveness of online education found that many research questions were qualitative, rather than quantitative, in nature. This in turn impacted on the type of research identified for the literature review as well as on the nature of the primary research they intended to carry out. In framing the question, you need to consider most carefully the outcomes that you are hoping to identify. For instance Belfield et al. (2001) identifies five levels of effectiveness to measure effectiveness in education: outcomes, behaviour, learning, reaction and participation, and discusses these levels within the context of research evidence for education within the medical profession. The Evidence Based Education Centre in the UK highlights the prominence of the first of these: Central to evidence-based practice is the combining of professional expertise, insight, experience and leadership with the ability to collect, interpret, and integrate valid, important and applicable user-observed and research-derived evidence to ensure significant outcomes' (E-BEUK, 2002, 1). While concluding that student learning and student learning outcomes are: 'too important to allow [them] to be determined by unfounded opinion, whether of politicians, teachers, researchers or anyone else' (E-BEUK, 2002, 1).

A pilot study into using systematic reviews to explore the effectiveness of Problem Based Learning (PBL) illustrates how educational research question(s) can be framed with intervention, comparison and outcomes all clearly delineated (Newman, 2003). Work undertaken to identify questions in librarianship reflected many in the area of educational interventions (Eldredge, 2001) (Box 15.1). For the information professional several types of education question will be relevant to practice. Not to be overlooked are those relating to the continuing professional development of yourself and your staff e.g. 'Is mentoring an effective form of continuing professional development?'

> ## Box 15.1 Questions asked within the educational activities domain
>
> - Do students who have been taught information skills perform better academically (as measured by exams and other assessment) than those who haven't?
> - Are students who have been taught information skills more or less likely to continue to further study?
> - Does teaching information skills at a distance (e.g. web based delivery) have a better or worse outcome than face-to-face?
> - Do library resource classes have an impact on student learning/achievement? If not, is there a better approach than the traditional one-off, 50-minute session that faculty usually allows us?
> - How do we assess the impact of our teaching?
> - Does problem-based learning enhance the students' skills in information seeking?
> - How do we assess library contributions to the practice of continuous learning?
> - How can librarian/searchers contribute to self-directed learning? What more can we contribute, based on evidence in other endeavours (such as higher education) that has been demonstrated to be effective?
> - How do we assess that students actually improve their critical appraisal and search skills once they've participated in informatics programmes?

Finding the evidence

What are the sources of evidence in education, and how good are they? Chapter 7 identified a preliminary range of sources of evidence for the domain of educational questions, although many more exist. Databases that list systematic reviews of education research include Educational Resources Information Center (ERIC), complemented by the newer International ERIC, covering the UK (Evans, Sharp and Benefield, 2000). Difficulties in harnessing the ERIC database are highlighted by Hertzberg and Rudner (1997). PsycInfo – the American Psychological Society's international database of the literature in psychology – provides some education coverage (Evans, Sharp and Benefield, 2000), as do Current Educational Research in the UK (CERUK), and the Campbell Collaboration's Social, Psychological, Educational, and Criminological Controlled Trials Register (SPECTR) database (Smith 2002). Begun by the Cochrane Collaboration, responsibility for SPECTR was subsequently handed over to the Campbell Collaboration based at the University of Pennsylvania (www.campbellcollaboration.org/). With more than 10,000 randomized and quasi-randomized trials, SPECTR is still at an early stage in its development (Evans, Sharp and Benefield, 2000).

The Evidence for Policy and Practice Information and Co-ordinating Centre (EPPI) Centre at the Social Science Research Unit, University of London (EPPI 2003b) has compiled a Research Evidence in Education Library (REEL). REEL is an electronic database of completed reviews of educational research evidence (EPPI 2003a). This database is located at the home site of the Centre for Evidence-

Informed Policy and Practice in Education, commissioned by the Department for Education and Skills, England. The Centre aims to provide a centralized resource for people wishing to undertake systematic reviews of research in education and those wishing to use reviews to inform policy and practice. References for all completed and ongoing systematic reviews are included in the database which currently contains over 700 records (http://eppi.ioe.ac.uk/EPPIWeb/home.aspx).

Evans, Sharp and Benefield (2000) observe that databases that serve education are 'far less developed than those found in medical and health care research'. In comparison with MEDLINE and its 'highly sophisticated searching strategies', they bemoan the absence of facilities that allow 'insertion of quality strings (or evidence-based quality filters – EBQFs) into the searching strategy'. As mentioned previously, these are designed to limit searches in various ways, either by type of intervention or type of publication.

Databases alone are insufficient for capturing all the evidence on topic areas. This was the case when searching for all available evidence on the effectiveness of online education (Greenhalgh et al., 2003). The authors also attended education conferences and retrieved old conference papers as well as enrolling on courses in order to ensure that they had a full list of existing research. Much education research sits in the 'grey literature'.

The evidence base

Table 15.1   Research methods of importance in educational activities

Research methods of particular importance within this domain
Systematic reviews
Qualitative research

What types of evidence exist in education research, and how good is it? There are some RCTs but a large part of education research is qualitative. As stated above, evidence is highly dependent on the research question being asked and may require compromises in the name of pragmatism. Greenhalgh et al. (2003) refined their own research question when assessing their online learning programme, from evaluating their course from the perspective of 'student effectiveness' to considering 'what is a high quality online learning experience for postgraduate students of primary health care?' This helped to mitigate the trickier problems of attribution faced in educational research.

The gap between the questions that need to be answered in practice and the research undertaken is clear. Dolmans et al. (2000) report that in higher education there is a difference in attitude between university staff as teachers and as researchers – on the one hand they are happy to see evidence guiding the development of the discipline at large, but evidence on teaching and learning hardly ever affects their role as individual teachers. Unfortunately much published literature describes what needs to be done to boost the education evidence base, while very little appears to contribute to it.

Systematic reviews

Davis et al. (1995), in a systematic review of 150 RCTs of different methods of continuing medical education, found the following interventions to be effective:

- mini-sabbaticals
- sensitive personalized feedback
- patient education
- computer-assisted decision-making, providing reminders and easy access to guidelines
- on-the-job training of practical skills
- use of opinion leaders or 'educational influentials'.

Greenhalgh et al. (2003) write about the transferability of evidence-based medicine to evidence-based educational quality using a systematic review and case study of an online course. As noted above, the authors had to adjust their research questions during the course of the research as they came across a paucity of research evidence. Newman (2003) concludes that systematic reviews for some education interventions are possible. He was able to use standard systematic review and meta-analysis processes to examine the research literature on problem based learning. However, studies included did not define specific interventions they were employing under the rubric of PBL, limiting the ability to compare across studies. While not an insurmountable problem, it is clear that broad educational interventions such as PBL require a more focused definition of what is meant.

Webb (1999) suggests that the systematic review process can be made more useful by:

- inclusion criteria including rigorous observational studies
- inclusion criteria focusing on both the quality of the research design and the quality of the intervention
- the review process being more transparent to readers
- the review process being acknowledged as subjective in terms of how data is interpreted.

Smith (2002) looks at systematic reviewing as a methodology for educational interventions which can then be reported in a way that permits end users to make evidence informed decisions. Within information practice systematic review methods are in their infancy. One is reported in the special topic following this chapter (Brettle, 2003). Others include those by Winning and Beverley (2003) and Wagner and Byrd (2003).

Randomized controlled trials

Examples of randomized controlled trials (RCTs) are also rare, although some RCTs, identified by Eldredge (2003), supplemented by a recent addition by Cheng (2003), are given in Table 15.2.

Table 15.2 Some RCTs in LIS educational activities

	Population	Intervention (comparison)	Outcomes
Marshall & Neufeld (1981)	8 healthcare teams randomly selected from a pool of 20 teams	Clinical librarians providing information services	Meeting of information needs
Erickson & Warner (1998)	31 obstetrics and gynaecology residents	Individual 1-hour MEDLINE tutorial	Satisfaction with instruction and hands-on training
Foust et al. (1999)	67 MLIS degree programme students and 133 gifted high school students	Web-based tutorial	Effectiveness
Cheng (2003)	800 Hong Kong clinicians	Three-hour educational workshop (No training)	Satisfaction; learning; knowledge; change in searching skills; change in attitude; change in behaviour; search time; perceived burden of searching and success in clinical problem solving

Qualitative research

White (2002) identifies a 'widespread lack of skills for collecting and analysing quantitative data' within education which, combined with a historic preference for small-scale 'qualitative' studies, has created an imbalance in the type of methods employed in educational research.

Critically appraising the evidence

Can the tools developed by CASP be applied to educational research? An appraisal checklist for the appraisal of educational literature (Box 15.2) has been developed by Morrison et al. (1999). The checklist consists of nine questions. Initial results showed that this instrument was feasible, allowing the reader to critically appraise reports of educational interventions and supporting the practice of evidence-based education.

Box 15.2 Nine-question checklist for critically appraising educational research:

1 Is there a clear question which the study seeks to answer?
2 Is there a clear learning need which the intervention seeks to address?
3 Is there a clear description of the educational context for the intervention?
4 Is the precise nature of the intervention clear?
5 Is the study design able to answer the question posed by the study?
6 Are the methods within the design capable of appropriately measuring the phenomena which the intervention ought to produce?
7 Are the outcomes chosen to evaluate the intervention appropriate?
8 Are there any other explanations of the results explored in the study?
9 Are any unanticipated outcomes explained?

There is a need to develop skills both in critical appraisal and conduct of research (Egan, 1999).

Acting on the evidence

Acting on the evidence, or implementing evidence in practice, is probably the most difficult step in evidence-based practice. Even overwhelming evidence of the positive effects of changing practice is not sufficient to encourage individuals to change, and organizational and individual factors need to be taken into account (Iles and Sutherland, 2001). So how does education evidence get put into practice - or does it, even? What are the barriers to acting on the evidence?

The Campbell Collaboration, a sibling organization to the Cochrane Collaboration, aims to promote the development of systematic reviews of evidence about educational and social policy issues, and to make these readily available to practitioners (Davies and Boruch, 2001). Early work has uncovered numerous RCTs and it is likely that systematic reviews of RCTs to support decision making about education will become more plentiful together with specific evidence concerning the education of health professionals and information professionals.

One way of embedding education research evidence into practice is by ensuring greater involvement of practitioners themselves in the research process. The more that teachers, lecturers and others become involved in carrying out their own research to answer pressing questions related to their practice, the more likely they are then to transform their results into action. There is similarly a need for concise summaries of evidence (see Box 15.3). Davies et al. (2000) describe a situation in education where the research and practice communities are riven with disputes as to what constitutes appropriate evidence, there is relatively little experimentation (especially compared with healthcare), and divisions between qualitative and quantitative paradigms run deep.

In discussing the relationship between cost and continuing professional development, although methods shown to be more effective could be seen to increase costs, it has been suggested that the true cost of failing to offer effective education, and continuing to spend at current levels on techniques of unproven effectiveness, needs to be examined (Gray, 2001).

Hammersley (2001) suggests that the evidence-based practice movement makes false and dangerous promises – some aspects warrant transfer from health to education, others do not. He implies that evidence from research should not be rated too highly over other sources, with a lack of clarity about how such evidence should be integrated when making practical judgements. Another problem cited is thinking that research can make practice transparently accountable, and that attempting to achieve this will have undesirable consequences. Morrison (2001) strongly supports arguments against reliance on randomized control trials and systematic reviews, finding eight possible problems with relying on RCTs.

Box 15.3 Towards Experimental Research Syntheses in Education (TERSE) Reports

A TERSE Report summarizes the most important information about an educational experiment including details of the design, context, intervention and results of the experiment, under structured headings. A TERSE Report, essentially a structured abstract, closely resembles the Critically Appraised Topic advocated by proponents of evidence-based healthcare. TERSE Reports were originally devised by Carol Taylor Fitz-Gibbon for the journal *Evaluation and Research in Education* in 1998.

TERSE reports aim to make short, succinct summaries of small-scale experiments in education available to a wide and non-specialist audience. Its format offers many advantages: the length is enough to convey the important information about an experiment, but short enough to make it easily absorbed. It is not intended to provide enough information to enable the reader to replicate the study, so where possible it provides references to more extended reports. The structured format, seen in many journals in medicine, psychology, etc, has been shown to aid comprehension. The length and structure allow even small-scale studies to be reported and accessed. TERSE Reports to date include:

Coe, Robert (1999) *The Effects of Giving Performance Feedback to Teachers: a randomised controlled experiment.*

(continued)

Box 15.3 *(continued)*

Dowson, Val (1999–2000) *Time of Day Effects on Children's Learning.*
Fitz-Gibbon, Carol and Defty, Neil (2000) *Effects of Providing Schools with Names of Under-aspiring Pupils.*
Goodson, Vicky (1999) *Effects of Different Testing Environments on Children's Performance and Attitudes.*
http://cem.dur.ac.uk/ebeuk/research/terse/default.htm.

Espousing chaos theory, he states that even the same teacher teaching the same curriculum using the same methodology in the same setting, will achieve different outcomes. Morrison argues that it is often the extraneous factors that RCTs try to control for that are of key importance to understanding 'what works' in education.

Future research priorities

Several authors suggest areas ripe for research. Wolf et al. (2001), in meetings with medical research directors, identified four main areas requiring further research to inform medical education:

- curricular design: e.g. the impact of discipline-related versus integrated curriculum
- learning and instructional methods, e.g. the relative effectiveness of problem-based learning versus active learning (Newman, 2003)
- testing and assessment, including the effects of testing on what is learned
- outcomes, especially what outcomes should be used to evaluate medical education.

Conclusion

The evidence base for education is limited, particularly within LIS. Information practitioners rarely have a grounding in pedagogic theory or an understanding of the needs of adult learners.

To date, little emphasis has been given to identifying the most successful search strategies, or to critically appraising evidence from the educational knowledge base. Evidence on effective education strategies is not being systematically integrated into practice. Educational policy and practice still tend to be influenced by political factors or by individual professional judgement, rather than by evidence of best or effective practice. This belies the impression conveyed by enlightened centres that argue that policy and practice 'should be capable of being justified in terms of sound evidence about the likely effects' (E-BEUK, 2002, 1).

In the information science literature, the emphasis on evidence-based education has emerged from the healthcare sector, although traditionally higher education library services have had a more defined role in user education and involvement in teaching and learning.

We also need to consider how best it can be promoted, and whether there is an existing body of knowledge that can inform practice, how we can access it, and under what conditions such knowledge might impact on practice.

References

Belfield, C., Thomas, H., Bullock, A., Eynon, R. and Wall, D. (2001) Measuring Effectiveness for Best Evidence Medical Education: a discussion, *Medical Teacher*, **23** (2), 164–70.

Brettle, A. (2003) Information Skills Training: a systematic review of the literature, *Health Information and Libraries Journal*, **20** (Suppl 1), 3–9.

Cheng, G. Y. T. (2003) Educational Workshop Improved Information-seeking Skills, Knowledge, Attitudes and the Search Outcome of Hospital Clinicians: a randomised controlled trial, *Health Information Libraries Journal*, **20** (Suppl 1), 22–33.

Coe, R., Tymms, P. B. and Fitz-Gibbon, C.T. (2000) Promoting Evidence-Based Education: the role of practitioners. Roundtable presented at the British Educational Research Association annual conference, Cardiff, September 2000, www.leeds.ac.uk/educo.

Davies, P. (1999) What is Evidence-based Education?, *British Journal of Educational Studies*, **47** (2), 108–21.

Davies, H. T. O., Nutley, S. M. and Smith, P. C. (eds) (2000) *What Works? Evidence-based policy and practice in public services*, Bristol, The Policy Press.

Davies, P. and Boruch, R. (2001) The Campbell Collaboration. Does for public policy what Cochrane does for health, *BMJ*, **323**, 294–5.

Davis, D. A. et al. (1999) The Impact of Formal Continuing Medical Education: do conferences, workshops, rounds and other traditional continuing education activities change physician behavior or health care outcomes?, *JAMA*, **282** (9), 867–74.

Davis, D. A., Thomson, M., Oxman, A. and Haynes, B. (1995) Changing Physicians' Performance, *JAMA*, **274**, 700–5.

Dolmans, D. H. J. M., Scherpbier, A. J. J. A. and van der Vleuten, C. P. M. (2000) The Need for Evidence in Education, *Medical Teacher*, **22** (3), 246–50.

E-BEUK (2002) Evidence-Based Education, UK. Durham University's Curriculum, Evaluation and Management Centre, http://cem.dur.ac.uk/ebeuk/manifesto.htm.

Egan, B. A. (1999) Effective Teaching and the Ineffective Study. *Paper presented at the British Educational Research Association Annual Conference*, University of Sussex at Brighton.

Eldredge, J. (submitted on behalf of the Evidence-Based Librarianship Implementation Committee) (2001) The Most Relevant and Answerable Research Questions Facing the Practice of Health Sciences Librarianship, *Hypothesis*, 15 (1), 9–17, http://gain.mercer.edu/mla/research/hypothesis.html.

Eldredge, J. D. (2003) The Randomised Controlled Trial Design: unrecognized opportunities for health sciences librarianship, *Health Information and Libraries Journal*, 20 (Suppl 1), 34–44.

EPOC (2003) *Cochrane Collaboration Effective Practice and Organization of Care Group*, www.epoc.uottawa/ca/index.htm.

EPPI (2003a) *Research Evidence in Education Library*, http://eppi.ioe.ac.uk/reel/.

EPPI (2003b) *The Evidence for Policy and Practice Information and Co-ordinating Centre* (EPPI-Centre), http://eppi.ioe.ac.uk/EPPIWeb/home.aspx.

Erickson, S. and Warner, E. R. (1998) The Impact of an Individual Tutorial Session on MEDLINE use Among Obstetrics and Gynaecology Residents in an Academic Training Programme: a randomized trial, *Medical Education*, 32 (3), 269–73.

Evans, D. and Haines, A. (2000) *Evidence, Effectiveness and the Experience of Implementation*, Oxford, Radcliffe Press.

Evans, J., Sharp, C. and Benefield, P. (2000) *Systematic Reviews of Educational Research: does the medical model fit? Paper presented at the British Educational Research Association Conference, Cardiff University, 7–10 September*, National Foundation for Educational Research.

Fitz-Gibbon, C. T., Tymms, P. B. and Coe, R. (2000) *Promoting Evidence-based Education: the role of practitioners. Paper presented at the British Educational Research Association Annual Conference*, Cardiff University.

Foust, J.E., Tannery, N. H. and Detlefsen, E. G. (1999) Implementation of a Web-based Tutorial, *Bulletin of the Medical Library Association*, 87 (4), 477–9.

Gray, J. A. M. (2001) *Evidence-based Healthcare: how to make health policy and management decisions*, Edinburgh, Churchill Livingstone.

Greenhalgh, T., Toon, P., Russell, J., Wong, G., Plumb, L. and Macfarlane, F. (2003) Transferability of Principles of Evidence Based Medicine to Improve Educational Quality: systematic review and case study of an online course in primary health care, *BMJ*, 326 (7381), 142–5.

Griffith, J. R. (2000) Towards Evidence-based Health Administration Education: the tasks ahead, *J Health Adm Educ.*, 18 (2), 251–62.

Hammersley, M. (2001) *Some Questions About Evidence-based Practice in Education*, British Educational Research Association Annual Conference, Leeds University.

Hargreaves, D. H. (1996) Teachers, Educational Research and Evidence-based Teaching, *Education Review*, **10** (2), 46–50.

Hargreaves, D. H. (1997) In Defence of Research for Evidence-based Teaching: a rejoinder to Martyn Hammersley, *British Educational Research Journal*, **23** (4), 405–19.

Hart, I. R. and Harden, R. M. (2000) Best Evidence Medical Education (BEME): A plan for action, *Medical Teacher*, **22** (2), 131–41.

Hertzberg, S. and Rudner, L. (1997) The Quality of Searchers' Searches of the ERIC Database, *Education Policy Analysis Archives*, **7** (25), (August), epaa.asu.edu search; http://epaa.asu.edu/epaa/v7n25.html.

Iles, V. and Sutherland, K. (2001) *Managing Change in the NHS: organisational change – a review for health care managers, professionals and researchers*, London, London School of Hygiene and Tropical Medicine.

Marshall, J. G. and Neufeld, V. R. (1981) A Randomized Trial of Librarian Educational Participation in Clinical Settings, *Journal of Medical Education*, **56** (5), (May), 409–16.

Morrison, E. H. and Hafler, J. P. (2000) Yesterday a Learner, Today a Teacher too: residents as teachers in 2000, *Pediatrics*, **105** (1), 238–42.

Morrison, J. M., Sullivan, F., Murray, E. and Jolly, B. (1999) Evidence-based Education: development of an instrument to critically appraise reports of educational interventions, *Medical Education*, **33** (12), 890–3.

Morrison, K. (2001) Randomised Controlled Trials for Evidence-based Education: some problems in judging what works, *Evaluation and Research in Education*, **15** (2), 69–83.

Newman, M. (2003) *A Pilot Systematic Review and Meta-analysis on the Effectiveness of Problem Based Learning*, Newcastle, Learning and Teaching Support Network.

Oakley, A. (2002) Social Science and Evidence-based Everything: the care of education, *Educational Review*, **54** (3), 277–86.

Perkins, E., Simnett, I. and Wright, L. (1999) *Evidence-based Health Promotion*, Wiley and Sons, Chichester.

Schon, D. A. (1991) *The Reflective Practitioner: how professionals think in action*, Aldershot, Ashgate-Arena.

Smith, P. (2002) *Systematic Reviews in Education*, British Educational Research Association, University of Exeter.

Todd, R. (2001) Transitions for Preferred Futures of School Libraries: knowledge space, not information place; connections, not collections; actions, not positions; evidence, not advocacy. Keynote address: *International Association of School Libraries (IASL) Conference*, Auckland, New Zealand, 2001. Keynote paper, *IASL conference 2001 virtual session*: paper from Ross Todd, www.iasl-slo.org/virtualpaper2001.html.

Todd, R. (2002a) Evidence-based Practice I: The sustainable future for teacher-librarians, *Scan*, **21** (1), 30–7.

Todd, R. (2002b) Evidence based Practice II: Getting into the action, *Scan*, **21** (2), 34–41.

Todd, R. (2003) Keynote Paper: *Learning in the Information Age School: Opportunities, Outcomes and Options*, International Association of School Librarianship (IASL) 2003 Annual Conference Durban, South Africa, 7–11 July 2003

Wagner, K. C. and Byrd, G. D. (2003) *Evaluating the Effectiveness of CML Programs: a systematic review of the literature*, Presented paper. MLA Annual Meeting, May.

Webb, D. (1999) Current Approaches to Gathering Evidence. In Perkins, E., Simnett, I. and Wright, L. (eds), *Evidence-based Health Promotion*, Wiley and Sons, Chichester.

White, P. (2002) *A Shifting UK Educational 'Research Culture'? Paper presented at the Annual Conference of the British Educational Research Association*, University of Exeter, England, 12–14 September 2002.

Winning, M. A. and Beverley, C. A. (2003) Clinical Librarianship: a systematic review of the literature, *Health Information and Libraries Journal*, **20** (Suppl 1), 10–21.

Wolf, F. M., Shea, J. A. and Albanese, M. A. (2001) Toward Setting a Research Agenda for Systematic Reviews of Evidence of the Effects of Medical Education, *Teaching and Learning in Medicine*, **13** (1), 54–60.

Special topic (B)
How can I train my users?
(Evidence Digest)

Alison Brettle

Why is it important?

Finding evidence is an essential skill for students and practitioners. With increasing numbers of end-users independently searching electronic resources there is a need to acquire information skills to support lifelong learning. Librarians and information professionals, with their knowledge of sources and searching, are well placed to teach these skills.

Evidence-based healthcare requires clinicians to find information to keep up-to-date in order to make better informed treatment decisions. They need skills in asking the right questions, identifying sources and selecting the best quality evidence (Hicks, 1998). Accessing research evidence in electronic databases also requires new skills in information technology (Pyne et al., 1999). Research has shown that medical professionals are less effective at searching than librarians, finding less relevant information and missing important information, for example conflicting conclusions about treatment effectiveness (Haynes et al., 1990). Optimizing search skills is therefore a worthwhile goal (Erickson and Warner, 1998). Information skills training can help practitioners recognize and use evidence, and make more efficient use of their time (Hicks, 1998).

This chapter draws on evidence from the health sector. However, it is likely that the lessons and experiences learned are relevant and transferable to other sectors.

What is required?

Teaching methods

Teaching information skills, or user education, is undertaken in a wide variety of settings, using a range of methods (Brettle, 2003; University Health Sciences Librarians Group, 2001). These include:

- didactic sessions
- demonstration of techniques
- hands-on sessions
- one-to-one sessions
- small and large groupwork
- interactive web packages
- sessions delivered via e-mail
- various combinations of the above.

However, a systematic review of career grade doctors (Davis et al., 1995) concluded that training using enabling or reinforcing elements is more effective in improving outcomes than are formal and didactic teaching methods. Teaching strategies used in evidence-based medicine (question formulation, searching for evidence, critical appraisal, implementing evidence and evaluation of performance) have also been shown to be effective (Rosenberg and Donald, 1995; Rosenberg et al., 1998).

The NHS Executive (1999) advises that education providers should: consider access to ICT facilities; allow individuals to set their own learning objectives (as they have better ownership and motivation towards learning than those whose objectives are set for them); establish fixed areas of learning and flexibility to respond to individual needs; enable clinicians to use new information skills to reinforce and retain them; and take the clinicians' normal environment into account when developing programmes.

Curriculum

For some trainee clinicians, information skills training is a formal part of the curriculum (University Health Sciences Librarians Group, 2001). Training can be provided at different times during the course: at the beginning; as part of key skills; later in the course; embedded throughout; or at induction plus a follow-up session (Brettle, 2003; University Health Sciences Librarians Group, 2001). Librarians are involved to a greater or lesser extent with curriculum development, although problem-based learning methods necessitate that students develop effective information retrieval and handling skills (University Health Sciences Librarians Group, 2001).

For practising clinicians, training is provided by libraries at the place of work or by regional or professional bodies as part of continuing professional development (Hicks, 1998; Fox et al., 1999). Again, content varies and courses can be provided on their own or as part of evidence-based practice or research methods training.

There is no formally established curriculum for trainee or practising clinicians. The NHS Information Authority (2001) has set out guidance on skill and knowledge levels in information management, and on information and communications technology for NHS staff, but little guidance is included on content or style of teaching. A competency framework proposed by Pyne et al. (1999) puts forward the following technical competencies:

- basic computer skills and database familiarity
- key sources of information
- familiarity with indexing and referencing systems
- ability to design and employ sound searching strategies
- formulation of appropriate and focused questions.

These skills are seen as the basis on which to access, adopt and implement evidence-based practice.

Likely cost consequences

No evidence could be found on the costs of providing information skills training. Staff time should be taken into consideration including involvement in curriculum planning; developing supporting materials; developing, organizing and undertaking sessions; supporting students in the library; follow-up support. Other resources may include database resources; internet access; computer terminals and training suites; providing workbooks or other training materials.

Evidence

A recent systematic review (Brettle, 2003) examined whether information skills training is effective and whether some training methods are more effective than others. Taking a pragmatic approach to analysing the studies and interpreting the results, there was very limited evidence to show that training improves search skills. The heterogeneity of the studies meant that it was impossible to compare methods across studies. Therefore no conclusions were drawn regarding effective training methods. In view of this a summary of the studies included and their coverage is provided below.

Randomized controlled trials

Erickson and Warner (1998) aimed to ascertain the impact of an individual one-hour tutorial session on Medline use amongst obstetric and gynaecology residents training at an academic medical centre. They reported a non-significant increase in Medline usage and self-reported improvement in skills following the intervention. Rosenberg et al. (1998) demonstrated the effectiveness of a three-hour interactive session, which covered question formulation and MEDLINE searching, to small groups of medical students.

Experimental

Verhoeven et al. (2000) evaluated different methods of training general practitioners in the use of controlled vocabulary, subheadings and free-text searching.

Quasi experimental

Ghali et al. (2000) evaluated a mini EBM course for third-year medical students and demonstrated an improvement in skills.

Cohort

- Dorsch et al. (1990) describe how an EBM course was integrated into the curriculum, and presented formal and informal feedback.
- Verhey (1999) described, implemented and evaluated an information literacy programme in a nursing undergraduate curriculum.
- Fox et al. (1999) described and evaluated an information programme delivered via a virtual classroom.
- Grant et al. (1996) evaluated the impact of a literature searching course that focused on teaching search principles and systematic approaches.
- Sowinski et al. (2000) developed and evaluated a literature searching module delivered via the internet for pharmacy students.
- Burrows and Tylman (1999) evaluated the adequacy of MEDLINE instruction given routinely to students at the beginning of their course, by testing their searching ability at the end of their course.
- Fox et al. (1996) evaluated the effectiveness of an information literacy programme integrated into a nursing curriculum.

- Gibson and Silverberg (2000) developed and implemented an intensive introductory course in computers as a tool for managing information.
- Vogel et al. (2002) developed and evaluated the effectiveness of a MEDLINE workshop in finding high-quality clinical information as part of EBM training.
- Poyner et al. (2002) developed and evaluated an intensive information skills training programme delivered to psychiatry trainees in their homes.

Observational

Brandt and Lehman (1995) compared traditional versus web-based literature searching during a session that aimed to teach lifelong searching skills.

Qualitative

- Martin (1998) introduced a reflective essay as part of user education, and evaluated its impact.
- Martindale (1995) investigated whether teaching the search process was more effective compared with more practical skills.
- Lambert-Lanning (2000) evaluated a literature-searching workshop with different components.
- Richwine and McGowan (2001) described the development and initial impact of providing access and training to a virtual health library.

References

Brandt, K. A., Lehmann, H. P. and Welch, W. H. (1995) Teaching Literature Searching in the Context of the WWW, *Proceedings of the Annual Symposium on Computer Applications in Medical Care*, 888–92.

Brettle, A. (2003) Information Skills Training: a systematic review of the literature, *Health Information and Libraries Journal*, **20** (Suppl 1), 3–9.

Burrows, S. C. and Tylman, V. (1999) Evaluating Medical Student Searches of MEDLINE for Evidence Based Information: process and application of results, *Bulletin of the Medical Library Association*, **87** (4), 471–6.

Davis, D. A., Thomson, M. A. and Oxman, A. D. (1995) Changing Physician Performance: a systematic review of the effect of continuing medical education strategies, *JAMA*, **274**, 700–5.

Dorsch, J. L., Frasca, M. A., Wilson, M. L. and Tomsic, M. L. (1990) A Multidisciplinary Approach to Information and Critical Appraisal, *Bulletin of the Medical Library Association*, **78** (1), 38–44.

Erickson, S. and Warner, E. R. (1998) The Impact of an Individual Tutorial Session on MEDLINE use Among Obstetrics and Gynaecology Residents in an Academic Training Programme: a randomized trial, *Medical Education*, **32** (3), 269–73.

Fox, L. M., Richter, J. M. and White, N. E. (1996) A Multidimensional Evaluation of a Nursing Information Literacy Program, *Bulletin of the Medical Library Association*, **84** (2), 182–90

Fox, N. J., Dolman, E. A., Lane, P. et al. (1999) The WISDOM Project: training primary care professionals in informatics in a collaborative 'virtual' classroom, *Medical Education*, **33** (5), 365–70.

Ghali, W. A., Saitz, R., Eskew, A. H., Gupta, M., Quan, H. and Hershman, W. Y. (2000) Successful Teaching in Evidence Based Medicine, *Medical Education*, **34**, 18–22

Gibson, K. E. and Silverberg, M. (2000) A Two Year Experience Teaching Computer Literacy to First-year Medical Students using Skill Based Cohorts, *Bulletin of the Medical Library Association*, **88** (2), 157–64.

Grant, K. L., Herrier, R. N. and Armstrong, E. P. (1996) Teaching a Systematic Search Strategy Improves Literature Retrieval Skills of Pharmacy Students, *American Journal of Pharmaceutical Education*, **60** (3), 281–6.

Haynes, R. B., McKibbon, K. A., Walker, C. J. et al. (1990) On-line Access to MEDLINE in Clinical Settings: a study of use and usefulness, *Annals of Internal Medicine*, **112**, 78–84.

Hicks, A. (1998) Developing Information Skills Training for National Health Service Personnel: experiences at the Trent Institute for Health Services Research, *Program*, **32** (2), 123–36.

Lambert-Lanning, A., Watson, L. and Evans, M. F. (2000) Integrating Medical Informatics into the Undergraduate Curriculum, *Bibliotheca Medica Canadiana*, **21** (3), 16–19.

Martin, S. (1998) Reflections on a User Education Session with Nursing students, *Health Libraries Review*, **15**, 111–16.

Martindale, K. (1995) Teaching Information Skills on CD-ROM: a conceptual approach, *Learning Resources Journal*, **11** (2), 37–40.

Maynard, S. (2002) *A Survey of NHS Libraries 2000–2001*, Loughborough, Library and Information Statistics Unit.

NHS Executive (1999) *Learning to Manage Health Information: a theme for clinical education*, London, Department of Health.

NHS Information Authority (2001) *Health Informatics Competency Profiles for the NHS*, Birmingham, NHS Information Authority.

Poyner, A., Wood, A. and Herzberg, J. (2002) Distance Learning Project – Information Skills Training: supporting flexible trainees in psychiatry, *Health Information and Libraries Journal*, **19**, 84–9.

Pyne, T., Newman, K., Leigh, S. et al. (1999) Meeting the Information Needs of Clinicians for the Practice of Evidence-based Health Care, *Health Libraries Review*, **16**, 3–14.

Richwine, M. and McGowan, J. J. (2001) A Rural Virtual Health Sciences Library Project: research findings with implications for next generation library services, *Bulletin of the Medical Library Association*, **89** (1), 37–44.

Rosenberg, W. and Donald, A. (1995) Evidence Based Medicine: an approach to clinical problem-solving, *BMJ*, **310**, 1112–16.

Rosenberg, W. M. C., Deeks, J., Lusher, A., Snowball, R., Dooley, G. and Sackett, D. (1998) Improving Searching Skills and Evidence Retrieval, *Journal of the Royal College of Physicians of London*, **32** (6), 557–63.

Schilling, K., Ginn, D. S., Mickelson, P. et al. (1995) Integration of Information Seeking Skills and Activities into a Problem-based Curriculum, *Bulletin of the Medical Library Association*, **82** (2), 176–83.

Sowinski, K. M., Scott, S. A. and Carlstedt, B. C. (2000) An Internet Training Module for Traditional and Non-traditional Doctor of Pharmacy Students: content and evaluation, *American Journal of Pharmaceutical Education*, **64** (1), 15–19.

University Health Sciences Librarians Group (2001) *Making a Difference: contributions of higher education library and information professionals to the Government's nursing, midwifery and health visiting strategy*, University Health Sciences Librarians Group, 12–15.

Verhey, M. P. (1999) Information Literacy in an Undergraduate Nursing Curriculum: development, implementation and evaluation, *Journal of Nursing Education*, **38** (6), 252–9.

Verhoeven, A., Boerma, E. J. and Meyboom de Jong, B. (2000) Which Literature Retrieval Method is Most Effective for GPs?, *Family Practice*, **17** (1), 30–5.

Vogel, E. W., Block, K. R. and Wallingford, K. T. (2002) Finding the Evidence: teaching medical residents to search MEDLINE, *Journal of the Medical Library Association*, **90** (3), 327–30.

16

An evidence-based approach to collection management

Andrew Booth

Introduction

This chapter outlines the main components of collection management within the increasingly popular concept of the 'hybrid' collection which brings together both paper and electronic sources. It identifies a range of questions that management of such collections needs to address. The evidence base is characterized in terms of useful sources and important research studies. This chapter is followed by a special topic examining the research evidence on managing the electronic/paper mix in connection with journal holdings.

What is evidence-based collection management?

The third domain identified by Crumley and Koufogiannakis (2002) is *Collections* by which they refer to the activity of: 'building (and we could add maintaining) a high-quality collection of print and electronic materials that is useful, cost-effective and meets the users' needs'.

The broad term 'collection management' includes collection development, maintenance and withdrawal. Collection development involves 'planning, goal-setting, decision-making, budgeting, and acquiring materials and evaluating them' (Gessesse, 2000). Richards and Eakin (1997) emphasize the centrality of this domain to information practice: 'The library's collection is its heart because it is the collection that is the central information resource upon which most library activities rely . . . . Today's vision of the collection must incorporate both a broader range of materials . . . and a greater sense of connectivity'.

The first impression on reviewing this domain is the tremendous spectrum encompassed, from management-oriented tasks of collection development to the physical (or even electronic) sciences involved in preservation or restoration of printed or electronic materials. Some observers identify the specific field of archive management as one of the most unequivocally 'evidence-based' areas of information practice. On the other hand, Scott Plutchak, in reviewing collection development, affirms that 'as with so much else in librarianship (and medicine, for that matter), [it] remains more of an art than a science' (Plutchak, 2003). If evidence-based information practice is the science of making decisions then our view of evidence-based collection management has to be reconciled with the observation of Richards and Eakin (1997) that: 'Librarians make decisions about collections . . . . Some claim these decisions are primarily an art; others argue that they are, or should be, grounded in scientific methods'.

Collection management also includes investigation of subject access via catalogues. Whereas the technical performance of retrieval methods falls more properly within information access and retrieval (see Chapter 18), fundamental assumptions made when providing subject access might be considered central to collection management.

The broader context of collection management also includes the evidence base regarding purported measures of quality – for example citation and impact factors and the processes involved in facilitating subject access (i.e. evidence-based cataloguing and classification!)

Asking the question

Tenopir (2003) identifies questions arising within the specific subdomain of electronic publishing:

- How is the change to digital information sources affecting the scholarly work of college and university students?
- How do differences between separate article and full journal databases affect the way research is done?
- What are the implications for scholarship of decisions being made about what publishers publish and what librarians purchase?

before posing the concluding question: 'finally, are librarians – as intermediaries to the search process – still necessary in a digital age?'

Illustrative questions identified from a worldwide survey of evidence-based practitioners (Eldredge, 2001) include (Box 16.1).

> **Box 16.1 Questions posed from within the domain of collection management**
>
> - How can we predict the future usability of a print monograph collection in an electronic environment?
> - What are the currently most popular/successful models for planning, predicting, and budgeting for non-print collections?
> - How could we determine user preferences for journals (and choices between print, electronic or hybrid collections)?
> - Do students who use electronic library resources have better or worse outcomes than those who use physical libraries? Outcomes of interest would include academic results, workload, use of time, user satisfaction, drop out rates. Also compare with those who don't use library resources at all?
> - How will desk-top access to databases and full text affect library organization, personnel, and work flow patterns in medical libraries?
> - Is a just-in-time policy more effective in terms of user satisfaction than a just-in-case policy?
> - How do we decide which print journal subscriptions to retain in our collections where an electronic version is also available?

Finding the evidence

In contrast to other domains, collection management is almost exclusively populated from within the library literature. By 'library literature' we admit the wider scope offered by museum and archival activities. Sources for such literature include the main library bibliographic databases covered in Chapters 7 and 8. In addition, collection development and acquisitions has accumulated its own resources:

- *AcqWeb* is a 'gathering place for librarians and other professionals interested in acquisitions and collection development'. It documents 'resources of interest to staff involved in selecting and purchasing books, serials and related information resources for libraries'.
- *ACQNET*, a managed listserv, sister service to AcqWeb, targets librarians interested in acquisitions work to exchange information and ideas, and to find solutions to common problems.
- The appearance in 2002 of Collections and Acquisitions Research OnLine (CAROL) (Anonymous, 2002), a clearing house for projects related to library research for collections and acquisitions, purportedly at http://128.253.121.98/carol/start/, has yet to be confirmed by more recent sightings.

The evidence base

Table 16.1　Research methods of importance within collections management

Research methods of particular importance within this domain
Systematic reviews and meta-analyses
Cohort (comparative studies)
Surveys
Bibliometric studies

What evidence exists in collection management and how good is it? This domain carries a long tradition of practitioner-based research (Brophy, 2001). In a review of topical research in technical services (1988–1991) Simpson (1992) found 'two-thirds of the research represents field studies and one-fifth represents survey research, with the rest comprising experiments, methodologies and models'. Simpson also found cost studies and case studies.

Plutchak (2003) reminds us that although 'the evidence-based movement pushes us in the direction of measurable goals and objectives', we must be 'careful, however, not to confuse measurement with efficacy'. This echoes the wider distinction within evidence-based practice as a whole between 'efficacy' (the ability to demonstrate an effect in optimal laboratory conditions) and 'effectiveness' (the ability to achieve this effect in real world conditions). Increasingly there is interest in outcomes assessment which is seen to complement other assessment techniques in assisting information organizations to enhance their decisions when providing information services and resources (Bertot and McClure, 2003).

In theory, collection management is one of the more straightforward areas of information practice within which to conduct empirical research. Textbooks, electronic titles or journal issues are all 'mute' subjects for research and can be arbitrarily constituted into samples or cohorts. Numbers of volumes are usually of a magnitude that permits fairly straightforward generation of valid sample sizes. Similarly, acquisition and processing of stock, though still required to be timely, is not as 'time-critical' as reference or enquiry services. To illustrate, Kairis (2000) describes how 77 gift books were added to the collection of a medium-sized academic library in the course of a year, after an evaluation and collection development process. The library investigated whether these items were used more or less than items the library purchased in the same year. For comparison they took the first 77 items purchased and added to the general collection in the following July, and tracked usage (circulation, renewal or in-house use) for a year. They found that the non-gift books had an average usage per book of 1.38 and the gift books an average of 0.87. So the non-gift books were used more, on average.

Systematic reviews

There are few systematic reviews within this domain. One of these is a qualitative systematic review examining the controversy regarding journal impact factors (Pratt et al., 2001). The authors searched the MEDLINE and Science Citation Index databases and employed manual methods to identify over 20 articles, editorials, commentaries, and letters to the editor discussing use and misuse of impact factors. These were reviewed and major ideas synthesized.

Shelley and Schuh (2001) conducted a meta-analysis examining the relationship between writing quality, readability and selectivity within 17 education journals. They concluded that general interest journals are significantly more selective in what they publish than those publishing in a specialized field. Olson and Schlegl (1999) performed an analysis of critiques of subject access standards as found in the library literature. In particular they looked for discussions of biases (e.g. gender, sexuality, ethnicity, language and religion). In their meta-analysis they analysed five quantitative variables and then supplemented this with a textual analysis (or meta-synthesis).

Randomized controlled trials

Eldredge (2003) has identified only one unpublished study within the domain of collection management. Perhaps unsurprisingly, given the observed difficulty in identifying such a study design from abstracts, the exhibit in question is from his personal experience. In a study of the effect of weeding a collection on its subsequent use by users at an academic health sciences library, he and his colleagues matched three pairs of monograph ranges according to similarities in size, decade-long growth, and usage. One monograph range from each pair was randomly selected to be weeded according to strict criteria. Outcome measures were usage and greater use of unique items. An important methodological point from this study is the small sample size that it employed. Although, as mentioned above, studies of book collections are relatively easily able to conduct, the power of the study was reduced by making the classmark range the unit of analysis (n=6) rather than harnessing large numbers of monographs (Eldredge et al., 2002).

Cohort studies

In reviewing cohort studies in health librarianship, Eldredge (2002) documents numerous applications of the study design within the domain of collections. Most common are the book or journal usage study. The earliest of these dates from 1939 with a steady supply of such studies through the 1950s and early 1960s. Eldredge (2002) hypothesizes that: 'This usage studies genre of cohort studies endures, because it answers many practical – and sometimes a few theoretical – research questions'. For an example of their practicality see Box 16.2. Such studies usually relate to usage, with Eldredge (2002) arguing that these act as a proxy for a more detailed chronicle of the users' behaviour in the same way that laboratory results and case notes are a proxy for patients. Eldredge supports the above-mentioned observation that such studies: 'offer the practical advantage [over studies in other domains] . . . of not normally requiring approval from human subjects research committees, because individuals are not linked to their confidential usage data'. His brief compilation of illustrative cohort designs from this domain has been adapted in Table 16.2.

Table 16.2   Collection resources cohort studies (from Eldredge, 2002)

Defined population	Exposure or non-exposure	Outcomes
Users at the University of Southern California Norris Medical Library	194 journal titles available in print or electronic media versions	Most heavily used print versions also most heavily used in electronic versions (Morse and Clintworth, 2000)
User population at 36 various sized hospital libraries in US	Journal collections at these 36 hospital libraries	Lack of commonality in most popular titles across different collections (Dee et al., 1998)
User population at the University of New Mexico academic health sciences library	Monographs purchased during 1993	84% of monographs circulated; a total of 91% used after five years (Eldredge, 1998)
User population at the University of Illinois at Chicago academic health sciences library	Monographs added during the 1994 to 1995 period	81% circulated within three years; monographs had longer than expected active shelf life (Blecic, 2000)
Users at a teaching hospital in the UK	Two free MEDLINE CD-ROMs	CD-ROMs were popular despite less than optimal search strategies (Dyer and Buckle, 1995)
Diverse users at the Massachusetts General Hospital Library	Access to hospital library monographs and journal collections	Usage led to monograph and journal retention or weeding decisions (Schneider et al., 1995)
Stratified sample of 622 faculty members in biochemistry or medicine departments at 126 US medical schools who published during 1990 and 1991	Access to various sized journal collections at academic health sciences libraries	Size of journal collection at faculty members' institutions correlated neither with number of articles published nor with articles cited (Byrd, 1999)

(continued)

Table 16.2   *(continued)*

Defined population	Exposure or non-exposure	Outcomes
Patients desiring more information from their healthcare professionals	'Info Scripts' to resources at Consumer Health Information Center in Ontario	Patients with certain personality traits used the information center (Farrar and Bang, 1998)
Users of the National Library of Medicine's DOCLINE system during two fiscal years	Access to collection resources at libraries in the system via DOCLINE	1.93 million filled requests; 76% of individual articles requested only once (Lacroix, 1994)
Publishers of 300 core medical journals	'Free' access to electronic version with print subscriptions	Publishers of free online bundling raised prices above average print-alone publishers' subscription prices (Ball, 2000)
Seventy-eight (93% of total) users at Institute for Biodiagnostics, Nova Scotia	New electronic resources supplementing more traditional on-site services and resources	Large numbers still valued and utilized traditional on-site services and collections (Colborne et al., 1999)
Patients, laypersons, and healthcare providers	Web access to the Digital Health Sciences Library (DHSL) comprised digitized books and	Patients and laypersons were most frequent visitors, although they more often accessed resources intended for healthcare providers (D'Alessandro et al., 1998)

Practical decisions between library suppliers provide a ready means for conducting an empirical study. A decision between two subscription agents could be piloted over a year by matching titles according to publishers and frequency. Rouzer (1993) describes a controlled study of vendor performance according to order-fill rate, vendor efficiency and cost-effectiveness. The sample population was stratified to ensure the accuracy of the study thereby permitting subsequent tests for statistical significance.

Box 16.2 Example: a simple comparative study

Experimental studies do not have to be expensive and complex to be applicable, as the following illustrates (Flowers, 1995):

In a controlled trial aimed at studying whether books were damaged by the book chutes fitted to public libraries to enable borrowers to return books when the library is closed, sets of five identical books were employed at eight libraries, each with a book chute of different design. The hypothesis, that book chutes damage books, was confirmed. Worst damage was caused when the book chute failed to function correctly and books became caught by or between parts of the chute or when books landed where they were not meant to. Six out of eight book chutes revealed design faults with the potential to cause damage.

Surveys and bibliometric studies

Collection management reflects the predominance of pragmatic methods such as surveys and bibliometric studies within LIS research as a whole (Schlachter and Thomison, 1982). Stevens (1999) describes a survey to characterize acquisitions departments at the forefront of book acquisitions. Benaud et al. (1999) surveyed cataloguing departments to determine which cataloguing standards exist in academic libraries.

The ease with which bibliometric studies are conducted makes them prime candidates for student dissertations or small-scale research projects. They may therefore be heavily represented in conference papers, proceedings and ephemeral publications such as newsletters. Recent attention has focused on the application of bibliometrics to the new contexts and contents of the world wide web.

A significant body of literature tackles 'evidence-based publishing' and this bears a tangential relationship to evidence-based collection management. For this reason this chapter has focused on the consumption, as opposed to production, end of the journal 'supply chain'. Notwithstanding the plethora of studies available within the field of collection management, very few address the 'holy grail' of impact. A pertinent question was raised in the international survey of evidence-based practitioners (Eldredge, 2001): 'Do students who use electronic library resources have better or worse outcomes (in terms of academic results, workload, use of time, user satisfaction, dropout rates) than those who use physical libraries?'

Critically appraising the evidence

Critical appraisal within the domain of collection management has the potential for considerable confusion. In implementing collection development policies a number of appraisal tools are used in evaluating book purchases, journal selection and websites, to name but a few. However, what is being referred to here, instead, is critical appraisal of research studies describing collection management techniques. A primary concern here is generalizability, as much collection management research is very context-sensitive. No tools have been identified specifically to address collection management studies although some aspects may be covered by either a generic survey instrument or by the CriSTAL information use studies tool.

Acting on the evidence

In looking to act on the evidence within the domain of collection management we would do well to heed the cautions of Todd (2003). Drawing on the views of Bertram Brookes, one of the founders of information science in the 1970s, he reminds us: 'that while the collection, organization and access to information sources were essential to professional practice, they were not the focus of professional practice; rather, the intent of such organization and access was the transformation of information into personal knowledge'. That is to say, Brookes: 'saw libraries, not in terms of their collections, access structures and staffing, but in terms of people's knowledge undergoing transformation through a dynamic interaction with information' (Todd, 2003).

In heeding this warning the practitioner will do well not to be beguiled by the apparent ease with which research within this domain can be performed and its findings implemented. Clearly, such research needs to target people-centred outcomes and, once implemented, must achieve *real* impact (Bertot and McClure, 2003).

Future research

Interesting questions in collection management await future researchers. Firstly, where is the evidence that particular contents or methods of creation of collection development policies are particularly effective? How useful are they, and in what ways? Secondly, how does input relate to outcomes – which specific collection factors affect reference service efficiency, as measured by accuracy and speed of librarians' answers to questions and by patrons' ease of use of reference works? This is once more a cross-domain issue.

Outcomes assessment has emerged as a major concern within the networked environment. Bertot and McClure (2003) have suggested that it has the potential to complement other assessment techniques and to assist information in making decisions on the provision of information services and resources. However, they conclude that much work remains before libraries can implement outcomes assessment successfully.

Finally, how has web-based access to electronic journals and databases impacted upon usage of hard copy collections? Certainly collection management, a traditional and unique domain of librarian responsibility, continues to generate enduring and pertinent questions to act as a stimulus for further investigation.

References

Anonymous (2002) Announcement: Collections and Acquisitions Research OnLine, *Library Collections, Acquisitions and Technical Services*, **26**, 193–4.

Benaud, C. L., Bordeianu, S. and Hanson, M. E. (1999) Cataloging Production Standards in Academic Libraries, *Technical Services Quarterly*, **16** (3), 43–68.

Bertot, J. C. and McClure, C. R. (2003) Outcomes Assessment in the Networked Environment: research questions, issues, considerations, and moving forward, *Library Trends*, **51** (4), 590–613.

Brophy, P. (2001) The Historical Context of eLib: practice-based library research in the UK, *Library Management*, **22** (1/2), 15–18.

Crumley, E. and Koufogiannakis, D. (2002) Developing Evidence-based Librarianship: practical steps for implementation, *Health Information and Libraries Journal*, **19** (4), 61–70.

Eldredge, J. (submitted on behalf of the Evidence-Based Librarianship Implementation Committee) (2001) The Most Relevant and Answerable Research Questions Facing the Practice of Health Sciences Librarianship, *Hypothesis*, **15** (1), 9–17, http://gain.mercer.edu/mla/research/hypothesis.html.

Eldredge J (2002) Cohort Studies in Health Sciences Librarianship, *Journal of the Medical Library Association*, **90** (4), 380–92.

Eldredge, J. D. (2003) The Randomised Controlled Trial Design: unrecognized opportunities for health sciences librarianship, *Health Information and Libraries Journal*, **20** (Suppl 1), 34–44.

Eldredge, J. D., Mondragon, K. L. and Fierro, C. (2002) Does Weeding a Monographs Collection Increase Subsequent Usage of Unweeded Titles? A Randomized Controlled Trial. Poster # 84, *Hypothesis*, **16** (2), 6–7.

Flowers, L. (1995) Book Chute Damage, *Australasian Public Libraries and Information Services*, **8** (2), 78–85.

Gessesse, K. (2000) Collection Development and Management in the Twenty-first Century with Special Reference to Academic Libraries: an overview, *Library Management*, **21**, 365–72.

Kairis, R. (2000) Comparing Gifts to Purchased Materials: a usage study, *Library Collections, Acquisitions, and Technical Services*, **24**, 351–9.

Olson, M. A. and Schlegl, R. (1999) Bias in Subject Access Standards: a content analysis of the critical literature. In Turner, J. (ed.), *Information Science: where has it been, where is it going? Proceedings of the 27th Annual Conference of the Canadian Association for Information Science, University of Sherbrooke, June 9–11*, Montreal, CAIS/ACSI, 236–47.

Plutchak, T. S. (2003) The Art and Science of Making Choices, *Journal of the Medical Library Association*, **91** (1), 1–3.

Pratt, G., Hutchins, R. and Kier, K. (2001) *Impact Caveats: the growing controversy surrounding journal impact factors. Paper presented at Tri-Chapter Meeting of the MLA, October 24th–28th 2001, New Orleans*.

Richards, D. T. and Eakin, D. (1997) *Collection Development and Assessment in Health Sciences Libraries*, (Current practice in health sciences librarianship, v.4.), Lanham, MD, MLA and Scarecrow Press.

Rouzer, S. M. (1993) A Firm Order Vendor Evaluation Using a Stratified Sample, *Library Acquisitions: Practice and Theory*, **17** (3), 269–77.

Shelley, M. C. and Schuh, J. H. (2001) Are the Best Higher Education Journals Really the Best? A meta-analysis of writing quality and readability, *Journal of Scholarly Publishing*, **33** (1), 11–22.

Schlachter, G. A. and Thomison, D. (1982) *Library Science Dissertations 1973–1981: an annotated bibliography*, Littleton, CO, Libraries Unlimited.

Simpson, C. W. (1992) Technical Services Research, 1988–1991, *Library Resources and Technical Services*, **36**, 363–408.

Stevens, P. H. (1999) Who's Number One? Evaluating acquisitions departments (suggested evaluation criteria; presented at the 1998 Feather River Institute), *Library Collections, Acquisitions, and Technical Services*, **23** (1), 79–85.

Tenopir, C. (2003) Electronic Publishing: research issues for academic librarians and users, *Library Trends*, **51** (4), 614–35.

Todd, R. (2003) Keynote Paper: *Learning in the Information Age School: Opportunities, Outcomes and Options*, International Association of School Librarianship (IASL) 2003 Annual Conference, Durban, South Africa, 7–11 July, 2003.

Special topic (C)
Electronic or paper: how do I manage my journal collection? (Evidence Digest)

David Peacock

Question

To what extent should library and information services move from providing a physical printed journal collection to providing access to remote and distributed electronic journals?

Why is it important?

Initially librarians viewed e-journals as supplementary to the print title but increasingly a hybrid mix of journal formats is seen as complementary. Few library and information services have replaced print titles with an electronic-only option, arguing that their users expect easy, anytime, anywhere access (Goodman, 2002). Most examples are in the academic and corporate sectors. In asking whether 'replacing print journals with electronic versions is either feasible or, indeed, desirable for the end-user' this topic excludes associated issues regarding managing the serials acquisition process. It focuses on studies published between 2000 and 2002.

What is required?

Users are assumed to prefer electronic access to print resources. A *small* international survey of all types of libraries revealed relatively few standardized or best practices. A *larger* survey of all types of library users is required.

Likely cost consequences

It is frequently assumed that e-journals are cheaper to produce and distribute than paper counterparts. In reality, the cost of electronic-only subscriptions ranges considerably from between 85% and 115% of the paper price (Bevan et al., 2001). Another assumption is that availability of e-journals allows geographically separate sites/campuses to share the cost of single deals and reduce the cost of duplicating titles. In reality, this will depend on the definition of 'site' and access restrictions by individual publishers.

Publishers make it difficult for libraries to take electronic-only options (Bevan et al., 2001). At the present, the primary issue concerns the additional cost of obtaining electronic access over and above the existing print subscription. Online access can range from being completely free and unrestricted to costing up to 50% more and with various access restrictions.

Drexel University, which has moved to purchase only the electronic version whenever possible, has not yet proven that converting to the electronic version lowers costs over paper versions. The universities *per title* subscription costs are lower for e-journals, but the University has maintenance costs. Although several mainly clerical tasks were eliminated, new tasks were created for more highly skilled staff (Montgomery, 2000). Despite the costs of binding and physically storing paper archives, electronic archiving still has 'considerably higher' costs (Drewes and Guzi, 2001).

Who is involved?

Librarians, information and knowledge workers, library users, subscription agents, and publishers and vendors of print and electronic journals.

Evidence

Current 'evidence' comes largely from case studies.

Can and should libraries replace print journals with electronic-only access?

Several case studies describe an accelerated transition to an all-electronic journal collection (Montgomery, 2000; Goodman, 2002; Bevan et al., 2001). At Princeton University Library, electronic-only access is considered preferable, where the financial advantage is significant, where browsing use is trivial, and where the stability and performance of the publisher is trusted (Goodman, 2002).

Bevan et al. (2001) describes the situation at Cranfield University (UK). Reasons to replace paper journals with electronic included improved access for users (both on- and off-campus), and shared costs over different sites. The article quotes a very small survey of PhD students, accessing e-journals heavily from outside the library.

Drewes and Guzi (2001), examining the archival standpoint, identify several issues: Is the electronic version the version of record? Is the indexing adequate? What are the retention policies of the vendors?

Evidence suggests no clear right or wrong answer. A rational decision depends on several considerations:

- *Organizational issues.* Has the organization got the ICT infrastructure to support this transition? Issues include network bandwidth, numbers of network terminals, and computer literacy of end-users (Montgomery, 2000).
- *Subject-based issues.* For some subject areas the transition is easier than others. Science, Technology and Medicine (STM) traditionally has led development of e-journals, while arts-based areas may have limited titles available. Case studies considered above are all university libraries supporting STM subjects.
- *User needs and expectations.* Is the move to electronic journals what library users *really* want? A small survey of PhD students from the STM academic community found electronic journals were preferred to print. A similarly small survey of graduate trainees within the same subject area found that 66% preferred print journals. Preferences and use may differ by type and level of user (Bevan et al., 2001).
- *Available method(s) of accessing e-journals.* Options include: a single list, a publisher list or via the web OPAC. Surveys quoted by Bevan et al. (2001) found two-thirds of students used and preferred library web pages over using the OPAC.

How do libraries handle hybrid access to paper and electronic journals? Is there a best practice to follow?

Jordan and Kisley (2002) undertook an international survey of all types of libraries, establishing how they manage access to e-serials. Quantitative results show diverse ways of managing e-serials, and a lack of standards and best practices. Libraries are fairly equally divided between providing access to e-journals either outside or from within their library catalogues. Access methods included database driven approaches and hand-maintained web pages. Cranfield chose the OPAC access method (Bevan et al., 2001), although consensus is that multiple methods of access should be provided.

References

Bevan, S., Nieminen, S., Hunn, R. and Sweet, M. (2001) Replacing Print with e-journals: can it be done? – a case study, *Serials*, **14** (1), 17–24.

Drewes, J. and Guzi, G. (2001) To Bind or Not to Bind: managing electronic and paper serials in a sea of change, *The Serials Librarian*, **40** (3/4), 409–14.

Goodman, D. (2002) A Year without Print at Princeton, and what we plan next, *Learned Publishing*, **15** (1), 43–50.

Jordan, M. and Kisley D. (2002) How Does your Library Handle Electronic Serials? A general survey, *Serials*, **15** (1),41–6.

Montgomery, C. H. (2000) Measuring the Impact of an Electronic Journal Collection on Library Costs, *D-Lib Magazine*, **6** (10), www.dlib.org/dlib/october00/montgomery/10montgomery.html.

17

Towards evidence-based management

Andrew Booth

Introduction

This chapter characterizes management in terms of its main functions before identifying common types of question and approaches used to resolve them. From here the chapter considers sources to yield answers to such questions. Key management studies are identified and assessed together with implications for practice. The chapter concludes by identifying research priorities with most promise for management. This chapter is followed by two special topics examining the evidence relating to the measurement of service impact and charging for services.

What is evidence-based management?

In the fourth of their domains, Management, Crumley and Koufogiannakis (2002) include 'managing people and resources within an organization'. Stewart (2001) adopts a broad definition of 'evidence-based management' as: 'The conscientious, explicit and judicious use of current best evidence in making decisions'.

Claiming that it is 'more difficult to practise evidence-based management than evidence-based medicine' she asserts that if managers were required to search and appraise evidence for themselves, opportunities for evidence-based practice would be very rare indeed. Barriers are more to do with the slim likelihood that managers will acquire skills in searching and appraising the literature than the paucity of management evidence.

Asking the question

Management research is a relatively young field, far less developed in terms of question formulation than healthcare. There tends to be low consensus concerning key research questions in management research. Studies in the field rarely address identical problems, share a research agenda, or more importantly, ask the same questions. As a result the extent to which meta-analysis, or its qualitative equivalent, meta-ethnography, can be used to group and synthesize findings has been questioned within management research. Replication studies are extraordinarily difficult to find within management research. Consequently, management research often addresses questions at a broad, overarching, organizational level rather than examining the causes of particular problems or specific policies (Tranfield et al., 2002).

Finding the evidence

Management, as a domain, simultaneously lies within the information literature and yet subsumes it. Layzell Ward (2002) observes that: 'One of the surprising aspects of this year's review has been an increase in the quantity and quality of writing about the management of services within the sector. This review contains more citations than before – and still a higher number of interesting items were rejected. This is in contrast to the general literature of management where fewer interesting papers were retrieved'. However, she qualifies this with the following: '. . . but, as ever, the *Harvard Business Review* was the most productive for readable papers on topics of current interest to managers across the globe. This should be required reading for all managers in all sectors'. The challenge is to create management research which is theoretically sound, methodologically rigorous and relevant to practitioners (Starkey and Madan, 2001).

Aside from the library-specific literature, data sources for management evidence fall within three categories:

1   General management databases such as ABI-Inform and the Emerald full-text collection
2   Sector-specific management databases, such as the Health Management Information Consortium (HMIC) database for health management
3   Databases covering a specific facet of management (e.g. marketing, financial management or human resource management).

The internet is assuming increasing prominence as full-text management reports and academic papers become more plentiful. Layzell Ward (2002) observes: 'One of the areas of concern for anyone wanting to get an overview of the total output of sources of information about the ILS sector is necessarily the coverage of the secondary services. The old model of covering the journal literature does not necessarily provide a total overview of print and electronic publishing and time delays exacerbate the problem'. The author then observes that, with 'an increasing number of students producing interesting case studies as part of their masters studies . . . useful information often goes unrecorded and unnoticed', before lamenting 'as evidence-based practice becomes of increasing importance to managers this loss will be regretted'.

Searching for evidence in management is made more difficult by the lack of specificity of indexing, even for 'research' in general without even getting as far as specific study design-types. There is also a tension between the comparative design, required for assessing relative effectiveness or advantage, and the case study beloved of management researchers. Spell (1999) further characterizes the evidence base in management, employing a bibliometric analysis to observe that management fashions appear in the popular press long before the academic literature.

Management questions identified from an international survey of evidence-based practitioners (Eldredge, 2001) include (Box 17.1):

Box 17.1 Questions from the LIS management domain

How do we apply outcomes-based evaluation to services in order to realistically demonstrate the impact of what we do?

How do we identify/measure competencies for library job roles so that new posts can be assessed with regard to salary grades?

How do you determine when you have enough information to make a decision?

How can we best measure customer satisfaction with library services such as circulation, reserves, photocopying, and interlibrary loan?

Do student employees at service desk (circulation, information, reference, etc.) provide an effective and efficient service when compared to the time needed to hire, train, and supervise them?

Is it most efficient to have a combined circulation/photocopying service desk or separate desks and staff for each function?

How do we measure the appropriateness and effectiveness of performance management tools in libraries: e.g. KPIs, benchmarks, best practice scorecards?

The evidence base

Table 17.1   Research methods of significance within management

Research methods of particular importance within this domain
Qualitative systematic reviews
Case studies
Mixed methods research
Qualitative research

In his book *Evidence-based Healthcare* Muir Gray (1997) exhorted 'the compleat manager' to base practice on research evidence and to apply evidence in decision making. This idealistic model of rational planning counterpoints his claims that the secondary journal *Evidence Based Health Policy and Management* is the 'slimmest journal known to mankind'. Herein lies a fundamental paradox. Management is a well researched area with much from which managers can benefit. On the other hand, there are few randomized controlled trials, or indeed cohort studies, to populate the knowledge base. The fundamental building blocks of management research are the 'case study' and 'field research' (Eisenhardt, 1989). Such studies often lack the detail required to sustain synthesis. Case studies in management are scattered across numerous sectors and the usable literature is distributed across many databases.

Production is only one side of the equation. Managers prefer informal, personal information sources to formal bibliographic resources. The management evidence base shares many characteristics with that of information systems. Specific methodologies within both domains, such as operational research, action research and performance indicators, share a 'management science' pedigree. Both domains look for research that solves specific problems. While this makes an evidence-based approach more immediate and attractive for the predominantly practical library manager this has repercussions with regard to applicability.

The fragmented and divergent nature of management research has received considerable analysis and discussion. Like librarianship, management research is a 'practically oriented social science' (Whitley 1984a; Whitley 1984b). Commentators have identified a considerable and widening divide between academics and other stakeholders (Whitley, 2000) leading to 'irrelevant theory and untheorized and invalid practice' (Hodgkinson et al., 2001). Management research has been characterized as 'soft' rather than 'hard', 'applied' rather than 'pure', 'rural' rather than 'urban', and 'divergent' rather than 'convergent' (Tranfield and Starkey, 1998). A lack of consensus makes it difficult to establish standards or guidelines for management work.

Systematic reviews

Within management research few studies address the same research question. Meta-analysis is considered rare (Tranfield et al., 2002). Nevertheless, a proliferation of case studies has yielded materials for meta-analysis as a tool for combining their findings. Jensen and Rodgers (2001) describe the knowledge generated in this way as 'intellectual gold'. Beinhocker and Kaplan (2002) evaluated the strategic planning process of 30 companies. They concluded that strategic planning often yields few new ideas or insights and companies may be better channeling their efforts towards 'more creative' activities. Management information systems (MIS) are particularly suitable for meta-analysis – Hwang et al. (2000) tested a system success model using 82 empirical studies in a meta-analysis to produce guidelines for future research.

Such examples excluded, however, the most promising approach seems to lie in a two-stage synthesis. The first level is the 'epidemiological survey of the literature'. How many studies are there on a particular topic? In which settings have they been conducted? From which countries do they originate? What are the characteristics of the organizations involved? The output is typically a broad descriptive account of the field with specific exemplars and an audit trail, justifying conclusions (Tranfield et al., 2002).

At the second level is 'thematic analysis', outlining what is known and looking for consensus or conflict (Tranfield et al., 2002). Key emerging themes and research questions emerge, supported by a detailed audit trail back to the core contributions. A thematic systematic review draws conclusions from study findings, rather than study data (Clarke and Oxman, 2001). The methods for conducting a thematic analysis are a further challenge to developing systematic reviews in management research.

Randomized controlled trials

The two reported instances of randomized controlled trials within the library management domain (Eldredge, 2003) concern providing access to the MEDLINE database. Thirty-eight senior physicians and one resident, quasi-randomized by alphabetical last name, were assigned either to free, unlimited access to PaperChase or to access to manual searches of *Index Medicus* or to searches by a hospital librarian. Costs for both groups were similar (Wolffing, 1990). In the following year Haynes and colleagues (1991) examined the search practices of 85 clinical physicians where users either paid for or received free MEDLINE searches. Free MEDLINE users searched more often although the quality of searches was about the same.

Cohort studies

Concern with online charges, as addressed by the aforementioned RCTs, had been a major preoccupation for almost a decade prior to these studies. In 1983 a less rigorous, opportunistic cohort design reportedly addressed the question 'Do user charges affect online searching behaviour?' (Fidel, 1983). Increasingly rigorous designs can thus be used to address a similar question, with cohort studies having proved valuable in exploring a tentative hypothesis. Having tentatively identified evidence that charging user fees for online searches encourages efficient searching, the author compared searching behaviour of searchers in fee-charging settings with counterparts in free settings.

Other research designs

Surveys too make a major contribution to the evidence base while the use of the Delphi technique and of focus groups, methods derived from marketing and strategic planning, may also address practical management concerns. Kao (1997) describes the use of the Delphi technique in systematically allocating library staff and budget for a university library in Taiwan. The technique was claimed to have saved 3.5 FTE staff and 520,000 New Taiwan dollars. Within a health context, Higa-Moore et al. (2002) describe their use of focus groups to feed into their library's strategic planning.

Critically appraising the evidence

Growing interest in the contribution of qualitative research findings has made critical appraisal of management research more realizable. Several authors suggest questions to judge the quality of qualitative studies (Greenhalgh and Taylor, 1997; Popay et al., 1998; Mays and Pope, 2000; BSA Medical Sociology Group, 1996). Popay and colleagues (1998) suggest that quality assessment includes the following:

- A primary marker: is the research aiming to explore the subjective meanings that people give to particular experiences and interventions?
- Context sensitive: has the research been designed in such a way as to enable it to be sensitive/flexible to changes occurring during the study?
- Sampling strategy: has the study sample been selected in a purposeful way shaped by theory and/or attention given to the diverse contexts and meanings that the study is aiming to explore?
- Data quality: are different sources of knowledge/understanding about the issues being explored or compared?
- Theoretical adequacy: do researchers make explicit the process by which they move from data to interpretation?
- Generalizability: if claims are made to generalizability do these follow logically and/or theoretically from the data?

Traditionally, management researchers assess quality at the level of the journal or source, rather than the article or research study itself. Difficulties in specifying and conducting quality assessments of studies constitute a major challenge in developing a systematic review methodology for management research (Tranfield et al., 2002).

Acting on the evidence

Evidence-based practice recognizes that managers should use personal experience and problem-solving skills rather than relying solely on the results of systematic reviews (Rosenberg and Donald, 1995; Bero and Rennie, 1995). Values, resources and judgement all contribute to the interpretation and application of research findings (Macdonald, 1999). In fact the UK Government Cabinet Office goes further, describing evidence as: 'Expert knowledge; published research; existing statistics; stakeholder consultations; previous policy evaluations; the Internet; outcomes from consultations; costings of policy options; output from economic and statistical modelling' (Strategic Policy Making Team, 1999).

Evidence-based management has a major contribution to make in acknowledging that evidence alone is often insufficient and incomplete, only informing decision making by reducing uncertainty (Nowotny et al., 2001). Increasingly, systematic reviews of management research aim to improve the precision of a reliable evidence base and effect more sensitive judgements by policy makers and practitioners. Nevertheless the gap between having the evidence and implementing it continues to elude managers (Farmer, 2001).

Evidence suggests that when managers make decisions they are more likely to be influenced by relationships and historical patterns of service provision (Laing and Cotton, 1996). Even where recourse is made to the literature, managers, more than any other sector, debate whether lessons from one organization are transferable and applicable to another within the same sector, let alone in other sectors. This 'more similar than different' (homogeneous) or 'more different than similar' (heterogeneous) tension poses a particular challenge to the development of evidence-based practice.

The Museums, Libraries and Archives Council (MLA) (www.mla.gov.uk) attests to the value of a wide definition of 'evidence' to policy making:

> Increasingly, hard data (typically quantitative data, or 'numbers') are required to make the case to Government . . . and other funding bodies for more support for the sector . . . to inform decision making; establish, develop and evaluate policies; identify trends; measure the progress that the sector is making; measure the impact MLA is having; support advocacy; and, to facilitate the sector's operational effectiveness. Soft data (typically qualitative data) are also required to support, develop and enrich our understanding of these issues; indeed, a number of key aspects of our sector's work cannot be measured simply using statistics, numbers and ratios.

Conclusion

Despite a slow but perceptible growth in the number of librarians with management qualifications, questions from this domain seem under-represented in the lists compiled from practitioners. In actuality the management domain is so pervasive that it underpins many of the domains in Crumley and Koufogiannakis's typology (2002). So an apparent collections question: 'What is the best method for evaluating the cost-effectiveness of print versus electronic journals?' (Eldredge, 2001) is driven by management concerns. In addition, many would situate 'Marketing and Promotion', within the management domain. In resisting the temptation to make the management domain all-inclusive or, alternatively, to subsume management within all other library domains, we recognize the importance of questions that are not context-specific, such as 'What is the most efficient system of budgetary management?' and 'What procedures for staff recruitment and selection maximize the likelihood of a satisfactory result?' Clearly, a significant management research agenda remains to be answered within an evidence-based practice paradigm.

References

Beinhocker, E. D. and Kaplan, S. (2002) Tired of Strategic Planning?, *The McKinsey Quarterly*, special edition, 49–57.

Bero, L. and Rennie, D. (1995) The Cochrane Collaboration: Preparing, maintaining and disseminating systematic reviews of the effects of health care, *JAMA*, **274**, 1935–8.

BSA (British Sociological Association) Medical Sociology Group (1996) Criteria for the Evaluation of Qualitative Research Papers, *Medical Sociology News*, **22** (1), 69–71.

Clarke, M. and Oxman, A. D. (eds) (2001) *Cochrane Reviewers' Handbook*, 4.1.4 (updated October 2001), Oxford.

Crumley, E. and Koufogiannakis, D. (2002) Developing Evidence-based Librarianship: practical steps for implementation, *Health Information and Libraries Journal*, **19** (4), 61–70.

Eisenhardt, K. M. (1989) Building Theories from Case Study Research, *Academy of Management Review*, **14** (4), 352–550.

Eldredge, J. (submitted on behalf of the Evidence-Based Librarianship Implementation Committee) (2001) The Most Relevant and Answerable Research Questions Facing the Practice of Health Sciences Librarianship, *Hypothesis*, **15** (1), 9–17, http://gain.mercer.edu/mla/research/hypothesis.html.

Eldredge, J. D. (2003) The Randomized Controlled Trial Design: unrecognized opportunities for health sciences librarianship, *Health Information and Libraries Journal*, **20** (Suppl 1), 34–44.

Farmer, J. (2001) Impact of the Evidence-based Health Care 'Movement' on Health Service Strategic Planning 1995–1998, *Third International, Inter-disciplinary Evidence-Based Policies and Indicator Systems Conference*, July 2001.

Fidel, R. (1983) Do User Charges Affect Online Searching Behaviour? *Productivity in the information age: proceedings of the 46th ASIS Annual Meeting 1983.* In Vondran, R. F., Caputo, A., Wasserman, C. and Diener, R. A. V. (eds), White Plains, New York, Knowledge Industry Publications, Inc. for American Society for Information Science, 1983 volume 20, Washington, D. C.

Gray, J. A. M. (1997) *Evidence-based Healthcare: how to make policy and management decisions*, Edinburgh, Churchill Livingstone.

Greenhalgh, T. and Taylor, R. (1997) Papers That Go Beyond Numbers (Qualitative Research), *British Medical Journal*, **315**, 740–3.

Haynes, R. B., Ramsden, M. F., McKibbon, K. A. and Walker, C. J. (1991) Online Access to MEDLINE in Clinical Settings: impact of user fees, *Bulletin of the Medical Library Association*, **79** (4), 377.

Higa-Moore, M. L., Bunnett, B., Mayo, H. G. and Olney, C. A. (2002) Use of Focus Groups in a Library's Strategic Planning Process, *Journal of the Medical Library Association*, **90** (1), 86–92.

Hodgkinson, G. P., Herriot, P. and Anderson, N. (2001) Re-aligning the Stakeholders in Management Research: lessons from industrial, work and organizational psychology, *British Journal of Management*, **12**, Special Issue, S41–8.

Hwang, M. I., Windsor, J. C. and Pryor, A. (2000) Building a Knowledge Base for MIS Research: a meta-analysis of a systems success model, *Information Resources Management Journal*, **13** (2), 26–32.

Jensen, J. L. and Rodgers, R. (2001) Cumulating the Intellectual Gold of Case Study Research, *Public Administration Review*, **61** (2), 235–46.

Kao, C. (1997) The Delphi Technique for Personnel and Budget Allocation, *Libri*, **47** (4), 256–60.

Laing, A. W. and Cotton, S. (1996) Purchasing Health Care Services: information sources and decision criteria, *Journal of Marketing Management*, **12**, 783–802.

Layzell Ward, P. (2002) Management and the Management of Information, Knowledge-Based and Library Services 2001, *Library Management*, **23** (3), 135–65.

Macdonald, G. (1999) Evidence-Based Social Care: wheels off the runway?, *Public Money and Management*, **19**, 25–32.

Mays, N. and Pope, C. (2000) Assessing Quality in Qualitative Research, *BMJ*, **320**, 50–2.

Nowotny, H., Scott, P. and Gibbons, M. (2001) *Rethinking Science: knowledge and the public in an age of uncertainty*, Oxford, Blackwell.

Popay, J., Rogers, A. and Williams, G. (1998) Rationale and Standards for the Systematic Review of Qualitative Literature in Health Services Research, *Qualitative Health Research*, **8** (3), 341–51.

Rosenberg, W. and Donald, A. (1995) Evidence Based Medicine: an approach to clinical problem solving, *BMJ*, **310** (6987) 1122–6.

Spell, C. S. (1999) Management Fashions: where do they come from, and how long do they stay?, *Journal of Management History*, **5**, 334–48.

Starkey, K. and Madan, P. (2001) Bridging the Relevance Gap: aligning stakeholders in the future of management research, *British Journal of Management*, Special issue 1, S3–S26.

Stewart, R. (2001) *Evidence-Based Management: a practical guide for health professionals*, Oxford, Radcliffe.

Strategic Policy Making Team (1999) *Professional Policy Making for the Twenty First Century*, London, The Cabinet Office.

Tranfield, D., Denyer, D. and Smart, P. (2002) *Developing an Evidence-based Approach to Management Knowledge Using Systematic Review*, Submitted to EURAM, Stockholm, April 2002.

Tranfield, D. and Starkey, K. (1998) The Nature, Social Organization and Promotion of Management Research: towards policy, *British Journal of Management*, **9**, 341–53.

Whitley, R. (1984a) The Fragmented State of Management Studies: reasons and consequences, *Journal of Management Studies*, **21** (3), 331–48.

Whitley, R. (1984b) The Scientific Status of Management Research as a Practically-Oriented Social Science, *Journal of Management Studies*, **21** (4), 369–90.

Whitley, R. (2000) *The Intellectual and Social Organisation of the Sciences*, 2nd edn, Oxford, Oxford University Press.

Wolffing, B. K. (1990) Computerized Literature Searching in the Ambulatory Setting using PaperChase, *Henry Ford Hospital Medical Journal*, **38** (1), 57–61.

Special topic (D)
How do I measure the impact of my service? (Guideline)

Christine Urquhart

Statement of the question under consideration

This guideline examines how to measure the impact of your service, with an emphasis on impact studies from the health sector. It seeks to identify what works and what is less successful and to translate general lessons to other sectors (See also Wavell et al., 2002).

Impact measurement has a long history. Reports by Flowerdew and Whitehead (1974) and King Research Inc. (1984) may appear old-fashioned but arguments about cost-benefit analysis for information services, the value of information, and the cost of user time, remain fresh. Although the social impact of public libraries is now seen in terms of community identity, lifelong learning and support for local business and culture (Kerslake and Kinnell, 1998), the social impact (Harris, 1998), or the social audit (Linley and Usherwood, 1998) of public libraries is not a new concern.

In the education sector, the impact of the information and library service on learning is often taken for granted. It is only when new electronic information services require an investment in hardware support, networking, additional licences, and new ways of working, that such assumptions are questioned. In the UK, the eVALUEd project reviewed a variety of manuals useful to those evaluating digital library services (Thebridge and Hartland-Fox, 2003), including American (Bertot et al., 2001; Hernon and Dugan, 2002; Lindauer, 2000; Shim et al. 2001), UK (Crawford, 2000) and European manuals (EQUINOX). The JUSTEIS project (Urquhart et al., 2003) (and its companion JUBILEE project at Northumbria University) is part of the monitoring and evaluation framework set up by the Joint Information Systems Committee to assess how electronic information services affect the information behaviour of staff and students in higher and further education. Its remit covers possible impacts on learning, teaching and research.

Health library services operate within a wide variety of organizational structures, with various funding sources. They may serve undergraduate students; postgraduate students; staff undertaking formal and informal continuing professional development; clinical and biomedical researchers; health service managers and administrators; and patients and their carers. A library in an NHS Trust must consider impacts on staff learning and clinical research activities, as well as the direct and indirect impacts on improved quality of patient care. Increasingly, it needs to consider its social impact, through services designed to liaise with patients, providing information and advice on their condition, its treatment and appropriate support services.

Measuring the impact of any information service is difficult, as the questions concern:

- *type of impact* – is the effectiveness of the service related to the costs of delivery? For example, are you interested in softer, social impacts or are you concerned with assessing benefits to the organization in monetary terms? Are you concerned with more expensive, newer services, or with a holistic view of the impact of your service?
- *impact on whom* – which user groups matter, and how do their priorities differ? It is easy to focus on groups who use your services most, but it is important to learn about the impact on less frequent users.
- *timescale* – is this short-term impact or longer term? For example, are you concerned with immediate satisfaction, immediate learning or future actions taken as a result of reading and reviewing information provided by your service?
- *location of impact* – do services delivered remotely require different impact measures from those for services provided by paper or in the library building?

Performance measurement largely focuses on the easy-to-measure, such as service inputs (human resources, materials), or service outputs (e.g. documents supplied, training sessions delivered). Relating outputs to service inputs provides a measure of service efficiency. The effectiveness of the service should relate service outcomes to service inputs. Outcomes are, essentially, how the users use library service outputs to help them provide better quality services or products. In a library serving the health service, outcomes relate to the quality of patient care. Performance of the service should be measured in terms of what matters to the users (Urquhart, 1997), not what library staff think users should do:

➤ INPUTS➤LIBRARY➤ OUTPUTS➤USER➤OUTCOMES.

Efficiency = Outputs/Inputs

The more outputs (interlibrary loans, database accesses) the library produces for the same inputs (human resources, materials), the more efficient the library is.

Effectiveness = Outcomes/Inputs

The greater the outcomes (useful actions by the user) in relation to the same inputs, the more effective the service is.

Library services tend to overlook the time users spend in accessing and using services. Such services may be provided free at the point of access to the users, but users still 'pay' in terms of their time to use these services. Providing access to a full-text journal is worthwhile only if users value the contents and are willing to spend some time reading.

To assess the impact of their service, librarians need to ask:

- Am I interested in assessing the impact of the service as a whole? How can we relate our contribution to the mission of our parent organization, for example?
- Am I interested in assessing whether service element A is more effective than service element B? For example, if I need to make cuts to the service, should I cut back on journals or the interlibrary loans?
- Am I interested in assessing whether mode of delivery X is more effective than mode of delivery Y for service element C? For example, is delivery of full-text electronic journals more valuable to users than print journals plus interlibrary loans?

It is important to identify before you start what your impact questions are and what you intend to do as a result of the impact assessment.

Options for 'diagnosis'

Users value outcomes (what they do with the outputs of your service) and ideally impact is measured directly as outcomes. Often that is very difficult, as users will not usually tell us unless we ask. For most health library impact studies, impact on patient care can only be measured indirectly in terms of helping health staff improve the quality of care.

Quality is elusive, but we need to capture what it means for library users, when applied to their work and their organizational policies. Ways in which care might be improved, from the perspective of both patient and health practitioner with the corresponding impact question are shown in Table D.1. Other types of library will require variants but are likely to share an emphasis on supporting learning, professional development, research and development, product or service support, and corporate governance.

Table D.1   Linking quality of care to library impact questions

Quality of care questions	Impact questions
Is the care provided evidence-based, as far as possible?	Is the library service providing an appropriate mix of evidence-based resources and support in using those resources?
Do the health practitioners have appropriate support in professional development to maintain high quality of care?	Is the library service supporting professional development aimed at improving the quality of care?
Do the services supplied match the needs of the user population, and is staff time used cost-effectively?	Is the library service providing a service that saves time for the user, compared to other means of obtaining necessary information?
Is a system of governance in place to ensure that appropriate action is taken to minimize risk?	Is the library service reaching key decision makers? Does the library service have an impact on clinical decision making, and if so, how? Is the service attuned to governance needs?

Many impact questions require subjective judgements and this seems to affect the answers obtained (Urquhart and Hepworth, 1995a, 1995b). The value of information provided to a user depends on the situation of need and the prior knowledge of the user, and what is valuable to one user may not necessarily be valuable to another. The value of the information, or services, may be affected by the user's attitudes towards the service and the staff. If the users appreciate a service they are more likely to accord it a high value. Overall impact assessments may not account for important differences in benefits obtained for particular user groups (O'Connor, 2002), and it is important to be aware how your user groups are segmented.

Subjective judgements of the value of information provided are valuable but often you need to provide objective assessments of impact. You may be able to show:

- savings in staff time (networked databases save time as users do not need to travel to the library)
- decisions and actions that save the organization money (choice of treatment may be cheaper and safer)
- information skills of users have improved (training has increased knowledge of searching techniques and critical appraisal).

These examples from health libraries have equivalents elsewhere. Time savings, for library users, are relevant in many types of library. Decisions may relate to the type of building to be constructed, or whether a product line is viable. What matters to the library user may be something they have learnt, or something they need to learn. Some impacts are less formal and may relate to helping library users to feel part of a community, and to be good citizens. An education library may view information skills provision quite formally, whereas a public library may view impact on information skills as part of its mission to promote social inclusion.

Review of methods used in impact studies

Impact studies of health library services are usually cross-sectional surveys, retrospective studies of the user population. Klein et al. (1994) used a case-control design to compare the costs of care for patients with similar conditions. Patients for whom a literature search was done were compared with those for whom there was no literature search. This technique could be adapted to other sectors making it possible to hypothesize the costs of doing without a library service and to calculate the costs of obtaining the same information for users in other ways. Though not quite the same as calculating the impact directly it is occasionally useful (see examples in Urquhart et al. (2001, Section 3.3)).

Most impact surveys are based on self-reporting questionnaires, interviews, or a mix of both (Table D.2).

Table D.2 Examples of impact studies

Methods used	Number of responses	Sample	Notes	Reference
Questionnaire survey	184 (176 usable)	310 health - professionals, Chicago hospital	Users asked to make a mediated search request first	King (1987)
Questionnaire survey	543 (usable)	2101 health professionals, Kentucky hospital	Part of a TQM survey	Fischer and Reel (1992)
Questionnaire survey	227 (208 usable)	448, from 15 hospitals, 3 physician groups in Rochester, NY	Users asked to make a mediated search request first. A few follow-up interviews conducted	Marshall (1992)
Critical incident interview	552	1160, mostly US medical staff	Use of NLM's MEDLINE service	Lindberg et al. (1993) Wilson et al. (1989)

(continued)

Table D.2 (*continued*)

Methods used	Number of responses	Sample	Notes	Reference
Questionnaire survey	799	3877, all medical staff at five university hospitals in Spain	Based on Marshall (1992)	Casado Uriguen et al. (1995)
Questionnaire survey, supplemented by interviews	486	713 (227 end-user searches, 212 interlibrary loans, 47 mediated searches) from 11 hospital sites in the UK, with 10% sample of various medical staff groups used for the inform-ation behaviour element	Based on Marshall (1992) but the study also included a background study on the information behaviour of medical staff	Urquhart and Hepworth (1995a, b)
Questionnaire survey	295 (290 usable)	372 (requests or searches) from medical staff in regional hospitals	Based on Marshall (1992)	Burton (1995)
Questionnaire survey	278 (document) delivery, 82 (searches)	745 (document delivery requests), 226 searches, all hospital staff, one hospital	Based on Marshall (1992) but searches not solicited	Scolaro (1995)
Questionnaire survey, supple-mented by interviews	311	776 (nursing staff from 18 sites throughout UK)	Based on Urquhart and Hepworth (1995a, b)	Davies et al. (1997)
Questionnaire survey	127 (98 usable)	288 (medical staff – specialists and registrars, Canberra)	Based on Marshall (1992), study conducted 1994 to 1995	Ali (2000)

(*continued*)

Table D.2   *(continued)*

Methods used	Number of responses	Sample	Notes	Reference
Interview and questionnaire surveys	137 interviews, 331 questionnaires	7 virtual outreach services in England – all health professionals included. Questionnaire response c.40% on average	Methodology varied according to site requirements. Included a cost study at one site	Yeoman et al. (2001)
Interview and questionnaire surveys, with some analysis of web server statistics	41 interviews, 179 online questionnaires. Seven month's log file analysis (web server statistics)	Evaluation of the pilot National electronic Library for Health (NeLH). Formative evaluation study	Based partly on Yeoman et al. (2001)	Urquhart et al. (2001)
Online survey	98 responses	Clinical Access Information Program, NSW, Australia	Commentary on planned evaluation of CIAP	Wyatt (2001)

Critical appraisal of the evidence

Although a case-control study is appropriate for assessing whether a literature search led to a better patient care outcome, it has several disadvantages when assessing impact. Firstly, it is complicated to set up, dependent on the data quality in the clinical information system and the diagnostic resource group system used. Secondly, timing of literature searching affects the results obtained. Thirdly, the design does not allow for the fact that more experienced and knowledgeable doctors might not need a literature search. Fourthly, the design raises the question: who should do the literature searching – doctors or librarians? For other library services, in calculating the costs of doing without the conventional service, there are often too many unknowns in trying to calculate how users would obtain the information in other ways. It may be necessary to check whether the priorities of the service accord with the priorities of the service users, using the PAPE methods (Broadbent and Lofgren, 1993) or SERVQUAL (e.g. Martin, 2003).

Early impact studies, modelled on the Rochester design, assessed the impact on patient care of searches carried out by librarians for medical staff. Although librarians continue to conduct mediated searches, interest is more likely to focus on the effect on patient care of searches conducted by health staff themselves, using networked services provided by the library, and for which appropriate support and training have been provided. In many educational, research and workplace libraries, librarians may be part of a research or a learning support team, and may provide specialist searching skills, but more commonly they are a facilitator or trainer, supporting effective use of services by users themselves.

Results obtained in impact studies based on the Rochester design vary. Reasons for this are unclear. Possibly the impacts are genuinely different, but the results may be affected by how the research is conducted. Practical design questions for those planning impact studies are:

- Who are the service users? Does my proposed sampling method exclude groups of staff that should be included? Am I only seeking the views of faithful library users? Will an online survey be representative?
- Am I asking appropriate questions for the user group? Is the impact evidence being sought of relevance to the group? How should I determine membership of the group? Is it better to consider job roles, type of work situation, educational or social setting, or professional group?
- What type of data will be most helpful – quantitative, qualitative or a mix of both? If I need qualitative data how can I best obtain that – by interviews or focus groups or a mixture of both? For a questionnaire, am I asking questions that will provide the information that I need?
- Are my professional assumptions about the service I provide likely to bias interpretation of the findings? Do I need to re-assess the aims and objectives of the study?

Looking for immediate patient care impacts may not be productive. Studies of the way information is actually used in clinical decision making (Urquhart, 1998) suggest that the personal knowledge and experience of the clinician is important, and that will affect not just the type of impacts perceived, but whether the impact is immediate (just in time) or long-term (just in case). There may be an immediate impact on knowledge (in confirming that a supposition was correct), but the long-term impact on patient care may depend on other organizational changes or events or availability of other information which affect implementation. The impact of your service in other sectors may be similarly hard to quantify particularly where outcomes depend on factors outside your control.

Recommendations – graded according to strength of evidence

Evidence from impact studies largely comprises cross-sectional surveys and barely registers on conventional evidence hierarchies (e.g. SIGN guidelines, 2001). It is probably better to accept the limitations of such studies and to replicate with care, trying to reduce bias and building in some mechanism to facilitate learning from the survey. An impact study should not just demonstrate an impact but also provide clues on how service improvements might enhance the impact. An aim might be an action research philosophy of practical-deliberative action research (McKernan, 1991), where researchers and practitioners identify potential problems, underlying causes, and possible interventions (Hughes, 2001).

The indications from the existing evidence are:

- *Quantity of evidence* has grown considerably. Information provided by the library has a positive impact, mostly indirectly, on patient care, but a stronger positive impact on the learning (of new knowledge, or substantiation of existing knowledge) of the clinician.
- *Quality of evidence* is problematic, as response rates to questionnaire surveys rarely exceed 50%. It is difficult to target the 'non-respondent' and, given the growth in networked services and use of online surveys, to judge realistic response rates is problematic. It may be better to complement any questionnaire survey with a small interview survey, (preferably) with a randomly selected group of users.
- *Consistency of evidence* is variable. Questions concerning cost savings, for example reducing the length of stay in hospital, produce different results, and are inevitably subjective. Such questions are difficult to frame without it being obvious to the respondent what type of answers are desired.
- *Cost* questions might be easier framed in terms of savings in time (Yeoman et al. 2001, Urquhart et al. 2001).

Discussion of practical points – resource and geographical considerations

Methods used for an impact study should be sensitive to variations in organizational culture. A user group that values quantitative methods is unlikely to be convinced by a wholly qualitative impact study.

Existing impact studies suggest that you should:

- expect a target 45–50% response rate from a population of a couple of hundred as realistic for a questionnaire survey. Increasing the sample size appears to reduce the response rate markedly

- use appropriate impact questions for your situation (see Table D.1, and review questions used in situations similar to your own, using Table D.2 to help you with appropriate questions for your service)
- include a qualitative interview element to help in taking action to improve services, and target the 'non-users'.

Good practice point

Best practice will use a combination of quantitative and qualitative techniques: quantitative to convince funders of the impact of your service, and qualitative to show how the impact of your service can be enhanced.

Acknowledgements

Patrick O'Connor and Alison Yeoman provided valuable advice and support for the production of this guideline.

References

Ali, I. (2000) Library Provided Information and Clinical Decision Making: a study of two hospitals in Canberra, *Australian Academic and Research Libraries*, **31** (1), 30–45.

Bertot, J. C., McClure, C. R. and Ryan, J. (2001) *Statistics and Performance Measures for Public Library Networked Services*, Chicago, American Library Association.

Broadbent, M. and Lofgren, H. (1993) Information Delivery: identifying priorities, performance and value, *Information Processing and Management*, **29** (6), 683–701.

Burton, J. E. (1995) The Impact of Medical Libraries and Literature on Patient Care in New Zealand, *Bulletin of the Medical Library Association*, **83** (4), 425–30.

Casado Uriguen, M., Garcia Martin, M. A., La Torre, P. M., Montes del Olmo, M. I., Mas Vilardell, T. and Ribes Cot, M. (1995) Importance of Hospital Library Facilities to Clinical Decision Making by Medical Staff. In McSean, T., Van Loo, J. and Coutinho, E. (eds), *Health Information – New Possibilities: Proceedings of the 4th European Conference of Medical and Health Libraries, 28 June–2 July 1994*, Oslo, Dordrecht, Kluwer for EAHIL, 126–8.

Crawford, J. (2000) *Evaluation of Library and Information Services*, 2nd edn, London, Aslib.

Davies, R., Urquhart, C. J., Massiter, C. and Hepworth, J. B. (1997) *Establishing the Value of Information to Nursing Continuing Education: report of the EVINCE project*, British Library Research and Innovation Report no. 44, Boston Spa, Wetherby, British Library Document Supply Centre.

Fischer, W. W. and Reel, L. B. (1992) Total Quality Management (TQM) in a Hospital Library: identifying service benchmarks, *Bulletin of the Medical Library Association*, **80** (4), 347–52.

Flowerdew, A. D. J. and Whitehead, C. M. E. (1974) *Cost Effectiveness and Cost/benefits Analysis in Information science*, Report to OSTI on project s1/97/03, London, LSE.

Harris, K. (1998) *Open to Interpretation. Community Perceptions of the Social Benefits of Public Libraries*, British Library Research and Innovation Report no. 88, Boston Spa, Wetherby, British Library Document Supply Centre.

Hernon, P. and Dugan, R. E. (2002) *An Action Plan for Outcomes Assessment in Your Library*, Chicago, American Library Association.

Hughes, I. (2001) Action research, http://casino.cchs.usyd.edu.au/arow/reader/hughes5.htm.

Kerslake, E. and Kinnell, M. (1998) Public Libraries, Public Interest and the Information Society: theoretical issues in the social impact of public libraries, *Journal of Librarianship and Information Science*, **30** (3), 159–67.

King Research Inc. (1984) *A Study of the Value of Information and the Effect on Value of Intermediary Organizations, Timeliness of Services and Products and Comprehensiveness of the EDB*, NTIS Report DE85-003670.

King, D. N. (1987) The Contribution of Hospital Library Information Services to Clinical Care: a study in eight hospitals, *Bulletin of the Medical Library Association*, **75** (4), 291–301.

Klein, M. S., Ross, F. V., Adams, D. L. and Gilbert, C. M. (1994) Effect of Online Literature Searching on Length of Stay and Patient Care Costs, *Academic Medicine*, **69** (6), 489–95.

Lindauer, B. G. (2000) *Measuring What Matters: a library/LRC outcomes assessment manual*, Fairfield, CA, Learning Resources Association of California Community Colleges.

Lindberg, D. A. B., Siegel, E. R., Rapp, B. A., Wallingford, K. T. and Wilson, S. R. (1993) Use of MEDLINE by Physicians for Clinical Problem Solving, *Journal of the American Medical Association*, **269** (4), 3124–9.

Linley, R. and Usherwood, B. (1998) *New Measures for the New Library: a social audit of public libraries*, British Library Research and Innovation Report no.89, Boston Spa, Wetherby, British Library Document Supply Centre.

Marshall, J. G. (1992) The Impact of the Hospital Library on Clinical Decision Making: the Rochester study, *Bulletin of the Medical Library Association*, **80** (2), 169–78.

Martin, S. (2003) Using SERVQUAL in Health Libraries Across Somerset, Devon and Cornwall, *Health Information and Libraries Journal*, **20** (1), 15–21.

McKernan, J. (1991) *Curriculum Action Research. A handbook of methods and resources for the reflective practitioner*, London, Kogan Page.

O'Connor, P. (2002) Determining the Impact of Health Library Services on Patient Care: a review of the literature, *Health Information and Libraries Journal*, **19** (1), 1–13.

Scolaro, T. (1995) Assessing the Impact of Information Provided by the Library, In Keyword Editorial Services (ed.) *Synergy in Sydney. Proceedings of the Sixth Asian Pacific Specials, Health and Law Librarians Conference*, Canberra, Australian Library and Information Association, 95–109.

Shim, W. J., McClure, C., Fraser, B. T. and Bertot, J. C. (2001) *Data Collection Manual for Academic and Research Library Network Statistics and Performance Measures*, Washington, D.C., Association of Research Libraries.

SIGN (Scottish Intercollegiate Guidelines Network) (2001) *SIGN 50: A Guideline Developer's Handbook*, Edinburgh, Scottish Intercollegiate Guidelines Network.

Thebridge, S. and Hartland-Fox, Rebecca. (2003) Evaluating in the Electronic World, *Update (Library + Information Update)*, **2** (3), 48–9.

Urquhart, C. (1997) Performance Measurement in Library and Information Services: health advice from the Value and EVINCE studies, *Library and Information Briefings* (71).

Urquhart, C. (1998) Personal Knowledge: a clinical perspective from the Value and EVINCE projects in health library and information services, *Journal of Documentation*, **54** (4), 420–42.

Urquhart, C.J. and Hepworth, J.B. (1995a) *The Value of Information to Clinicians: a toolkit for measurement*, Aberystwyth, Open Learning Unit, Department of Information and Library Studies, University of Wales Aberystwyth.

Urquhart, C. J. and Hepworth, J. B. (1995b) *The Value to Clinical Decision Making of Information Supplied by NHS Library and Information Services*, British Library R and D Report 6205, Boston Spa, Wetherby, British Library Document Supply Centre.

Urquhart, C., Yeoman, A., Cooper, J. and Wailoo, A. (2001) *NeLH Pilot Evaluation Project. Final report to NHS Information Authority*, NeLH, www.nhsia.nhs.uk/nelh/pages/documents/aber.doc.

Urquhart, C., Thomas, R., Armstrong, C., Fenton, R., Lonsdale, R., Spink, S. and Yeoman, A. (2003) Uptake and Use of Electronic Information Services: trends in UK higher education from the JUSTEIS project, *Program* (to appear).

Wavell, C., Baxter, G., Johnson, I. and Williams, D. (2002) *Impact Evaluation of Museums, Archives and Libraries: Available Evidence Project*, London, Resource.

Wilson, S. R., Starr-Schneidkraut, N. and Cooper, M. D. (1989) *Use of the Critical Incident Technique to Evaluate the Impact of MEDLINE*, AIR-646000-9/89-FR, NLM/OPE-90/01, Palo Alto, American Institute Behavioral Sciences.

Wyatt, J. (2001) *Development of an Evaluation Methodology for the NSW Health Clinical Information Access Program*, Sydney, New South Wales Health Department, www.health.nsw.gov.au.

Yeoman, A., Cooper, J., Urquhart, C. and Tyler, A. (2001) *The Value and Impact of Virtual Outreach Services: report of the VIVOS project*, LIC 111, London, Re:source: The Council for Museums, Archives and Libraries.

Websites

ARL data collection
   www.arl.org/stats/newmeas/emetrics/phase3/ARL_Emetrics_data_Collection_manual.pdf
eVALUEd
   www.cie.uce.ac.uk/evalued/
JUBILEE
   http://online.northumbria.ac.uk/faculties/art/information_studies/imri/
JUSTEIS
   www.justeis.info.uk (to be launched)
Scottish Intercollegiate Guidelines Network
   www.sign.ac.uk

Special topic (E)
Should I charge and, if so, what should I charge for? (Evidence Briefing)

Lynette Cawthra

What are my objectives in charging?

'Before introducing charges for any service it is essential to consider where the service sits within your long-term objectives and priorities and establish that: there is a need for the service; there is a willingness to pay; and you have the appropriate resources and skills to take it forward' (Webb, 2003). You must decide what your objectives are in charging. For instance:

- are you trying to produce value-for-money outcomes? (Cooper, 1997)
- are you attempting to make a profit, recover costs or control excessive use? Libraries are often more concerned to recover costs than to make money, e.g. 'cost-minus pricing', providing subsidized services below costs (Snyder and Davenport, 1997)
- is the charged-for service peripheral (e.g. a service to 'non-core' users) or integral to what the library offers (e.g. passing on costs to internal users)?

Answers to such questions will generate very different pricing strategies (Ward et al., 2002).

Libraries should establish a pricing mechanism only after determining the implications of such a policy on performance and utilization of library services (elasticity analysis) (Olaisen, 1992).

What are my motives?

Possible reasons for charging include:

- to generate revenue
- to recover costs, in whole or in part
- to benefit from users' ability and willingness to pay
- to control usage (Snyder and Davenport, 1997) e.g. by 'non-core' users
- conversely, as outreach to 'non-core' users (Ward et al., 2002)
- to bring a service in line with 'competitor services' (Ward, 1997)
- to provide 'value-added' services e.g. a new or upgraded service. If a service benefits only a small proportion of library users, they may be expected to pay (Snyder and Davenport, 1997)
- to create a measure of value, aiming to demonstrate – e.g. to funding bodies – that information (and by extension the information expert! (Webb, 2003, 5)) is viewed as a valuable commodity
- as the only way to afford some services at all (Snyder and Davenport, 1997).

What services might I charge for?

Table E.1 suggests possible services that might be charged for:

Table E.1   Services that might be charged for

Item	Comment	Identified by
Access to the library		
Document supply	Copyright law requires libraries to cover their complete costs when photocopying documents plus an additional element towards library running costs	
Printing	Providing free printing from electronic resources but charging for photocopies encourages users to select information based on format rather than quality or relevance	(Park 1997, 150)
Loans, overdues and reservations		
Literature searches, reading lists and current awareness services		
User education/training		
Services for distance learners		
Access to externally-produced online or CD-ROM services	This may penalize users whose needs are served by resources not held by the library	

(continued)

Table E.1 *(continued)*

Item	Comment	Identified by
Other 'value-added' services, offering advantages such as speed, depth, tailoring or packaging of information.	Deciding what constitutes a 'basic service' which may be free, and 'non-core' services which may be priced, is not straightforward	(Webber, 1993, 216; Webber, 2001, 17)
Expanded services benefiting the individual rather than the public		(Park, 1997, 149)
Consultancy; selling floppy disks, stationery; selling off old stock or indeed new books; room hire		(Webber, 1993, 213)

You should not introduce charges randomly for existing, unchanged, previously free services (Webb, 2003). Previous demand from existing users does not necessarily convert into sales. You may need to look more broadly and recruit new clients (Webb, 1994). When providing services to a group of users you could use the following pricing strategies:

* producing a 'fixed price quote' to cover all members of that group for an agreed level of service demand
* quoting a 'variable price' where activity triggers charges
* providing an agreed minimum level of activity at a fixed price with further activities at a variable, pay-as-you-go price (Cooper, 1997).

What do I need to do?

Key elements in deciding what services to offer at what price, resources required, and procedures to put in place include (Webb, 2003):

* Do not launch a product unless you can quantify demand for it. Undertake market research to be sure the needs of potential customers are understood in advance; this may include a competitor analysis (Ward et al., 2002; Webb, 2003). Involve front-line staff with a good grasp of users' requirements, and address any issues they raise promptly (Gourlay, 1999).
* Use such research to inform a succinct business plan (Ward, 1997). This requires compiling best estimates of financial outcomes (MacKintosh, 1999).
* When setting charges, consider not 'What should the price be?' but rather 'Have we addressed all the considerations that will determine the correct price?' (Dolan, 1995). Gather and analyse cost information to provide an evidence base for decisions on charging. Collect sufficient data to gauge the range of

potential demands upon a service at various price levels (Snyder and Davenport, 1997).
- Use cost accounting to determine the monetary cost of certain activities (Forrest and Cawasjee, 1997).

You also need to categorize:

- *fixed and variable costs*: not understanding the difference can lead to under-estimating costs of increased levels of provision of a service. Pricing to cover only variable costs maximizes the use of the service to customers, as they do not contribute to fixed costs which are being incurred anyway (Jones and Nicholas, 1993). Pricing at full cost provides the best chance of recovering the cost of assets used to provide a service.
- *direct and indirect costs*: it is difficult to identify strong cause and effect relationships in library activities, when working out how to allocate indirect costs (overheads). Such decisions have important implications for the pricing of services (Snyder and Davenport, 1997).

Other factors include:

- Different costing models suit different settings, e.g. for-profit and non-profit environments. Check if there is a locally-preferred method for calculating costs (Ward, 1997). Undertaking a break-even analysis is always important (Cooper, 1997; Olaisen, 1992; Snyder and Davenport, 1997). Do not skimp on staff costs, as knowledgeable staff are the backbone of any information service (Tanton, 1997). Be aware when pricing staff time on research-based activities that you can probably charge directly only for between two and four hours a day of each information specialist's time (Ward, 1997).
- Costs can be lowered by compiling standard packages of information to be delivered repeatedly (Gourlay, 1999). Designing different versions of a product, to meet the needs of different groups of customers, can decrease costs by a lesser extent but also increase possible income, e.g. by differential pricing. Personalized information packages cost the most to produce, but your market research may demonstrate that you can price them accordingly (Shapiro and Varian, 1999). If undertaking market-driven pricing ensure that you can establish a monetary value for your information, and that you know your markets (Snyder and Davenport, 1997).
- Record reasons for every decision in determining costs to ensure consistency and to counter external challenges to your decision-making process (Forrest and Cawasjee, 1997).

- Ensure service-level agreements or formal contractual arrangements specify services to be provided to whom and at what price (Tanton, 1997; Webb, 1994). Articulate a clear policy on charging: it can defuse opposition to fee-based services (Webb, 1994).
- Plan for expenditure on professional staff development, to ensure relevant skills are in place. Paying customers tend to be more alert to perceived failings (Ward, 1997; Webb, 1994).
- Check your liability for the accuracy of information (Ward, 1997), copyright (Webb, 2003), licensing restrictions and confidentiality (Ward, 1997).
- Make payment processes easy (Stratigos and Curtis, 2000). Pricing structures which include additional small amounts – e.g. for postage – are disliked by users (Fong, 1999; Ward, 1997).
- When undertaking an initial pilot project ensure it is of realistic duration (one year minimum); do not set prices below a cost-recovery point as this will lead to inaccurate conclusions and make later transition to higher prices difficult. Do not add to the duties of existing staff (Ward, 1997).
- Market the solutions and benefits the service can bring rather than listing the resources it offers (Ward, 1997).
- Once underway, evaluate value for money, impact and added value. Performance measures and continuous market research will be needed (Webb, 2003). Conduct periodic price reviews to consider whether you are still pricing appropriately and whether you are covering your costs (Cooper, 1997). Refine the service using feedback from client satisfaction surveys (Ward, 1997; Ward, 2000).

What are the potential benefits?

- Justifying the outcomes your library achieves, in relation to time and money spent. This can validate the service's worth and fortify against cutbacks (Cooper, 1997).
- Helping to communicate how resources are being used, and potential effects of budget increases/decreases (Virgo, 1992). Such data are useful for identifying inappropriate use of staff time (Forrest and Cawasjee, 1997). You may even conclude that it is not cost-effective to provide a particular service at all.
- Providing a service to non-core users without diminishing your ability to meet your primary obligations (Ward and Dugan, 1999). Charging high prices for specialist services can subsidize more popular services which do not generate income (Snyder and Davenport, 1997).
- Developing a greater depth of service (e.g. specialized skills) from a fee-based service which can be put to good use by the parent library (Ward,

1997; Ward and Dugan, 1999), or buying in extra reference sources or equipment which other departments can also use (Gourlay, 1999; Ward, 1997).
- Increasing efficiency and/or responsiveness of services if these are charged for. Paying for a service may heighten long-term commitment for both provider and user (Bailey, 1992; Olaisen, 1992; Webber, 2001).
- Possibly subsidizing staff or budget lines, at least until a new service reaches break-even point (Ward et al., 2002).
- Publicizing the library as a dynamic institution and enhancing the library's free services (Vavrek, 2000; Ward et al., 2002).
- Detering frivolous demands through nominal charges (Badenoch et al., 1994).

What are the possible pitfalls?
- Prices set too high can lead to a decrease – or a greater increase than desired – in library usage. Internet users increasingly expect their content free of charge (Stratigos and Curtis, 2000). Significant declines in usage of existing services occur if charges are introduced for them (Webber, 1993).
- Prices set too low can stimulate too high a demand (Snyder and Davenport, 1997). Your service may also be perceived as inferior to higher-priced 'competitor services' (Ward, 1997).
- Administrative overheads may not be sufficiently factored into the pricing structure (Dolan, 1995; Stratigos and Curtis, 2000).
- Users may fail to pay the charges requested. Debt collection must therefore be planned as an overhead (Tanton, 1997; Webber, 1993).
- Earning revenue will not be enough if costs of providing a service far exceed the income generated (Webb, 1994).
- Changes in the librarian/user relationship (Webber, 1993).
- Adverse effects on interlibrary loan co-operation over document supply (Webber, 1993).
- Such an entrepreneurial relationship may be easier with external commercial users than with other public sector users (e.g. an academic library providing services to NHS users) (Webber, 1993).

Where can I find examples of good practice?
- Snyder and Davenport (1997) give worked examples of traditional costing versus activity-based costing. Cooper (1997) gives examples in a health library setting. Fong (1999) illustrates cost accounting methodology.
- Ward et al. (2002) offer models for costing fee-based services to non-core users, including how to determine costs – direct and indirect – and how to set fees. Staffing, space and start-up funding are also covered.

- McGowan (2000) describes a programme offering healthcare professionals and others access to resources based on their specific information needs, and re-engineering library services to meet these needs. Fees charged were used to expand outreach activities.
- Jones and Nicholas (1993) examine functional cost analysis, whereby all costs are assigned to library functions which represent services to users. A more recent costing exercise in a health library is written up by Forrest and Cawasjee (1997).
- Webb (1994) illustrates decisions to be made, both at policy and operational levels. One service which ran into problems when relaunched as a subscription service made a further transition to a simpler charging system.
- Park (1997) includes principles for price-setting and collecting charges when charging for print-outs.

References

Badenoch, D. et al. (1994) The Value of Information. In Feeney, M. and Grieves, M. (eds), *The Value and Impact of Information*, London, Bowker Saur.

Bailey, S. J. (1992) Charging for Public Library Services. In Cronin, B., *The Marketing of Library and Information Services 2*, London, Aslib

Cooper, L. (1997) How Much Should it Cost?: an introduction to management use of costing information, *Health Libraries Review*, **14** (4), 209–17.

Dolan, R. J. (1995) How Do You Know When the Price is Right?, *Harvard Business Review*, (September/October), 174–83.

Fong, Y. S. (1999) Pricing and Costing in Fee-based Information Services. In Ward, S. M., Fong, Y. S and Nickelson Dearie, T. (eds), Information Delivery in the 21st Century: proceedings of the fourth international conference on fee-based information services in libraries, *Journal of Interlibrary Loan, Document Delivery and Information Supply*, **10** (1), 63–74.

Forrest, M. and Cawasjee, A.-M. (1997) Costing the Library Service: Cairns Library – a case study, *Health Libraries Review*, **14** (4), 219–32.

Gourlay, U. M. (1999) Know your Parent Organisation and Your Business Environment: criteria for success. In Ward, S. M., Fong, Y. S. and Nickelson Dearie, T. (eds), Information Delivery in the 21st Century: proceedings of the Fourth International Conference on Fee-based Information Services in Libraries, *Journal of Interlibrary Loan, Document Delivery and Information Supply*, **10** (1), 37–46.

Jones, L. and Nicholas, D. (1993) Costing Medical Libraries: the feasibility of functional cost analysis, *Health Libraries Review*, **10** (4), 169–201.

MacKintosh, P. J. (1999) Writing an Effective Business Plan for Fee-based Services. In Ward, S. M., Fong, Y. S and Nickelson Dearie, T. (eds), Information Delivery in the 21st Century: proceedings of the fourth international conference on fee-based information services in libraries, *Journal of Interlibrary Loan, Document Delivery and Information Supply*, **10** (1), 47–62.

McGowan, J. J. (2000) Health Information Outreach: the land-grant mission, *Bulletin of the Medical Library Association*, **88** (4), 355–61.

Olaisen, J. L. (1992) Pricing Strategies for Library and Information Services. In Cronin, B., *The Marketing of Library and Information Services 2*, London, Aslib.

Park, B. (1997) Charging for Print-outs, *The Bottom Line: Managing Library Finance*, **10** (4), 148–52.

Shapiro, C. and Varian, H. R. (1999) *Information Rules: a strategic guide to the network economy*, Boston, Harvard Business School Press.

Snyder, H. and Davenport, E. (1997) *Costing and Pricing in the Digital Age*, London, Library Association Publishing.

Stratigos, A. and Curtis, D. (2000) Chargebacks: solution or setback?, *Online*, **24** (3), 81–3.

Tanton, J. (1997) Charging for Information: costing and pricing, *Managing Information*, **4** (7), 36–7.

Vavrek, B. (2000) The Best Things in Life Have Fees, *American Libraries*, **31** (5), 75–6.

Virgo, J. A. C. (1992) Costing and Pricing Information Services. In Cronin, B., *The Marketing of Library and Information Services 2*, London, Aslib.

Ward, S. M. (1997) *Starting and Managing Fee-based Information Services in Academic Libraries*, Greenwich CT/London, JAI Press.

Ward, S. M. (2000) The Client Satisfaction Survey as a Tool for Evaluating Library Fee-based Information Services, *Journal of Interlibrary Loan, Document Delivery and Information Supply*, **10** (3), 63–76.

Ward, S. M., Fong, Y. S. and Camille, D. (2002) Library Fee-based Information Services: financial considerations, *The Bottom Line: Managing Library Finance*, **15** (1), 5–17.

Ward, S. M. and Dugan, M. (1999) Document Delivery in Academic Fee-based Information Services, *Reference Librarian* (63), 73–81.

Webb, S. P. (1994) *Making a Charge for Library and Information Services*, London, Aslib.

Webb, S. P. (with Winterton, J.) (2003) *Fee-based Services in Library and Information Centres*, London, Europa.

Webber, S. (1993) Charging for Library and Information Services in Medical Libraries: a review of the literature and a survey of current practice, *Health Libraries Review*, **10** (4), 202–23.

Webber, S. (2001) Getting What You Pay For?, *Information World Review*, (168), 16–17.

18

Evidence-based perspectives on information access and retrieval

Andrew Booth

Introduction

Information access and retrieval has generated significant research output over recent decades. This chapter examines issues in evaluating information retrieval systems and techniques. It then identifies issues involved in practical use of such systems. Sources from the information science and computing literature feature in addressing such issues. Illustrative studies are assessed for quantity and quality. The chapter concludes by describing priorities for future research. The chapter is followed by two special topics examining the research evidence on searching aptitudes and characteristics, and the merits of different interfaces.

What is evidence-based information access and retrieval?

In their fifth domain, Information Access and Retrieval, Crumley and Koufogiannakis (2002) consider 'creating better systems and methods for information retrieval and access'. Information retrieval (IR) is: 'the science and practice of identification and efficient use of recorded media. Although . . . traditionally concentrated on the retrieval of text from the . . . literature, the domain over which IR can be applied effectively has broadened considerably . . .'. (Hersh et al., nd).

Asking the question

Budd and Miller (1999) highlight three particular questions from this domain:

- How does technology affect the information-seeking behaviour of users?
- Do we think differently when using a print source and an electronic source?
- How should we evaluate information technology?

Evaluation of information technologies provides a particular challenge to evidence-based information practice. Frequently, innovative technologies are adopted uncritically as a 'good thing' and evaluation viewed as an unwelcome 'brake' to technological advance.

Marcum (2003) identifies several key questions for the digital library:

1 How are digital resource users best served? What resources will they want? How will they want to use them? And, what services will most enhance use?
2 What elements are required for a coherent preservation strategy covering resources both digital and traditional?
3 What kinds of education will 'librarians' of the future need?

The developing information environment and changing expectations and demands of library users have blurred the distinction between collection management and information access and retrieval, where digital libraries are concerned. Indeed, the third question, from the education domain, suggests that a holistic approach to question identification and subsequent resolution may be preferable. Such an interpretation is supported by Marcum's observation that we need to learn a lot more than we now know about the use of digital resources, their preservation, and the training needed for operating the library of the future.

Questions identified by evidence-based practitioners within information access and retrieval are shown in Box 18.1 (Eldredge, 2001).

Box 18.1 Questions from the domain of information access and retrieval

- How can we measure the effectiveness of the services for searching in databases provided via the internet?
- How do we measure searching skills?
- Has the shift to end-user searching over the last 15 years or so, and the huge increase in electronic information resources available to users, impacted positively on users?
- What are the relative advantages of precision and recall in using an internet search engine?
- What personality characteristics make a good or a bad searcher?
- What is the evidence that it is effective to provide current awareness services in comparison with on-demand literature searching?

Finding the evidence

Information retrieval research is increasingly inhabited by research into digital or electronic libraries (Chowdhury and Chowdhury, 2000). However, as Rowlands and Bawden (1999) observe: 'although more detailed typologies of searching and browsing are described in the information retrieval literature they do not seem to have been studied systematically in the context of the digital library.' Developments in digital libraries in the public (e.g. the National electronic Library for Health) and commercial sectors demonstrate disconcertingly little cross-fertilization from academic sector initiatives such as the Electronic Libraries (eLib) Programme (www.ukoln.ac.uk/services/elib/). As Bates (1999) summarizes: 'currently the wheel is being reinvented every day on the information super-highway', whereby, 'newcomers to information questions stumble through tens of millions of dollars of research and startup money to rediscover what information science knew in 1960.'

Trends in digital libraries are reported in online journals like D-Lib Magazine (www.dlib.org), Ariadne (www.ariadne.ac.uk), in professional journals and in published proceedings of conferences, such as the *ACM Digital Library Conferences*, *European Digital Library Conferences*, and in a number of institutional and personal websites (Chowdhury and Chowdhury, 2000). More broadly IR technologies are reviewed in the *Annual Review of Information Science and Technology* and studies of searching performance are found in the Cochrane Methodology Register.

The evidence base

Table 18.1   Research methods of particular importance within information access and retrieval

Research methods of particular importance within this domain
Systematic reviews and meta-analyses
Cohort (comparative studies)
Case study
Transaction log analysis
Mixed methods research
Qualitative research

Zmud (1998) discusses the tension between rigour and relevance when evaluating IR systems, arguing that rigour has had the upper hand: 'Studies considered rigorous are those which are aware of prior theoretical and empirical research on the topic being examined, effectively apply appropriate methods, and convincingly employ tight and concise reasoning in interpreting implications and conclusions', whereas 'Studies considered relevant are those which address current or enduring topics of interest to practice and which produce easily accessible, implementable outcomes, e.g., frames of reference, guidelines, prescriptions, etc.'

Systematic reviews

Longstanding recognition that information access and retrieval benefits from overviews of research (Borgman, 1986; Fenichel, 1980) has translated into recent interest in systematic reviews. Within this specific domain systematic reviews have a dual role. As in other domains, they provide a mechanism for synthesizing and summarizing the literature into manageable quantities. Unique to this domain is the stimulus that systematic review methods have provided for our knowledge of literature retrieval methods. As Pritchard and Weightman (2003) observe: 'information retrieval lies at the heart of an evidence-based healthcare movement that is committed to enabling patient care decisions to be well informed and based on up-to-date, reliable information and knowledge. For a review to be unbiased it is essential that a broad and sensitive literature search is conducted to retrieve the maximum number of randomised controlled trials and other relevant published and unpublished studies'. The proposed Information Retrieval Methods Group within the Cochrane Collaboration offers information professionals a forum within which they can 'systematize their provision of expertise, advice and support, conduct research and facilitate information exchange' (Pritchard and Weightman, 2003).

A key early systematic review (Dickersin, Scherer and Lefebvre, 1994) examined the sensitivity and precision of online searches conducted on the MEDLINE database for references to randomized clinical trials. This study recommended that all trials on MEDLINE be tagged retrospectively, and was a major driver of subsequent indexing activity within the Collaboration and at the National Library of Medicine.

Boynton et al. (1998) further illustrate the contribution that information professionals involved in systematic reviews may make to the evidence base. These researcher-practitioners conducted frequency analysis of words in the titles, abstracts and subject keywords of MEDLINE-indexed systematic reviews in order to derive a highly sensitive search strategy. Such work is heavily influenced by a seminal study by Haynes et al. (1994) which identified search strategies for obtaining MEDLINE references of high methodological quality. The contribution of information professionals as lead investigators in producing systematic reviews is attested to by the literature (Beverley, Booth and Bath, 2003). It is further evidenced by informatics-based systematic reviews by Urquhart et al. (2000) covering nursing record systems and telemedicine. Findings of these reviews confirm the importance of a holistic view of evaluation within this domain.

Other topics covered by systematic reviews include computer-based clinical decision support systems (e.g. Johnston et al., 1994) computer-based clinical reminder systems for preventive care (Shea et al., 1996) and computer-based approaches to patient education (Lewis, 1999).

Early application of meta-analysis to library and information science research examined publications about paper- or computer-based information retrieval (Trahan, 1993). Salang (1995–1996) applied the original meta-analysis technique of Glass to examining user needs in information retrieval. Recent examples of meta-analysis in information systems cover such topics as end-user perspectives on the uptake of computer supported co-operative working (Turner and Turner, 2002). Mahmood et al. (2000) analysed 45 end-user satisfaction studies published between 1986 and 1998 to establish the influence of nine variables on user satisfaction in widely divergent settings. A rare meta-analysis looking beyond usage to the holy grail of impact (Liao, 1999) found that hypermedia instruction is more effective in terms of student achievement than no instruction or video-tape instruction. Chan and Lim (1998) applied meta-analysis to studies involving natural language interfaces to explain previously inconsistent findings. Khalili and Shashaani's (1994) meta-analysis of 36 independent studies showed computer applications raised students' examination scores.

A systematic review by Hersh and Hickam (1998) reaffirms limitations to our domain-based approach. Its findings straddle both the information retrieval domain and the educational activities domain. Although the study indicates only a small difference in retrieval by physicians compared to that of medical librarians, this may in fact attest to the success of qualified information professionals in training end-users. If we reduced mediated information retrieval services on the basis of this evidence we might overlook how critical such a 'small difference' could be and underplay the importance of librarians in delivering end-user training or advice to end-users. Clearly a 'whole systems' approach is needed when applying evidence from this particular domain.

Randomized controlled trials

Heathfield et al. (1998) take issue with randomized controlled trials (RCTs) within this domain because of:

- high cost
- poor external validity
- lack of relevance of trial results beyond very specific applications
- limited coverage of a wide range of potential applications.

They quote McManus (1996): 'Can we imagine how randomised controlled trials would ensure the quality and safety of modern air travel . . .? Whenever aeroplane manufacturers wanted to change a design feature . . . they would make a new batch of planes, half with the feature and half without, taking care not to let the pilot know which features were present'.

Notwithstanding such cautions, Eldredge (2003) identifies one RCT within information access and retrieval. 103 general practitioners in the Netherlands were randomized to separate courses in *Index Medicus*, Grateful Med, or Silverplatter CD-ROM MEDLINE. Outcomes included precision, recall, and overall search quality. The *Index Medicus* group had the most effective, but not the most efficient performance (Verhoeven et al., 2000)

Heathfield et al. (1998) highlight an 'evaluation dilemma' – where randomized controlled trials fail, important projects may be prematurely abandoned, yet where decisions are based on unsubstantiated project reports precious resources may be wasted through inappropriate adoption.

Cohort studies

The potential for comparative studies in this domain is reflected in a large body of literature. The frame of reference is pivotal when critiquing comparative studies. Here a brief analogy with evidence-based healthcare is enlightening. Health economics recognizes at least four different types of comparison of costs and outcomes to use between competing technologies. At the most simple level there is the straightforward head-to-head cost comparison – which is the cheaper option? E.g. is manual searching cheaper or more expensive than machine-assisted searching? This assumes both techniques are equally effective. In practice we typically have to decide whether the 'added value' of a new technology is worth its additional expense. So, for example, if manual searching costs £50 and retrieves 50 relevant references, and an automated system costs £150 and retrieves 300 relevant references, then we must decide whether the extra 250 references we retrieve are worth the extra £100 we pay for them. From here it is only a slight analytical advance to handle a cost per unit analysis (i.e. the 50 manual references cost £1 each whereas the 300 automated references cost only 50p each). This assumes that the only measurable benefits are associated with the number of references retrieved. In reality the benefits may be realized across a number of domains and, in recognition of this, we might require the user to complete a satisfaction index to capture their utilities (preferences or values). Clearly, selecting a particular frame of reference has considerable bearing on the verdict.

Possible comparisons include:

- *Comparison between two different methods of searching* – for example Akeroyd and Rogers (1976) compared manual searching with machine searching and found a low correlation between sets of documents retrieved but a difference in search times.
- *Comparison between two different interfaces to the same dataset* – for example Vigil (1994) compared natural language (including relevance ranking) with Boolean retrieval with regard to ease of use versus complexity and cost considerations, in terms of precision and recall.
- *Comparison between two different resources with similar functions or coverage* – for example Sasikala and Patnaik (1999) compared Alta Vista with Excite using a set of ten queries and found AltaVista had higher scores for recall, precision and coverage.
- *Comparison between two types of users* – for example Haynes et al. (1990) conducted a study whereby searches by novice searchers were compared with the same searches performed by medical librarians and clinicians experienced with MEDLINE.

Clearly, information retrieval has considerable potential for the utilization of rigorous experimental designs.

Critically appraising the evidence

As illustrated above, the information access and retrieval domain contains numerous examples of the 'higher quality' study designs advocated by the evidence-based practice movement. This confirms the observation, made in Chapter 13, that this domain is the best populated and the highest quality of our six domains. Nevertheless an incomplete picture would result if we were to omit the contribution of three particular study-types:

- case studies
- qualitative studies
- transaction log analysis.

Case studies

Case studies are an accepted and useful method of information systems research (Klein and Myers, 1999). They aim to understand, or interpret, phenomena in terms of the subjective meanings people bring to them. Case study research brings an understanding of a complex issue or object and can extend what is already known through previous research. Case studies emphasize detailed contextual analysis of a limited number of events or conditions and their relationships.

Researchers have used the case study research method for many years across a variety of disciplines to examine contemporary real-life situations.

Critics of the case study method believe it cannot be used for establishing reliability or generality of findings. Others argue that intense exposure of the case opens it up to bias. Some dismiss case study research as useful only as an exploratory tool. Yet case study research, with its applicability across many disciplines, is an appropriate methodology for library and information science.

Much research focuses on the librarian or the customer. Researchers could use the case study method to further study the role of the librarian in implementing specific models of service. Case studies are complex because they generally involve multiple sources of data, may include multiple cases within a study, and produce large amounts of data for analysis. The advantages of the case study method are its applicability to real-life, contemporary, human situations and its public accessibility through written reports. Case study results relate directly to the common reader's everyday experience and facilitate an understanding of complex real-life situations.

Such prominence is acknowledged by Atkins and Sampson (2002) in developing an accessible and comprehensive checklist to evaluate 'the in-depth case study'. Their approach draws together related work from healthcare (particularly, Greenhalgh, 1997) and Information Systems (IS) on other qualitative methods. Twenty-nine questions are divided into five domains 'Way of Thinking', 'Way of Controlling', 'Way of Working', 'Way of Supporting' and 'Way of Communicating' and a selection of these questions is given in Box 18.2.

Box 18.2 Selected critical appraisal guidelines for single case studies (Atkins and Sampson, 2002)

- Are the philosophical stance and perspective of the authors stated?
- Have any opportunities for various forms of triangulation been exploited?
- Is the research process auditable?
- Are the criteria used to select the appropriate case and participants clearly described?
- Does the study describe an orderly process for the collection of data?
- Are limitations to the study acknowledged and described?
- Is sufficient detail given to allow readers to evaluate the potential transferability of the research to other contexts?
- Is the research presented in such a way that there is evidence of logical rigour throughout the study?
- Does the study place the findings in the context of IS practice?

Aside from the large number of questions, the major critique of an otherwise useful instrument is that, unlike most checklists, it does not appear to sequence its questions according to the order they would be encountered in a typical case study report.

Qualitative research

Although quantitative approaches provide strong indications of the potential of new technologies (what to adopt), it is qualitative research that answers questions about user acceptance, attitudes and expectations (how to adopt), (Fidel, 1993). Atkins and Louw (2000) state that, although some methods for evaluation are well accepted, qualitative methods are yet to be fully explored within an information systems context. Again this illustrates the complementarity of different research paradigms. Greenhalgh (1997) proposes nine questions for evaluating qualitative research. These guidelines are illustrated in Box 18.3.

Box 18.3 Nine guidelines for evaluating qualitative papers (after Greenhalgh, 1997)

1 Did the paper describe an important clinical problem addressed via a clearly formulated question?
2 Was a qualitative approach appropriate?
3 How were the setting and the subjects selected?
4 What was the researcher's perspective, and has this been taken into account?
5 What methods did the researcher use for collecting data, and are these described in enough detail?
6 What methods were used to analyse the data, what quality control measures were implemented?
7 Are the results credible, and if so, are they clinically important?
8 What conclusions were drawn, and are they justified by the results?
9 Are the findings of the study transferable to other clinical settings?

Transaction log analysis

Transaction log analysis (TLA) provides an unobtrusive way of monitoring users' interactions with retrieval systems (Tolle and Hah, 1985; Sewell and Teitelbaum, 1986; Ferl and Millsap, 1996). It thus enables librarians to investigate everything users have typed, examined, selected and printed. The log tracks every keystroke entered into the database system, with the time, date, length of the session, database being searched and results (Wood, 2001). Data obtained by TLA performs a similar function to epidemiological data concerning the prevalence of disease (i.e. it can be used to establish the extent of a problem, prior to devising a potential solution, or it can be used following an intervention to establish the extent of improvement). Finally, TLA may be used within 'critical incident analysis' where, rather than examining all data, only incidents of particular interest – (e.g. end-user errors (King, 1993)) – are analysed. Considerations when appraising a transaction analysis are similar to those for a survey or interviews – to what extent is the incident/user being described 'typical'?

Brophy and Craven (2002) used transaction analysis to examine information needs of visually impaired users. Keystrokes and mouse clicks were logged using on-screen data capture (Lotus ScreenCam), sound recording and note taking. These were supplemented by semi-structured interviews to provide data on emotion, feelings and experience. Data from searches and interviews were entered into Atlas.ti analysis software for content analysis and comparison. Sound recording was used to ascertain not only *what* the user had done, but also *why*, and *how* they felt about it.

Understanding the information needs of users has two potential benefits for designers of IR systems. Firstly, it helps in selection of content – identifying a 'typical user' helps to determine both coverage and content. Secondly, it allows designers to develop interfaces to handle users' questions. However, information retrieval is no mere technical process – it requires recognition of a 'complex set of social and political interactions and encounters' (May et al., 2000).

Acting on the evidence

Within information systems research Zmud (1998) advocates 'Practice-Oriented Literature Reviews' to provide a concise and accessible review of what is currently known, drawing on both scholarly and practitioner sources. Evidence should be 'implementable' (so that the reader can digest and apply concepts and findings) and possess multiple entry points (so the reader can access specific constituent studies). Methods developed by the Cochrane Collaboration could, with sensitive adaptation and modification, be applied to developing, evaluating and using ICT applications (Atkins and Louw, 2000).

Farkas and Farkas (2000) indicate the potential for guidelines with 12 guidelines for designing navigation within a website. In a departure from 'How to do it' checklists they accompany each guideline with an example and a synthesis of research, theory and expert opinion. This approach not only benefits the designer, but could be equally useful for evaluating existing websites.

One can detect an increasing confluence between the evidence-based practice movement's enthusiasm for practice guidelines and what the information systems community call 'prescriptions'. Zmud (1998), for example targets development of: 'a set of implementable prescriptions regarding a phenomenon . . . [so that] . . . compelling evidence be provided to readers that documents the effectiveness of the offered prescriptions . . .'.

User studies not only inform our understanding of the users themselves but also contribute to development of information retrieval systems. Paradoxically, while investigators are usually interested in the performance of the systems themselves, evidence-based practice is better served by the generalizability of results across different systems and interfaces. So, for example, the study by Hersh and

Hickam (1998) examined physicians' performance of information retrieval across a wide range of platforms. This debate, namely whether user behaviour is sufficiently similar (homogeneous) to be characterized across different technologies and across different time periods, or whether each interface should be analysed separately, is central to the conduct of systematic reviews in the field of information systems. This debate, with its precedents in systematic reviews of healthcare, is prosaically characterized as 'lumping versus splitting'.

Future research

Evaluation is particularly problematic when users, managers and, indeed, fellow professionals may apply pressure either for or against the introduction of new technologies (Wooton, 1998). How to ensure the relevance of information systems research without compromising its rigour has been a recurring concern of those involved in evaluation (Galliers, 1993). It is therefore not unusual for evaluation and innovation to be undertaken simultaneously whereby technologies are piloted within the context of ongoing evaluation. Even so, Jadad et al. (2000) observe that: 'most of our current research tools and methods cannot produce evaluations in 'real-enough time' to avoid disrupting the application development process. To succeed, researchers will need to modify existing methods or create new ones with sufficient flexibility and power to handle the complex, dynamic and rapidly expanding nature of the Internet'.

The challenge is to ensure that future projects benefit from 'retrospective insight'. Information retrieval is particularly suited to such investigation as it provides ready access to examples and accounts of projects. For example Chowdhury and Chowdhury (2000) scanned the current printed literature on twenty digital libraries and websites of various institutions engaged in digital library research around the world. They describe the features of the chosen libraries in terms of nature and content before looking at the information retrieval features of each digital library. This led to identification of unique features and of major areas of research to improve the information retrieval features of digital libraries of the future.

Evaluating information interventions requires recognition, not just of technical factors but also of societal and individual values and beliefs. Information technologies bring their own problems. Suppliers, and indeed potential users, of new ICT applications frequently pursue a position at the 'leading edge' of innovation (Jadad et al., 2000). Under such pressures evaluation becomes more, rather than less, important. With growing recognition of professional and organizational factors (Heathfield et al., 1998) multi-perspective, multi-method evaluations are being increasingly employed. As Atkins and Louw recognize (2000): 'The range of accepted research methods extends across a broad spectrum of paradigms taken from both scientific and social science disciplines. Indeed, rather than one research method being accepted as superior *per se*, some methods are considered to be more appropriate to certain types of research questions than others'.

Such multifaceted, multidisciplinary assessments require large-scale planning and co-ordination and involve researchers from backgrounds as diverse as social sciences, health economics, computer science, health service management and psychology (Heathfield et al., 1998).

Conclusion

Despite the ongoing reduction in relative costs of information technology, cost-effectiveness questions figure prominently in librarians' most asked questions. The emphasis may have changed; for example: 'should a library purchase a fully-operational commercial database product when a slimmed-down version of that service is available free on the Internet?', but the trade-off of cost and value continues.

Regardless of whether we are considering introduction of a new commercial information system or simply migrating to increased use of the internet, it is equally necessary to employ the tools and techniques of evidence-based information practice (Jadad et al., 2000). Notwithstanding the speed with which information is produced and accessed via the internet, the risks associated with inappropriate use of the internet for decision-making, when viewed in terms of both staff time and users' cognitive and affective information needs, place a heavy premium on evidence-based practice.

References

Akeroyd, J. and Rogers, R. (1976) *On-line Information Retrieval: a comparison of manual and machine searching*, Hatfield, Hatfield Polytechnic Library.

Atkins, C. and Sampson, J. (2002) Critical Appraisal Guidelines for Single Case Study Research. *Xth European Conference on Information Systems in Gdansk, Poland*, eta.ktl.mii.lt/~mask/varia/ECIS2002proceedings/clareatkins.pdf.

Atkins, C. and Louw, G. (2000) Building Bridges: constructing a framework for evidence-based information systems, *Health Informatics Journal*, **6**, 121–6.

Bates, M. J. (1999) The Invisible Substrate of Information Science, *Journal of the American Society for Information Science*, **50** (12), 1043–50.

Beverley, C. A., Booth, A. and Bath, P. A. (2003) The Role of the Information Specialist in the Systematic Review Process: a health information case study, *Health Information and Libraries Journal*, **20** (2), 65–74.

Borgman, C. L. (1986) Why are Online Catalogs Hard to Use? Lesson learned from information-retrieval studies, *Journal of the American Society for Information Science*, **37** (6), 387–400.

Boynton, J., Glanville, J., McDaid, D. and Lefebvre, C. (1998) Identifying Systematic Reviews in MEDLINE: developing an objective approach to search strategy design, *Journal of Information Science*, **24** (3), 137–54.

Brophy, P. and Craven, J. (2002) Non-Visual Access to the Digital Library: the use of digital library interfaces by blind and visually impaired people, *Hypothesis*, **16** (3), 3–4.

Budd, J. M. and Miller, L. K. (1999) Teaching for Technology: current practice and future direction, *Information Technology and Libraries*, **18** (2), 78–83.

Chan, H. C. and Lim, L. H. (1998) Database Interfaces: a conceptual framework and a meta-analysis on natural language studies, *Journal of Database Management*, **9** (3), 25–32.

Chowdhury, G. G. and Chowdhury, S. (2000) An Overview of the Information Retrieval Features of Twenty Digital Libraries, *Program*, **34** (4), 341–73.

Crumley, E. and Koufogiannakis, D. (2002) Developing Evidence-based Librarianship: practical steps for implementation, *Health Information Libraries Journal*, **19** (2), 61–70.

Dickersin, K., Scherer, R. and Lefebvre, C. (1994) Identifying Relevant Studies for Systematic Reviews, *British Medical Journal*, **309** (6964), 1286–91.

Eldredge, J. D. (2003) The Randomized Controlled Trial Design: unrecognized opportunities for health sciences librarianship, *Health Information and Libraries Journal*, **20** (Suppl 1), 34–44.

Eldredge, J. (submitted on behalf of the Evidence-Based Librarianship Implementation Committee) (2001) The Most Relevant and Answerable Research Questions Facing the Practice of Health Sciences Librarianship, *Hypothesis*, **15** (1), 9–17, http://gain.mercer.edu/mla/research/hypothesis.

Farkas, D. K. and Farkas, J. B. (2000) Guidelines for Designing Web Navigation, *Technical Communication*, **47** (3), 341–58.

Fenichel, C. H. (1980) The Process of Searching Online Bibliographic Databases: a review of research, *Library Research*, **2**, 107–27.

Ferl, T. E. and Millsap, L. (1996) The Knuckle-cracker's Dilemma: a transaction log study of OPAC subject searching, *Information Technology in Libraries*, **15** (2), 61–98.

Fidel, R. (1993) Qualitative Methods in Information Retrieval Research, *Library and Information Science Research*, **15**, 219–47.

Galliers, R. D. (1993) Research Issues in Information Systems, *Journal of Information Technology*, **8** (2), 92–8.

Greenhalgh, T. (1997) How to Read a Paper: the basics of evidence based medicine, *BMJ*, London.

Haynes, R. B., McKibbon, K. A., Walker, C. J., Ryan, N., Fitzgerald, D. and Ramsden, M. F. (1990) Online Access to MEDLINE in Clinical Settings, *Annals of Internal Medicine*, **112** (1), 78–84.

Haynes, R. B., Wilczynski, N., McKibbon, K. A., Walker, C. J. and Sinclair, J. C. (1994) Developing Optimal Search Strategies for Detecting Clinically Sound Studies in MEDLINE, *Journal of the American Medical Informatics Association*, **1** (6), 447–58.

Heathfield, H., Pitty, D. and Hanka, R. (1998) Evaluating Information Technology in Health Care: barriers and challenges, *BMJ*, **316**, 1959–61.

Hersh, W. R. and Hickam, D. H. (1994) Use of a Multi-application Computer Workstation in a Clinical Setting, *Bulletin of the Medical Library Association*, **82**, 382–9.

Hersh, W., Detmer, W. and Frisse, M. (No date) Chapter 15, Information Retrieval Systems in Medical Informatics, *Computer Applications in Health Care and Biomedicine*, http://smi-web.stanford.edu/textbook/Contents.html.

Hersh, W. R. and Hickam, D. H. (1998) How Well Do Physicians Use Electronic Information Retrieval Systems? A framework for investigation and systematic review, *JAMA*, **280** (15), 1347–52.

Jadad, A. R, Haynes, R. B., Hunt, D. and Browman, G. P. (2000) The Internet and Evidence-based Decision-making: a needed synergy for efficient knowledge management in health care, *CMAJ*, **162** (3), 362–5.

Johnston, M. E., Langton, K. B., Haynes, R. B. and Mathieu, A. (1994) Effects of Computer-based Clinical Decision Support Systems on Clinician Performance and Patient Outcome: a critical appraisal of research, *Annals of Internal Medicine*, **120** (2), 135–42.

Khalili, A. and Shashaani, L. (1994) The Effectiveness of Computer Applications: a meta-analysis, *Journal of Research on Technology in Education*, **27** (1), 48–61.

King, N. S. (1993) End-user Errors: a content analysis of PaperChase, *Bulletin of the Medical Library Association*, **81** (4), 439–41.

Klein, H. K. and Myers, M. D. (1999) A Set of Principles for Conducting and Evaluating Interpretative Field Studies in Information Systems, *MIS Quarterly*, **23** (1), 67–93.

Lewis, D. (1999) Computer-based Approaches to Patient Education: a review of the literature, *Journal of the American Medical Informatics Association*, **6** (4), 272–82.

Liao, Y. K. C. (1999) Effects of Hypermedia on Students' Achievement: a meta-analysis, *Journal of Educational Multimedia and Hypermedia*, **8** (3), 255–77.

Mahmood, M. A., Burn, J. M., Gemoets, L. A. and Jacquez, C. (2000) Variables Affecting Information Technology End-user Satisfaction: a meta-analysis of the empirical literature, *International Journal of Human-Computer Studies*, **52** (4), 751–71.

Marcum, D. B. (2003) Research Questions for the Digital Era Library, *Library Trends*, **51** (4), 636–51

May, C., Mort, M., Mair, F., Ellis, N.T. and Gask, L. (2000) Evaluation of New Technologies in Health-care Systems: what's the context?, *Health Informatics Journal*, **6**, 67–70.

McManus, C. (1996) Engineering Quality in Health Care, *Quality in Health Care*, **5**, 127.

Pritchard, S. J. and Weightman, A. L. (2003) Towards a Cochrane Information Retrieval Methods Group: a progress report, *Health Information and Libraries Journal*, **20** (Suppl 1), 69–71.

Rowlands, I. and Bawden, D. (1999) Building the Digital Library on Solid Research Foundations, *Aslib Proceedings*, **51** (8), 275–82.

Salang, M. M. C. (1995–1996) A Meta-analysis of Studies on User Information Needs and their Relationship to Information Retrieval, *Journal of Philippine Librarianship*, **18** (1–2), 36–56.

Sasikala, C. and Patnaik, K. R. (1999) A Comparative Study of Two Web Search Engines: AltaVista and Excite, *Academic libraries in the Internet era. Papers presented at the Sixth National Convention for Automation of Libraries in Education and Research (CALIBER 99)*, Nagpur, India, 18–20 February 1999. Kumar, P. S. G. and Vashishth, C. P. (eds), Ahmedabad, India, Information and Library Network Centre, 346–54.

Sewell, W. and Teitelbaum, S. (1986) Observations of End-user Online Searching Behavior Over Eleven Years, *Journal of the American Society for Information Science*, **37** (4), 234–45.

Shea, S., DuMouchel, W. and Bahamonde, L. (1996) A Meta-analysis of 16 Randomized Controlled Trials to Evaluate Computer-based Clinical Reminder Systems for Preventive Care in the Ambulatory Setting, *Journal of the American Medical Informatics Association*, **3**, 399–409.

Tolle, J. E. and Hah, S. (1985) Online Search Patterns: NLM CATLINE database, *Journal of the American Society of Information Science*, **36** (2), 82–93.

Trahan, E. (1993) Applying Meta-Analysis to Library and Information Science Research, *Library Quarterly*, **63** (1), 73–91.

Turner, P. and Turner, S. (2002) End-user Perspectives on the Uptake of Computer Supported Cooperative Working, *Journal of End User Computing*, **14** (2), 3–15.

Urquhart, C. J., Currell, R. A. and Wainwright, P. J. (2000) Evidence-based Policy Making in Health Informatics: indications from systematic reviews of nursing record systems and telemedicine, *Health Informatics Journal*, **6** (4), 204–11.

Verhoeven, A. A. H., Boerma, E. J. and Meyboom de Jong, B. (2000) Which Literature Retrieval Method is Most Effective for GPs?, *Family Practice*, **17** (1), 30–5.

Vigil, P. J. (1994) Associative and Boolean Retrieval: a comparative analysis, *Online Information 94. Proceedings of the 18th International Online Information Meeting,*

London, 6–8 December 1994, Raitt, D. I. and Jeapes, B. (eds), Oxford and New Jersey, Learned Information (Europe) Ltd, 57–62.

Wood, E. H. (2001) Transaction Log Analysis: what are they typing?, *Hypothesis*, **15** (1), 5 and 18.

Wooton, R. (1998) Telemedicine in the National Health Service, *Journal of the Royal Society of Medicine*, **91**, 614–21.

Yee, I. H. (1993) Effect of Search Experience and Subject Knowledge on the Search Tactics of Novice and Experienced Searchers, *Journal of the American Society for Information Science*, **44** (3), 161–74.

Zmud, R. W. (1998) Conducting and Publishing Practice-Driven Research. In Larsen, T. J., Levine, L. and DeGross, J. I. (eds) *Conference Proceedings of IFIP WG8.2 and WG8.6 joint working conference on Information Systems: Current Issues and Future Changes*, Helsinki, Finland Dec 10–13, www.ifip.or.at.

Special topic (F)
What are the characteristics of a good searcher? (Critically Appraised Topic)

Catherine Beverley

Indicative Title

Men may be more effective internet searchers than women.

Abstract

Abstracted from: Ford, N., Miller, D. and Moss, N. (2001) The Role of Individual Differences in Internet Searching: an empirical study, *Journal of the American Society for Information Science and Technology*, **52** (12), 1049–66.

Objective

This exploratory study aimed to investigate the role of 'individual differences' in internet searching. In particular, the authors wanted to determine whether there was any statistically based evidence that retrieval effectiveness is affected by:

(a) psychological differences between individuals, consisting of:
    (i) cognitive (cognitive styles and levels of experience)
    (ii) affective (internet and study attitudes and perceptions)
(b) demographic differences (age and gender).

Setting

Department of Information Studies, University of Sheffield, England.

Participants

Volunteers drawn from two cohorts (1999 and 2000 entry) of three taught Masters programmes (MA Librarianship, MSc Information Management and MSc Information Systems). The two cohorts consisted of 250 students.

Method

Students were asked to search for information on a prescribed topic using the AltaVista search engine via the Netscape Navigator browser. The following scenario was used:

A technician cuts his finger badly in the Information Studies departmental office. What are the legal implications of this for the university? Find relevant information on the web.

Searchers were free to choose the simple search option, which provides best match (or keyword) searching, and/or the advanced search option. A JavaScript front-end recorded all search data submitted to the search engine, and this was automatically sent to the researchers. There was no time limit or restriction on the number of queries students could submit.

Outcome measures

A 63-item self-completed 'individual differences' questionnaire, based on several different scales (e.g. Tait and Entwistle, 1995; Ford and Miller, 1996). Riding's (1991) psychometric measure, *Cognitive Styles Analysis*.

Details of age and gender were obtained via a form on the opening screen of the web-based search interface.

Data analysis

The first two screens of retrieved items resulting from each successive query were categorized using a dichotomous 'relevant/not relevant' classification. A single relevance estimate was calculated in relation to each participant's search across all queries. Multiple regression and factor analysis were applied to the data.

Main results

69 postgraduate students volunteered to participate; however, complete data were not available in all cases. 32% of the sample were male, and 68% female (N=68). All students had some experience of using search engines. A total of 228 queries were conducted (mean=3.35, SD: 2.37, range: 1–13). Gender differences

were significant only in the case of the number of terms per query in 'keyword only' queries, with males using more terms than females (t-test; p=0.030). Four separate factor analyses revealed that the principal components were 'approaches to studying', 'internet perceptions' and 'cognitive style, age and gender'. 'Experience' loaded separately from relevance, indicating there was no relationship. The best-fitting most statistically significant regression model accounted for 20% of the variance in relevance (14.6% when the R square was adjusted). Retrieval effectiveness (as measured by relevance scores) could be predicted to a statistically significant level by gender (p=0.018), and by feelings of being on target (p=0.047) and in control (p=0.047) when using the internet. The model as a whole was a significant predictor at the level of p=0.010.

Commentary

The authors conclude from this well-structured and reported exploratory study that retrieval effectiveness is linked to: male gender, low cognitive complexity, an imager (as opposed to verbalizer) cognitive style, and a number of internet perceptions and study approaches grouped together as indicating low self-efficacy. However, a detailed appraisal of the article, using the CriSTAL (Critical Skills Training for Librarians) user studies checklist (Booth, 2000), casts doubt on the robustness of these findings.

Although all students on the three courses were invited to participate in the study, the eventual sample was self-selected and comprised a fraction of the total population. No sample size calculation was performed, so the research may have been inadequately powered to detect statistically significant differences. All participants were strong academically and, by the nature of the courses they were undertaking, were confident in relation to ICT and information seeking. Students may even have been taught by researchers collecting and analysing the data. The searching exercise was conducted in a constrained environment (e.g. there was no time limit), and the use of only one prescribed topic could have been prohibitive to students. No reference is made to the validity or reliability of the 63-item 'individual differences' questionnaire used.

The response rate was very low (27.6%; n=69). This figure is based on the assumption that the total population was 250, although the text is ambiguous in this respect: 'the two cohorts consisted of 250 students' (p. 1054). In addition, data were missing for several students with respect to different analyses. There was also no consideration of non-responders. Why might people not volunteer to take part? Was it because they felt they had poor searching skills? All participants had used an internet search engine before. The ability to generalize the findings to the general population is, therefore, questionable. A crude measure of relevance was used and the ratings were not independently assessed or validated. In addition, relevance was based on retrieval results alone; retrieved documents were not opened and examined in detail.

As the authors note, 'a coherent picture does not emerge across the two types of analysis' (p. 1060): a number of relationships were identified using factor analysis that multiple regression did not subsequently identify as being statistically different. In addition, the factor analyses accounted for only a relatively small percentage of the variance in the variables used, suggesting that other factors may be involved. The rationale for using these analyses is not clear; multivariate analyses are prone to identifying spurious relationships.

To summarize, this exploratory study addresses a clearly focused question that builds upon existing research. The methods appear sound and any limitations have been acknowledged. However, the response rate was very low (27.6%), the sample size was small (N=69) and the representativeness of the sample was questionable, thereby casting doubt on the generalizability of the findings. Even the authors state that 'any generalization . . . should thus be drawn only with some caution' (p. 1062). In addition, the conclusions were not substantiated by the results. Further research which adopts a broader perspective of searching is, therefore, needed; for example, that which incorporates different search tasks and search engines in more naturalistic, less constrained conditions and in relation to a broader range of internet users. Such research may also benefit from taking into account information-seeking strategies, as well as search results (Ford et al., 2001).

References

Booth, A. (2000) Research, *Health Libraries Review*, **17** (4), 232–5.

Ford, N. and Miller, D. (1996) Gender Differences in Internet Perception and Use, In *Electronic Library and Visual Information Research, Papers from the 3rd ELVIRA conference, 30th April 1996*, London, Aslib, 87–202.

Ford, N., Miller, D. and Moss, N. (2001) The Role of Individual Differences in Internet Searching: an empirical study, *Journal of the American Society for Information Science and Technology*, **52** (12), 1049–66.

Riding, R. J. (1991) *Cognitive Styles Analysis*, Birmingham, Learning and Training Technology.

Tait, H. and Entwistle, N. J. (1995) *The Revised Approaches to Studying Inventory*, Edinburgh, Centre for Research on Learning and Instruction, University of Edinburgh.

Special topic (G)
Which database, which interface? (Guideline)

Maria J. Grant

Electronic databases have transformed access to information, previously only available in printed indexes. Size, content (both in subject and format) and depth of coverage varies from database to database. Each database is unique and should be considered on its merits. This special topic outlines issues to consider when selecting a database and search interface (see Table G.1).

Table G.1   Summary of evidence on which database, which interface?

Beneficial	Identifying the priorities of database users can inform decisions about the type of references required and how they prefer to access them. For some topics, there is evidence of an optimal combination of databases to search.
Likely to be beneficial	Selecting the right database or combination of database increases the likelihood that decisions made on the best available evidence. Selecting the right interface which meets the needs of database users enables effective searches to be undertaken.
Trade off between benefits and harms	Searching a single database increases the likelihood of missing relevant resources. Informed decisions require a range of databases to be searched. Service providers often provide access to a range of databases via a single search interface. This can assist searchers in undertaking effective searches easily.
Unknown effectiveness	There is no evidence to inform a core set of databases to which all library and information services should subscribe or have access.

(continued)

Table G.1 (continued)

Unlikely to be beneficial	If the right database or databases are not selected, the possibility of finding the most relevant information is reduced. This could be detrimental to the quality of subsequent decisions.
Likely to be ineffective or harmful	There is no evidence to suggest that searching a particular database or set of databases using a particular interface is ineffective or harmful. Searching a single database can miss relevant literature referenced in alternative sources. This could have a negative impact on decisions made.

Negative findings

Which database?

There is no evidence to inform a single formula nor a recommendation for the range or combination of databases to subscribe to or access.

Which interface?

There is no evidence to make general recommendations regarding one search interface in preference to another. A comparison of three search interfaces (SPIRS, WinSPIRS and OVID) for the MEDLINE database suggests that whilst all three interfaces have their strengths, none are perfect.[1]

Outcomes

Which database?

Complete directories list the myriad of databases available.[2, 3] Clarifying the subject area and type of material (book chapters, journal papers or conference proceedings) needed by database users will inform the choice of database subscriptions.

Available evidence is predominantly health-focused, and compares precision (percentage of relevant papers retrieved in relation to number of relevant papers retrieved), recall (percentage of relevant papers retrieved in relation to number of relevant papers published) and uniqueness (percentage of unique papers not indexed or retrieved by alternative databases).

MEDLINE is often the database of choice for health professionals and research indicates that, in some instances, this is appropriate. Okuma[4] compared eight identical free-text searches on MEDLINE and CINAHL for nursing literature and found that MEDLINE retrieved a higher number of relevant references. This finding was substantiated two years later by Brazier and Begley,[5] who conducted nine 'title word' searches on MEDLINE and CINAHL and found that, with the exception of information relating to the organization of nursing, MEDLINE retrieved twice as many relevant references (85% from MEDLINE compared with 41% from CINAHL). Of ten searches comparing MeSH and free-text searches of MEDLINE with free-text searches of PASCAL BIOMED, MEDLINE contained a larger proportion of relevant information,[6] unsurprisingly given that MEDLINE is the largest available biomedical database. However, the percentage of unique papers indexed by databases means that multiple database searching is important. In the Brand-de Heer study,[6] PASCAL BIOMED had up to 33% unique references (20% median) of references retrieved, whilst Okuma[4] retrieved 65.6% unique references from CINAHL.

The effect of coverage and indexing policies on MEDLINE retrieval performance was compared with four databases (Excerpta Medica, PsycInfo, SciSearch and Social SciSearch). MEDLINE achieved the highest recall levels overall (37%-median), although for certain queries ('learned helplessness' and 'Alzheimer's disease') citation databases (SciSearch and Social SciSearch) outperformed all three bibliographic databases.[7] Analysis suggested that the relatively low recall levels were due to coverage of journals, rather than indexing policy.

Mcdonald et al.[8] investigated database coverage of psychiatry journal titles. They found that 52% (n=506) of psychiatry journals cited in *Ulrich's International Periodicals Directory* are indexed by the four most frequently cited databases - BIOSIS, EMBASE, MEDLINE and PsycLIT. However, only 35% of the journals were indexed in just one of the four databases. The importance of searching a range of databases is a recurring theme. Mcdonald et al. found that the overall coverage of psychiatry journals was maximized (91%) when searching PsycLIT and EMBASE in conjunction. Complementary searches of SciSearch and MEDLINE are also beneficial when seeking to achieve comprehensive retrieval of literature in answer to a simple biomedical question.[9]

Whilst acknowledging MEDLINE's dominance, research indicates the appropriateness of alternative databases for specific topic areas. Kjellander et al.[10] involved oncologists in 16 cancer-related literature searches. Searches were repeated on CANCERLIT and MEDLINE. In 11 instances CANCERLIT retrieved a higher degree of relevant references, with a reported overlap between database coverage of 27%. This, combined with an expressed preference by the oncologists, led to the recommendation to search CANCERLIT in preference to MEDLINE. More recently, a report of literature retrieved for a systematic review on severe mental illness[11] recommended searching PsycLIT in preference to MEDLINE. Analysis indicated that PsycLIT retrieved 44% of papers included in the review, compared with 29% from MEDLINE.

Which interface?

Some search interfaces default to keyword/subject heading searching (OVID), whilst others default to free-text searching (SPIRS and WinSPIRS). However they broadly seek to facilitate the same tasks, and the ability to customize the interface to reflect the local environment should be highly valued.[1, 12]

Effects, not effectiveness

Which database?

Each database covers a subset of the resources potentially available. This can be useful if the search topic is narrow. However, to ensure an informed decision, particularly for broader search topics, information should come from across the evidence spectrum. To facilitate this, a range of complementary databases should accessed.[6–9]

Which interface?

The proliferation of database service and service providers (e.g. Dialog, OVID, SilverPlatter) has led to an abundance of search interfaces. A single interface can facilitate easy access across a range of databases, with database users having to familiarize themselves with only a single search interface.[13] However, the question of who has the power to determine the combination of 'bundled databases', whether the database producer or the purchaser, remains.[12]

Harms

Which database?

A single database is unlikely to contain the majority of relevant published literature on a topic area. This could lead to poor decisions based on a subset of the potential evidence base .[14]

Which interface?

Interfaces default to either keyword/subject heading or free-text searching. In general keyword/subject heading searching encourages a more targeted approach to searching, enhancing precision of searches with reasonable numbers of relevant references retrieved whilst mitigating retrieval of too many irrelevant references. The search can then be extended to include free-text searching. Free-text searching maximizes recall with reduced precision i.e. an increased number of references are retrieved although there is a greater likelihood of references not being relevant. Depending on the reason for searching, and the experience or knowledge of the searcher, the default search interface may or may not present a problem.

Information on cost

Which database?

Service providers often maintain databases remotely, freeing subscribers from maintenance issues and hardware costs. However, there are usually cost implications in accessing databases, whether it is an annual subscription, or a charge per the amount of time accessed or references downloaded. Service providers should be contacted directly for pricing scales. The most commonly used databases (Cochrane Library, MEDLINE etc.) are increasingly available free of charge.[15]

Which interface?

Service providers often offer a package of databases accessible via a single search interface. This may contain the overall cost of the purchase, but could restrict the range of databases available.

How to use the information

The above information is intended to be used in conjunction with other sources of information, such as identifying the personal preferences of database users,[1] to aid decision making.

Most research (65%) cited above has been published in the five years between 1998 and 2003. In acknowledging the rapid development of search interfaces, and of database indexing policies, caution is recommended in applying this evidence to inform decision making. Several of the identified research projects may benefit from being revisited.

References

1 Schoonbaert, D. (1996) SPIRS, WinSPIRS, and OVID: a comparison of three MEDLINE-on-CD-ROM interfaces, *Bulletin of the Medical Library Association*, **84** (1), 63-70.

2 Domoney, L., Carmel, S. and Sawers, C. (1996) *Directory of Health and Social Services Databases Based on Research Funded by the British Library Research and Development Department*, London, Library Association Publishing.

3 Nagel, E. (2002) *Gale Directory of Databases. Volume 1: online databases*, London, Gale Group.

4 Okuma, E. (1994) Selecting CD-ROM Databases for Nursing Students: a comparison of MEDLINE and the Cumulative Index to Nursing and Allied Health Literature (CINAHL), *Bulletin of the Medical Library Association*, **82** (1), 25–9.

5 Brazier, H. and Begley, C. M. (1996) Selecting a Database for Literature Searches in Nursing: MEDLINE or CINAHL?, *Journal of Advanced Nursing*, **24**, 868–75.

6 Brand-de Heer, D. L. (2001) A Comparison of the Coverage of Clinical Medicine Provided by PASCAL BIOMED and MEDLINE, *Health Information and Libraries Journal*, **18** (2), 110–16.

7 McCain, K. W., White, H. D. and Griffith, B. C. (1987) Comparing Retrieval Performance in Online Databases, *Information Processing and Management*, **23** (6), 539–53.

8 Mcdonald, S., Taylor, L. and Adams, C. (1999) Searching the Right Database: a comparison of four databases for psychiatry journals, *Health Libraries Review*, **16**, 151–6.

9 Brown, C. M. (1998) Complementary Use of the SciSearch Database for Improved Biomedical Information Searching, *Bulletin of the Medical Library Association*, **86** (1), 63-7.

10 Kjellander, E., Olsson, P. O. and Zajicek, E. (1985) Usefulness of the On-line Database CANCERLIT: an evaluation study based on consecutive searches in CANCERLIT and MEDLINE for oncologists, *Journal of the National Cancer Institute*, **74** (4), 1351–3.

11 Brettle, A. and Long, A. F. (2001) Comparison of Bibliographic Databases for Information on the Rehabilitation of People with Severe Mental Illness, *Bulletin of the Medical Library Association*, **89** (4), 352–62.

12 Allison, D., McNeil, B. and Swanson, S. (2000) Database Selection: one size does not fit all, *College and Research Libraries*, **61** (1), 56–63.

13 Joint Information Systems Committee (1999) *Adding Value to the UK's Learning, Teaching and Research Resources: the Distributed National Electronic Resource (DNER)*, www.jisc.ac.uk/pub99/dner_vision.html.

14 Brettle, A. and Grant, M. J. (2001) *Information for Evidence Based Practice: the health professional's guide to sources of information and how to use them*, Salford, University of Salford, Health Care Practice Research and Development Unit. Report Number 5.

15 NHS Information Authority (2002) *National Electronic Library for Health*, www.nelh.nhs.uk/.

19

Introducing an evidence-based approach to marketing and promotional activities

Andrew Booth

After defining evidence-based marketing this chapter considers questions that those marketing their service might need to answer. After briefly considering sources that address marketing and promotion, such as business and psychological databases, it critically examines studies that have examined this area. The chapter concludes with a look at the need for complementarity of research techniques within this domain.

What is evidence-based marketing and promotion?

By marketing and promotion, Crumley and Koufogiannakis (2002) refer to the activities of 'promoting the profession, the library and its services to both users and non-users'. In a recent article on 'information marketing' Rowley (2003) rehearses the following definition: 'Marketing is the management process, which identifies, anticipates and supplies customer requirements efficiently and profitably (Chartered Institute of Marketing).'

Although the library profession generally resists the term 'customer', preferring 'reader', 'user' or 'client', the recent expansion of marketing from goods and products to services has made business analogies more acceptable. This has opened the way for the domain of marketing and promotional activities to accommodate a wider knowledge base from the business and commercial literature.

Within its wider context marketing includes affecting behaviour (Rowley, 2003) and changing attitudes. In this sense marketing occupies a niche of perennial concern for libraries as a mechanism for raising awareness of a service amongst its stakeholders. Senior managers need to be convinced that they should spend resources on information services in preference to other activities or services. A prerequisite to successful marketing is 'premarketing' (Booth, 2003) (i.e. the identification of users' information needs). Hence this domain includes the information needs analysis or information (or marketing or communications) audit (Cram, 1995; Weingand, 1997).

Asking the question

As Rowley (2003) remarks: 'The large majority of the literature on the marketing of libraries and information services is in the form of either "how to" guides, or case studies of practice in specific contexts. This needs to be countered by an acknowledgement that there are unanswered, and possibly unanswerable questions relating to marketing.' This concisely highlights two key issues when applying evidence-based practice to this domain – first, the poor quality of usable literature, as already characterized in the broader, yet associated, domain of management and, second, the mismatch between questions addressed by the literature and those posed by the practitioner. Despite such an unpropitious verdict there is sufficient literature in marketing to merit consideration.

Eldredge's questions (Eldredge, 2001) contain marketing examples, albeit not as readily apparent as those in other domains (Box 19.1).

Box 19.1 Questions from the domain of marketing and promotion

How can we identify the non-users of [a library service], and what, if anything, can we do about them?

How can we best measure usability of our library web pages?

What is the lag time between the introduction of a new resource in an institution and widespread takeup of that resource?

What would be the impact of [making electronic tables of contents available] in terms of general library usage, utilization of the e-TACOS service, marketing benefits/aspects, etc.?

Finding the evidence

The marketing literature is extensive, with numerous journals devoted to the topic. Examples include:

* *International Journal of Market Research* : the journal of the Market Research Society
* *Marketing Research*
* *Journal of Consumer Policy*
* *Journal of Retailing*.

As illustrated above, a potential difficulty in accessing the evidence base lies in the closeness of the two distinct concepts 'market research' and 'marketing research'. The former applies to data collected to support marketing of a specific product or service while the latter is specifically methods of marketing as tested empirically. Nevertheless searches, particularly using internet search engines, tend to retrieve materials from both categories.

Two principal sources for marketing, with coverage of journals such as the above, are *ABI/Inform* and *Business Source Premier*. Both contain full-text materials and are most likely to be accessible to those working in academic or commercial libraries with a business agenda. *ABI/Inform* contains articles from 1971 to the present from major business journals, newsletters, and newspapers. It has a strong American focus. Similarly *Business Source Premier* contains 2710 full-text scholarly journals and business periodicals including such top management and marketing journals as *Harvard Business Review*, *MIT Sloan Management Review*, *Academy of Management Journal*, *Academy of Management Review*, *Journal of Management Studies*, *Journal of Marketing Management*, and others.

One database that may not come to mind so readily is PsycInfo. Covering psychology journals, books and dissertations, its strong international coverage means that it is considered a good place to find key marketing studies. It covers such important marketing-related concepts as consumer attitudes, consumer behaviour, consumer psychology, consumer research, consumer satisfaction, product design, consumer surveys, marketing and retailing. For related reasons those specifically looking at marketing information products, as opposed to library services, will find a wealth of materials in the databases of health promotion such as the Health Development Agency's HealthPromis. Indeed the concept of 'social marketing' is particularly germane and, because of its proximity to evidence-based healthcare, tends to exhibit more of the characteristics of a rigorous evidence base.

The evidence base

Table 18.1   Research methods of importance within marketing and promotion

Research methods of particular importance within this domain
Case studies
Surveys
Qualitative research

Systematic reviews

Perhaps surprisingly, given its apparent focus on case studies, examples of attempts at review and synthesis do exist within the marketing domain. For example,

Grunenwald and Traynor (1987) provided an early indication of the potential for synthesizing research on marketing services when they produced guidelines for the development of marketing plans, specifically in a law library.

The LISA database, covering related topics such as communication, includes meta-analytic reviews from the literature on the effects of persuasive messages (O'Keefe, 1999). Closer to home, Haug (1997) conducted an early attempt at meta-analysis in the library literature by summarizing the findings of the literature on physician's preferences for information sources. Although this article may justifiably be criticized for using a simplified ordinal ranking in presenting and interpreting its results it is deservedly recognized as an early application of evidence-based information practice. Finally, Beavers et al. (1996) examined studies related to the delivery of information services to agricultural scientists working at remote laboratories and in the field.

Randomized controlled trials

Eldredge (2003) identifies two similar RCTs located within the domain of marketing. A nursing librarian met face-to-face for 30–60 minutes with an intervention group of faculty nursing staff at the University of New Mexico, College of Nursing. Both intervention and control groups (n=28) were otherwise communicated with electronically. He reported that the intervention group seemed to experience greater numbers of changes in perception of and use of the library than those in the control group. When a pharmacy librarian was subject to a similar trial, Eldredge and Karcher (2002) found that one 30–60-minute length direct, in-person communication does not appear to affect pharmacy faculty members' perception or self-reported use of the library and informatics center.

Cohort studies

Eldredge (2002) also identifies at least one cohort study that falls within this domain. In this study all library users of the University of Texas Health Sciences Center at San Antonio (UTHSCSA) were subject to a public relations programme to introduce a new library building. A comprehensive quantitative evaluation demonstrated that the program increased user awareness (Eldredge, 1984).

Qualitative studies

As Weinreich (2003) identifies within the specific context of social marketing:

> rigorous quantitative research surveys do not necessarily provide all of the data needed to develop effective communications. Consequently, qualitative methods such as

focus groups and in-depth interviews, as well as less precise but useful semi-quantitative approaches, such as intercept surveys, have emerged as part of their research repertoire. In an ideal social marketing program, researchers use both quantitative and qualitative data to provide a more complete picture of the issue being addressed, the target audience and the effectiveness of the program itself.

This can be illustrated within the specific context of library service quality where the customer or user has been identified as the most critical voice in assessing service quality. Thus the LibQUAL+ project used qualitative research to measure the gaps between expected service and perceived service, thereby providing rich information about the users' own behaviours and their perceptions of what a library should provide (Cook and Heath, 2001).

Two qualitative techniques which command a particular position within the domain of marketing are the focus group and the Delphi technique.

Focus group

A focus group is a carefully planned discussion designed to obtain perceptions on a defined area in a non-threatening environment. It is conducted with approximately seven to ten people by a skilled interviewer. The discussion is comfortable and often enjoyable for participants as they share their ideas and perceptions. Group members influence each other by responding to ideas and comments in the discussion. (Krueger and Casey, 2000).

Welsh (2000) describes how focus groups were used in a pilot study of users' perceptions and attitudes to library and information services within the University of Wales Institute, Cardiff. The pilot established that some users were very aware of services and facilities, while others were vague about available support. All users required more and better computing facilities, longer opening hours and increased access to electronic resources, while staff were uniformly regarded as helpful. Robbins and Holst (1990) similarly used focus group interviews to evaluate a hospital library. Mullaly-Quijas et al. (1994) used focus groups in a regional marketing study of health professionals' information needs while Terman (1996) used them within the Brent public library service.

Notwithstanding numerous articles on the methodology of focus groups within a library environment (e.g. Widdows et al., 1991; Glitz, 1997; Glitz et al., 2001), and extensive coverage within the general research literature (e.g. MacDougall, 2001), the limitations of this method for evidence-based practice should be recognized. Focus groups reach limited numbers of people, who will ideally be relatively homogeneous and they require considerable time, effort, and expense. In particular very few people are interviewed so one cannot generalize about the larger population.

Delphi technique

Unsurprisingly, given its enthusiastic adoption within marketing in general, the Delphi technique figures prominently in the evidence base for library marketing. The Delphi process takes place in a series of rounds:

- Round 1: either relevant individuals are invited to provide opinions on a specific matter, based on their knowledge and experience, or the team undertaking the Delphi exercise expresses its opinions and selects suitable experts to participate in subsequent questionnaire rounds. Opinions are grouped together under a limited number of headings and statements, then circulated to all participants as a questionnaire
- Round 2: participants rank their agreement with each statement in the questionnaire. The rankings are subsequently summarized by the research team and included in a repeat version of the questionnaire
- Round 3: participants re-rank their agreement with each statement and can change their scores in view of the group's response.

Re-rankings are summarized and assessed for consensus: if an acceptable degree of consensus is obtained, the process may cease, with final results fed back to participants; if not, the third round is repeated. In addition to scoring their agreement with statements, respondents are commonly asked to rate the confidence or certainty with which they express their opinions.

The Delphi process has been used widely in research, particularly for education and training, priority setting, workforce planning, forecasting and service organization. The procedure enables a large group of experts to be contacted cheaply, usually by mail, using a self-administered questionnaire (though computer communications have also been used), with few geographical limitations on the sample. Within marketing, the Delphi technique is frequently used to predict future events and as a long-range planning tool for mapping broad trends likely to impact on a library service (Buckley, 1994). For example an expert panel comprising 45 scientists, publishers, librarians, periodical agents and consultants was constructed to look at issues regarding the future development of electronic journals (Keller, 2001a; Keller, 2001b). Other examples are given in Table 19.2.

However, Buckley (1995) describes it as a method 'more for preferences than for predictions' claiming that it can be used to focus on a specific component of an existing or proposed service. For example, it was used to explore the information needs of faculty for a programme of women's studies (Westbrook, 1997). Other examples are given in Table 19.3.

Table 19.2   Examples of Delphi technique for forward planning

Authors (Year)	Panel	Topic
Baruchson-Arbib & Bronstein (2002)	Israeli library and information science (LIS) experts	Future of the profession in light of the changes in information technology
Feret & Marcinek (1999)	23 key library experts from 10 countries	What will be the role of an academic library and skills of an academic librarian in the year 2005?
Holsapple and Joshi (2000)	31 recognized researchers and practitioners in the KM field	To develop a descriptive framework for understanding factors (managerial, resource, and environmental) that influence the success of knowledge management (KM) initiatives in an organization
Snoke & Underwood (2001)	105 academics from all Australian universities that offer IS under-graduate degree programmes of study and 53 members of the Australian Computer Society	To validate generic attributes of graduates of Australian undergraduate degree programmes with majors in Information Systems (IS)
Dwyer (1999)	34-member panel consisting of representatives of a wide range of health-related professions	Determining research priorities for health library and information services sector in the UK as to perceived value for the professional and impact on user needs, and to identify areas suitable for collaborative research
Khosrow-Pour & Herman (2001)	Panel of experts (unspecified)	To identify critical issues of web-enabled technologies in modern organizations
Hernon, Powell & Young (2002)	Directors and their immediate deputies of Association of Research Libraries (ARL) libraries	To develop a set of attributes that directors currently and in the near future will need to possess

Table 19.3   Examples of Delphi technique for service evaluation

Authors (Year)	Panel	Topic
Bremner (2000)	Students on Open University courses	How students use information and library services provided by both the Open University Library and other public and academic libraries nationally

(continued)

Table 19.3   (*continued*)

Authors (Year)	Panel	Topic
Chavez-Hernandez (1996)	Library experts	To assess the probability, desirability, and feasibility of developing and implementing a library networking model for the Caribbean region
Duffy (1995)	Group of expert USA technical editors	To identify needs of technical editors that might be supported by the use of computer-based tools; and to understand the editing process relevant to the design of these tools
Neumann (1995)	25 library media specialists (LMSs) from 22 secondary schools across the United States	Identifying high school students' most significant difficulties in using online and CD-ROM databases
Lipscomb et al. (1999)	Experts from faculty and employers	To evaluate five curricular models designed to improve education for health sciences librarianship
Gatfield, Barker & Graham (1999)	International students	To measure the effectiveness of University international advertising and promotional material
Green (2000)	Adult students	Evaluation of websites

Surveys

Mention marketing and most people envisage survey-based research, either in the street, by post or over a telephone. Much has been written on how best to conduct such research and this book will not address this specialist topic (e.g. Bell, 1999; Burton, 1990; Oppenheim, 1992; Russell and Shoolbred, 1995; Wilson, n.d.). It will suffice to give one brief case study on how such data might be used, particularly within the context of electronic services.

Case study

Directors of the Duke University Medical Center Library (Murphy et al., 2002) needed to generate data to support current and future funding. Realizing that gate counts, disparate e-resource figures and circulation statistics would not reflect the use of electronic resources, the staff identified a need to quickly generate data capturing the purpose and use of such resources. The Library decided to use web survey technology to reach its clientele. A survey instrument was designed to produce the relevant data. The survey had to be brief enough for patrons to take the time to complete it. By astute marketing, the Library generated a response rate of more than 2600 replies in less than two weeks! Survey data supported the Library's case for retaining its current level of funding.

Critically appraising the evidence

Few instruments exist specifically to appraise study designs such as Delphi techniques, focus groups and surveys. The former two study types may be subjected to generic appraisal using a qualitative research checklist. However, members of a Sheffield-based critical appraisal group have devised a tailored instrument for appraising a Delphi study (Figure 19.1).

Studies of information needs may be examined using the CriSTAL checklist for information needs analysis/information audit (Box 19.2).

Filter questions

1 Does the study provide sufficient detail of the methods of the consensus development process to allow assessment of its quality to take place?
☐ Yes
☐ No
☐ Do not know

2 Is the research question addressed by the study suitable for exploration by consensus development methods?
☐ Yes
☐ No
☐ Do not know

Detailed questions

3 Does the author make a case for the importance of the topic(s) under consideration?
☐ Yes
☐ No
☐ Do not know

4 Does the author provide sufficient detail of the questions being addressed?
☐ Yes
☐ No
☐ Do not know

5 Was the selection of participants appropriate to the topic being considered?
☐ Yes
☐ No
☐ Do not know

6 Is sufficient detail provided on the background and characteristics of participants to judge their credibility and whether they reflect a relevant range of opinion?
☐ Yes
☐ No
☐ Do not know

(continued)

Figure 19.1   Instrument for critically appraising a study describing a consensus development process

7 Were participants provided with sufficient information to complete the required group processes?	☐ Yes ☐ No ☐ Do not know
8 Was an appropriate method selected for structuring the group interaction?	☐ Yes ☐ No ☐ Do not know
9 Was an appropriate method selected for combining individual judgements?	☐ Yes ☐ No ☐ Do not know
10 Does it appear that the author has recorded the outcome of the group processes transparently and honestly?	☐ Yes ☐ No ☐ Do not know

Generalizability

11 Are the participants included in the study sufficiently similar to those in the local population?	☐ Yes ☐ No ☐ Do not know
12 Is it likely that the views expressed in the study are similar to those held within the local population?	☐ Yes ☐ No ☐ Do not know

Figure 19.1 (continued)

Reference: Murphy, M. K. et al. (1998) Consensus development methods, and their use in clinical guideline development, *Health Technology Assessment*, **2** (3).

Finally, appraisal of a survey will consider three key factors (Nelson, 1999)

- selection of the sample
- response rate
- characteristics of non-responders.

An example of a survey checklist (Ajetunmobi, 2002) includes the following:

- Is the chosen type of survey appropriate?
- Was the survey instrument piloted?
- Is the sampling frame justified?
- How was the sample size determined?
- What was the response rate?

Box 19.2 Twelve questions to help you make sense of an information needs analysis/information audit

A. Is the study a close representation of the truth?
  1. Does the study address a clearly focused issue?
  2. Does the study position itself in the context of other studies?
  3. Is there a direct comparison that provides an additional frame of reference?
  4. Were those involved in collection of data also involved in delivering a service to the user group?
  5. Were the methods used in acquiring data on information needs appropriate and clearly described?
  6. Was the planned sample of users representative of all users (actual and eligible) who might be included in the study?

B. Are the results credible and repeatable?
  7. What was the response rate and how representative was it of the population under study?
  8. Are the results complete and have they been analysed in an easily interpretable way?
  9. What attempts have been made to ensure reliability of responses?

C. Will the results help me in my own information practice?
  10. Can the results be applied to your local population?
  11. What are the implications of the study for your practice?
    • in terms of current deployment of services
    • in terms of cost
    • in terms of the expectations or attitudes of your users?
  12. What additional information do you need to obtain locally to assist you in responding to the findings of this study?

Acting on the evidence

Purists will bemoan the inclusion of opinion-based techniques such as Delphi processes, focus groups and market surveys in a book on evidence-based information practice. For justification it is necessary to return to definitions of evidence-based librarianship rehearsed earlier in the book. Firstly such practice is about the use of the 'best available' evidence. If this only exists in these 'lower' forms then at least a decision will be more informed than one with no evidence base at all. More importantly it should be highlighted that the function of these designs is to address primarily the dimension populated by 'user needs' and not necessarily that inhabited by research evidence. One function of marketing is to provide a toolbox by which, it is hoped, evidence-based techniques and interventions might be promoted and advanced. To this extent the complementarity of this primarily qualitative evidence with more 'rigorous' designs in other chapters is extremely apposite. The domain of marketing and promotion is one that primarily concerns implementation rather than intervention and as such we should welcome any evidence that may make our task easier and more realizable.

References

Ajetunmobi, O. (2002) *Making Sense of Critical Appraisal*, London, Arnold.

Baruchson-Arbib, S and Bronstein, J. (2002) A View to the Future of the Library and Information Science Profession: a Delphi study, *Journal of the American Society for Information Science and Technology*, **53** (5), 397–408.

Beavers, P. J., Russell, K. W. and Sibia, T. S. (1996) Supporting the Information Needs of Agricultural Research Scientists Working in Remote Locations: implications of recent studies and changes in technology and delivery mechanisms, *Quarterly Bulletin of the International Association of Agricultural Information Specialists*, **41** (2), 204–10.

Bell, J. (1999) *Doing your Research Project*, 3rd edn, Milton Keynes, Open University.

Booth, T. (2003) Pre-Marketing: Analysis of Information Needs, www.libsci.sc.edu/bob/class/clis724/SpecialLibrariesHandbook/booth.htm.

Bremner, A. (2000) Open University Students and Libraries Project 1999, *Library and Information Research News*, **24** (76), 26–38.

Buckley, C. (1995) Delphi: a methodology for preferences more than predictions, *Technical Communication*, **42** (2), (May), 262–77.

Buckley, C. C. (1994) Delphi Technique Supplies the Classic Result, *Australian Library Journal*, **43** (3), 158–64.

Burton, P. (1990) *Asking Questions: questionnaire design and question phrasing*. In Slater, M. (ed.), *Research Methods in Library and Information Studies*, London, Library Association, 62–76.

Chavez-Hernandez, M. T. (1996) The Establishment of a Library Networking Model for the Caribbean Region: a Delphi study, *Journal of Interlibrary Loan, Document Delivery and Information Supply*, **7** (2), 51–75.

Cook, C. and Heath, F. M. (2001) Users' Perceptions of Library Service Quality: a LibQUAL+ qualitative study, *Library Trends*, **49** (4), (Spring), 548–84.

Cram, L. (1995) The Marketing Audit: baseline for action, *Library Trends*, **43** (3), 326–48.

Crumley E and Koufogiannakis D. (2002) Developing Evidence-based Librarianship: practical steps for implementation, *Health Information and Libraries Journal*, **19** (4), 61–70.

Duffy, T. M. (1995) Designing Tools to Aid Technical Editors: a needs analysis, *Library Management*, **16** (7), 16–19.

Dwyer, M. (1999) A Delphi Survey of Research Priorities and Identified Areas for Collaborative Research in Health Sector Library and Information Services UK, *Health Libraries Review*, **16** (3), 174–91.

Eldredge, J. (1984) BobCats, Infestation, and a New Library, *College and Research Libraries News*, **45** (7), 336–40.

Eldredge, J. (2002) Cohort Studies in Health Sciences Librarianship, *Journal of the Medical Library Association*, **90** (4), 380–92.

Eldredge, J. D. (2003) The Randomized Controlled Trial Design: unrecognized opportunities for health sciences librarianship, *Health Information and Libraries Journal*, **20** (Suppl 1), 34–44.

Eldredge, J. D. and Karcher, C. T. (2002) Determinants of Effective Library Faculty – Pharmacy Faculty Communication. A Randomized Controlled Trial, *Hypothesis*, **16** (2), 10.

Eldredge, J. (submitted on behalf of the Evidence-Based Librarianship Implementation Committee) (2001) The Most Relevant and Answerable Research Questions Facing the Practice of Health Sciences Librarianship, *Hypothesis*, **15** (1), 9–17, http://gain.mercer.edu/mla/research/hypothesis.html.

Feret, B., Marcinek, M. (1999) The Future of the Academic Library And Librarian: a DELPHI study, IATUL Proceedings (New Series). 9 1999, CD-ROM Full Text Database *The Future of Libraries in Human Communication*. Twentieth Annual IATUL Conference 1999, Technical University of Crete, Chania, Greece, 17–21 May 1999.

Gatfield, T., Barker, M. and Graham, P. (1999) Measuring Communication Impact for University Advertising Materials, *Corporate Communications: An International Journal*, **4** (2), 73–9.

Gibbs, A. (1997) Focus Groups. Social Research Update, www.soc.surrey.ac.uk/sru/SRU19.html.

Glitz, B. (1997) The Focus Group Technique in Library Research: an introduction, *Bulletin of the Medical Library Association*, **85** (4), 385–90.

Glitz, B., Hamasu, C. and Sandstrom, H. (2001) The Focus Group: A Tool for Programme Planning, Assessment, and Decision-Making — An American View, *Health Information and Libraries Journal*, **18** (1), 30–7.

Green, J. W. (2000) Delphi Method in Web Site Selection: using the experts, *Reference Librarian*, (**69/70**), 299–310.

Greenbaum, T. L. (1993) *The Handbook for Focus Group Research*, New York, Lexington Books.

Grunenwald, J. P. and Traynor, K. (1987) A Marketing Plan for the Law Library, *Law Library Journal*, **79** (1), 93–101.

Haug, J. D. (1997) Physicians' Preferences for Information Sources: a meta-analytic study, *Bulletin of the Medical Library Association*, **85** (3), 223–32.

Hernon, P.;,Powell, R. R, and Young, A. P. (2002) University Library Directors in the Association of Research Libraries: the next generation, Part two, *College and Research Libraries*, **63** (1), (Jan), 73–90.

Holsapple, C. W. and Joshi, K. D. (2000) An Investigation of Factors that Influence the Management of Knowledge in Organizations, *Journal of Strategic Information Systems*, **9** (2–3), (September), 235–61.

Keller, A. (2001a) Future Development of Electronic Journals: a Delphi survey, *Electronic Library*, **19** (6), 383–96.

Keller, A. (2001b) Delphi Survey on the Future Development of Electronic Journals, *Serials*, **14** (2), 121–8.

Khosrow-Pour, M. and Herman, N. (2001) Critical Issues of Web-enabled Technologies in Modern Organizations, *Electronic Library*, **19** (4), 208–20.

Krueger, R. A. and Casey, M. A. (2000) *Focus Groups: a practical guide for applied research*, 3rd edn, Thousand Oaks, CA, Sage.

Lipscomb, C. E., Moran, B. B., Jenkins, C. G., Cogdill, K. W., Friedman, C. P., Gollop, C. J., Moore, M. E., Morrison, M. L., Tibbo, H. R., Wildemuth, B. M. (1999) Feasibility and Marketing Studies of Health Sciences Librarianship Education Programs, *Bulletin of the Medical Library Association*, **87** (1), 50–7.

MacDougall, C. (2001) Planning and Recruiting the Sample for Focus Groups and In-Depth Interviews, *Qualitative Health Research*, **11** (1), 117–27.

Mullaly-Quijas, P., Ward, D. H., Woelfl, N. (1994) Using Focus Groups to Discover Health Professionals' Information Needs: a regional marketing study, *Bulletin of the Medical Library Association*, **82** (3), 305–11.

Murphy, B., Peterson, R. A., Wardell, S. and Thibodeau, P. L. (2002) Capturing the Big D$: Dollars and Data, *Hypothesis*, **16** (2), 5.

Nelson, E. A. (1999) Questions for Surveys, *Nursing Times Learning Curve*, **3**, 5–7.

Neuman, D. (1995) High School Students' Use of Databases: results of a National Delphi study, *Journal of the American Society for Information Science*, **46** (4), 284–98.

O'Keefe, D. J. (1999) Variability of Persuasive Message Effects: meta-analytic evidence and implications, *Document Design*, **1** (2), 86–97.

Oppenheim, A. N. (1992) *Questionnaire Design, Interviewing and Attitude Measurement*, 2nd edn, London, Pinter Publications.

Robbins, K. and Holst, R. (1990) Hospital Library Evaluation Using Focus Group Interviews, *Bulletin of the Medical Library Association*, **78** (3), 311–13.

Rowley, J. (2003) Information Marketing: seven questions, *Library Management*, **24** (1/2), 13.

Russell, A. and Shoolbred, M. (1995) Developing an Effective Questionnaire – some thoughts on obtaining appropriate data and respecting the respondents, *Library and Information Research News*, **19** (63), 28–33.

Snoke, R. and Underwood, A. (2001) Generic Attributes of IS Graduates: a comparison of Australian industry and academic views, *Journal of Global Information Management*, **9** (2), 34–41.

Terman, K. (1996) Getting Things in Focus: the use of focus groups in Brent libraries, *Library Management*, **17** (2), 36–9.

Weingand, D. E. (1997) *Chapter 4: The marketing audit: using systems analysis to inform marketing research*, Future Driven Marketing, Chicago, American Library

Association, 47–61, www.ala.org/editions/samplers/sampler_pdfs/
wein_future.pdf.

Weinreich, N. K. (2003) Integrating Quantitative and Qualitative Methods in Social
Marketing Research (originally in the Winter 1996 issue of the *Social Marketing
Quarterly*), www.social-marketing.com/research.html.

Welsh, J. (2000) Focus Groups in Library and Information Services: report of a pilot
study, *New Review of Information and Library Research*, **6,** 93–111.

Westbrook, L. (1997) Information Access Issues for Interdisciplinary Scholars: results
of a Delphi Study on Women's Studies Research, *Journal of Academic
Librarianship*, **23** (3), 211–16.

Widdows, R., Hensler, T. A. and Wyncott, M. H. (1991) The Focus Group Interview:
a method for assessing users' evaluation of library service, *College and Research
Libraries*, **52** (4), 352–9.

Wilson, Tom, *Electronic Resources For Research Methods*,
http://InformationR.net/rm/RMeth21.html.

Special topic (H)
Determining the information needs of practising nurses post-registration in the UK from 1990 to 2003 (Evidence Digest)

Jennie Kelson

Why is it important?

Studies investigating the information needs of healthcare professionals have tended to focus on medical staff (Bunyan and Lutz 1991; Roddham 1995). Nurses learnt on the wards, which discouraged the use of research in practice (Wakeham et al., 1992) and led to the belief that nurses had no need of libraries (Wakeham 1992).

Since the early 1990s, the UK nursing profession has undergone radical changes that are expected to increase nurses' requirement for information and libraries (Roddham 1995; Yeoh 2000). These include the introduction of a more scholarly base for nursing (UKCC 1986; UKCC 1999), increasing emphasis on continuing professional development (UKCC 1994), the growing evidence-based healthcare movement and the extended role of nurses (Yeoh 2000).

Technological developments such as the internet and the NHSnet, and initiatives including the National electronic Library for Health (Yeoh 2000) and the increasing focus on electronic delivery of information are expected to impact on the information needs and information-seeking behaviour of practising nurses.

What is required?

Many NHS Trust libraries traditionally have provided services to a narrow range of clients, predominantly physicians and junior doctors in training (Capel 1998). Government initiatives to encourage NHS libraries to take on a multidisciplinary focus (Department of Health, 1997), coupled with the move of nursing education to the higher education sector (UKCC, 1986), have meant they are expected to provide services for different staff groups although they may have little experience or knowledge of their information needs.

Marketing techniques and strategies can be used to evaluate existing services and to plan new services (Bunyan and Lutz 1991). Products and services to meet the needs of a particular client group can then be developed and promoted.

The information needs of nurses are diverse, as the profession encompasses a variety of specialities including general, psychiatric, community, midwifery and children's nursing (Bawden and Robinson 1994). Nurses may work in acute care or within the community and, in addition to their role as carer, may undertake other roles including those of teacher, student, researcher or manager (Roddham 1995; Urquhart et al., 1997).

This digest describes existing research on the information needs and information-seeking behaviour of practising nurses post-registration from 1990 to 2003. As comparisons between studies conducted in different countries can be difficult owing to cultural, political, educational and working differences, only original research studies undertaken in the UK have been reviewed.

Who else is involved?

Library staff, users and non-users of nursing libraries, funding bodies such as the Workforce Development Confederations, NHS Trusts, higher education institutions, professional bodies such as the Nursing and Midwifery Council.

Evidence

Quality of evidence varies considerably although a poor quality rating may indicate incomplete reporting of methodology or results rather than poor study design.

Information needs and information-seeking behaviour

A survey of 433 incidences that generated an information need found that nurses most commonly sought information for personal updating and patient care (Davies et al., 1997). Needs most commonly related to patient care included details of specific drugs or treatments (39%) or administration of care (31%) (Davies et al., 1997). Information for research or publication each accounted for approximately 10% of requests. The majority of incidences involved more than one purpose (average 2.6).

Information needs expressed by nurses in acute settings differed slightly from those in community settings. Community nurses indicated slightly lower need for drug or treatment information for patient care and slightly higher need for patient education information and information for research or publication. However, these differences were not statistically significant (Davies et al., 1997).

An analysis of 501 completed questionnaires from nurses in Essex found that over 90% of respondents 'often' or 'sometimes' needed information to support patient care (Wakeham et al., 1992). Respondents said they 'often' needed information for personal interest (44.8%) and 42% said they 'often' needed information for course work. Information was least often sought for research or to prepare for a course or job interview. Differences in the expressed needs of nurses with differing qualifications or job role were observed but were not analysed for statistical significance.

An interview study found both midwives and psychiatric nurses expressed a need for multi-disciplinary information (Bawden and Robinson 1994). Midwives regularly cited use of specialist information services such as MIDIRS, libraries (local or other) and specialist midwifery journals as sources of information. Their use of databases such as MEDLINE and CINAHL was less common. In contrast, although psychiatric nurses cited little use of information services, most identified specific journals in their area and expressed needs for information related to mental health and social services.

A more recent survey (Fakhoury and Wright, 2000) of the communication and information needs of 110 community psychiatric nurses found that 76% of respondents identified information needs. Information needs on mental health law, state benefits and voluntary services were most common. Colleagues, especially medical professionals, were valuable conduits of information for these nurses.

Two studies investigated use of the internet. A self-selected group of 126 nurse internet users identified information pertinent to their speciality, news, access to bibliographic databases and peer-reviewed journals as being of high importance for a nursing web site (Ward, 2000). Job advertisements, local information and mailing lists were deemed less important (Ward, 2000). Community nurses in the Western Isles of Scotland reported that they wanted internet access to full-text journal articles related to specific conditions, CINAHL plus online discussion groups and e-mail to improve communication with colleagues (Farmer et al., 1997).

Wakeham et al. (1992) found that nursing colleagues (68.3%), ward-based collections (47.5%) and own journals (46.3%) were the resources 'often' used by nurses to address information needs concerning patient care. Libraries were most 'often' used to find information related to course work or research. Most respondents said they most 'often' found information in the library by asking the librarian (54%) or browsing the shelves (34.8%). Books were more commonly used in libraries than journal articles. Differences in the sources used by nurses with differing qualifications or job roles were observed but these were not analysed for statistical significance.

Ward-based information (60%), followed by colleagues (51%) and personal journal or book collections (50%) were the most common sources used by acute and community nurses (Davies et al., 1997). Use of colleagues was more common amongst community nurses and use of base or ward resources was significantly lower compared to acute nurses. Colleagues and ward-based information were most often used for patient care or personal updating. Course work and personal updating were primary reasons for using a library.

Colleagues, particularly clinical nurse specialists, were the main source of information used by nurses in acute settings (Thompson et al., 2001). Libraries were viewed as a resource to support continuing professional development and libraries or librarians were not perceived to be a resource for clinical problem solving. Audits of ward-based resources found that the average age of textbooks was more than 11 years and most were not research based. In 180 hours of observation, nurses consulted text-based research information infrequently. Local protocols or guidelines were used four times and the *British National Formulary* was consulted more than 50 times.

Analysis of nurses' information-seeking skills found that only 25% were confident information seekers whilst 20% showed limited information skills and knowledge of sources (Davies et al., 1997). An earlier study of trained nursing staff found that a third of respondents had low levels of information seeking skills (Urquhart and Crane, 1994). Informal sources such as colleagues were used equally, regardless of the level of information seeking skills (Urquhart and Crane, 1994). Those with better information-seeking skills were more likely to use a library.

A survey investigating use of the *Cochrane Pregnancy and Childcare Database* available on the labour ward found that 37% of midwives stated that they had used it at least once whilst 27% said that they used it regularly (Hillan and McGuire, 1998). Reasons given for non-use were lack of searching skills or lack of access.

The use of CINAHL, MEDLINE and the *Cochrane Database* to inform practice was investigated via a questionnaire survey completed by 82 nurses working on acute wards (Griffiths and Riddington, 2001). Whilst 66% said they were confident using CINAHL, only 27% reported using it at least monthly. In contrast, only 6% felt confident using the Cochrane Library. However, no respondents reported using it regularly. A statistically significant relationship was found between CINAHL usage and past or current experience of higher education. A highly significant relationship was found between home computer use and regular use of CINAHL or MEDLINE databases. Lack of awareness was the main reason why nurses did not use the *Cochrane Database*.

A study of nurse researchers found that 58% used a library once a week or more and that libraries were the main information source used, followed by their own collections of books and journals (Blair and Wakeham, 1995). Main reasons for using the library were to consult journals or books, use CD-ROMs for literature searching, other indexing or abstracting services and interlibrary loan services.

Nurses often used a single or core library for most needs and supplemented this with other libraries including other college libraries, specialist libraries such as the Royal College of Nursing or Family Planning Association and public libraries (Blair and Wakeham, 1995; Urquhart and Crane, 1995; Yeoh and Morrissey, 1996). The key factor in choice of library was availability of resources rather than convenience (Yeoh and Morrissey, 1996).

Many studies reported experiences of nurses using libraries (Wakeham et al., 1992; Blair and Wakeham, 1995; Yeoh and Morrissey, 1996; Farmer et al., 1997). Difficulties experienced included lack of time, inadequate library opening hours, restrictive access policies, insufficient or inappropriate stock, lack of funding to support nurses' needs, lack of confidence or skills in seeking information and travelling distance where a library was not on site.

Studies found nurses most commonly reported visiting a library after their shift or whilst on courses as they reported difficulty accessing the library during work hours. Two studies examined the most common times that nurses visited libraries (Urquhart and Crane, 1995; Yeoh and Morrissey, 1996). Yeoh and Morrissey (1996) found that most nurses used the library during normal office hours: however, 43% reported using the library in the evening and 21% used the library at weekends. The second study found that preferred times for using the library were from 12.00 to 4.30p.m. and from 4.30 to 7p.m. respectively (Urquhart and Crane, 1995).

Analyses of information needs and information-seeking behaviour of nurses have been used to develop marketing strategies for library services (Hernando, 1997) or to evaluate library provision to staff (Banwell et al., 1995).

Hernando (1997) found that fewer than 24% of potential users actually used the library. Of these, approximately two-thirds were not on an educational course. Nurses most commonly used the library to update their knowledge although teaching, publication or personal continuing education were also cited. Personal and departmental collections were important sources of information, as were colleagues. Printed resources in the library were consulted but computerized resources were rarely used.

Questionnaires, interviews and focus groups were used to determine library services available, use made of these services, information needs of staff groups and options for redesign of the library services to meet identified needs (Banwell et al., 1995). The results showed the library service was limited in coverage, did not reflect the multidisciplinary nature of work, did not meet changing user needs or emerging user groups and that additional investment should be made in electronic delivery options to enhance services to an increasingly geographically remote workforce. Library services needed to focus more on supporting information needs related to clinical practice and patient care rather than just supporting those on courses or doing research.

Future research areas

'Information gatekeepers' such as clinical nurse specialists are key conduits of information to nurse colleagues (Bawden and Robinson, 1994; Thompson et al., 2001), ensuring that nurses have access to high quality information at the point of care (Thompson et al., 2001). Further investigation of their role and impact on nurse's clinical decision making is needed.

References

Banwell, L. et al. (1995) Implications of the UNNDERPIN Study at St George's Hospital, Morpeth, Northumberland, *Health Libraries Review*, **12** (4), 279–93.

Bawden, D. and Robinson, K. (1994) *Information Systems for Nursing Specialities*, BRR&D report 6168, Boston Spa, Wetherby, British Library Document Supply Centre.

Blair, E. and Wakeham, M. (1995) *The Use of Libraries by Nursing Researchers*, BLR&D report 6207, Boston Spa, Wetherby, British Library Document Supply Centre.

Bunyan, L. E. and Lutz, E. M. (1991) Marketing the Hospital Library to Nurses, *Bulletin of the Medical Library Association*, **79** (2), 223–5.

Capel, S. (1998) Nurses' Access to Library and Information Services, *Nursing Standard*, **12** (25), 45–7.

Davies, R. et al. (1997) *Establishing the Value of Information to Nursing Continuing Education: report of the EVINCE project*, BLRIC report 44, Boston Spa, Wetherby, British Library Document Supply Centre.

Department of Health (1997) *Library and Information Services*, HSG (97)47, London, Department of Health.

Fakhoury, W. K. and Wright, D. (2000) Communication and Information Needs of a Random Sample of Community Psychiatric Nurses in the United Kingdom, *Journal of Advanced Nursing*, **32** (4), 871–80.

Farmer, J. et al. (1997) *Improving Access to Information for Nursing Staff in Remote Areas: the potential of the internet and other networked resources*, Aberdeen, Robert Gordon University.

Griffiths, P. and Riddington, L. (2001) Nurses' Use of Computer Databases to Identify Evidence for Practice – a cross-sectional questionnaire survey in a UK hospital, *Health Information and Libraries Journal*, **18** (1), 2–9.

Hernando, S. (1997) Promoting Library Services to Qualified Nurses: towards a market-led approach, *Health Libraries Review*, **14** (2), 105–19.

Hillan, E. M. and McGuire, M. M. (1998) Computers in Midwifery Practice: a view from the labour ward, *Journal of Advanced Nursing*, **27** (1), 24–9.

Roddham, M. (1995) Responding to the Reforms: are we meeting the need?, *Health Libraries Review*, **12** (2), 101–14.

Thompson, C. et al. (2001) The Accessibility of Reseach-based Knowledge for Nurses in United Kingdom Acute Care Settings, *Journal of Advanced Nursing*, **36** (1), 11–22.

UKCC (1986) *Project 2000: a new preparation for practice*, London, UKCC.

UKCC (1994) *PREP – Preparation for Education and Practice*, London, UKCC.

UKCC (1999) *Fitness to Practice*, London, UKCC.

Urquhart, C. and Crane, S. (1994) Nurses' Information-seeking Skills and Perceptions of Information Sources: assessment using vignettes, *Journal of Information Science*, **20** (4), 237–46.

Urquhart, C. and S. Crane (1995) Preparing for Post-registration and Practice (PREP): the support role of the library, *Nurse Education Today*, **15**, 459–64.

Urquhart, C. et al. (1997) Assessing How Nurses use Information Derived from Databases and the Internet, *Healthcare Computing*, 254–60.

Wakeham, M. (1992) Improving Library Services for Nurses, *Nursing Standard*, **6** (37), 37–9.

Wakeham, M., Houghton, J. and Beard, S. (1992) *The Information Needs and Information Seeking Behaviour of Nurses*, BLR&D report 6078, Boston Spa, Wetherby, British Library Document Supply Centre.

Ward, R. (2000) Nurses' Net Needs, *Health Informatics Journal*, **6** (4), 196–203.

Yeoh, J. (2000) Nursing Information Needs: what next?, *Health Libraries Review*, **17** (1), 14–16.

Yeoh, J. and Morrissey, C. (1996) Selection of Library Services by Post-registration Nursing, Midwifery and Health Visiting Students, *Health Libraries Review*, **13** (2), 97–107.

20

A future for evidence-based information practice?

Anne Brice, Andrew Booth, Ellen Crumley,
Denise Koufogiannakis and Jonathan Eldredge

This concluding chapter, bringing together perspectives from evidence-based information practice in the UK, US and Canada, takes stock of achievements so far. It considers the main challenges facing the movement as it gathers momentum, and suggests some short and long-term priorities. After defining progress made, both nationally and internationally, it records personal aspirations for the evidence-based practice paradigm, linked to some 'quick wins' to be achieved if such a culture is to develop and grow.

The EBIP journey

The successful planning, delivery and experience of the first Evidence Based Librarianship Conference in Sheffield in September 2001 may be viewed, in retrospect, as a major landmark in the progress of the movement (Eldredge, 2001). It brought together individuals from the UK, Canada and the USA, already pioneers in EBL, with a shared awareness of the potential activities and goals required by a global initiative. In charting the unique contribution of each country, alongside complementary developments already underway, the conference presented an opportunity to test EBIP with a broader audience, and to identify practical steps to be planned and taken forward internationally. These included agreement on planning a second conference.

Since then the EBIP movement has moved forward on sometimes divergent and sometimes parallel tracks, culminating in a second International Conference held in Edmonton, Canada in June 2003. Several key themes have emerged as a potential focus for future strategies and actions.

Any movement seeking 'critical mass' must be active in awareness raising and dissemination. Initiatives to date include publishing, community building and teaching and learning activities.

Publishing

A plethora of conceptual literature has been published, bringing EBIP to the forefront of professional concerns and generating interest in its development. Leading articles have promoted EBIP in the major health libraries journals and, perhaps more significantly, in generalist library journals (Booth and Haines, 1998; Koufogiannakis and Crumley, 2002; Marshall, 2003).

After several years of hosting a quarterly 'Research' column the editorial team of *Health Information and Libraries Journal* (formerly *Health Libraries Review*) decided that the principles of research-based practice were beginning to be integrated within the main body of the journal to the extent that a separate column was no longer required. Instead, 2003 saw the introduction of a 'Using research in practice' column, specifically focusing on the utilization of research. Mirroring this integration, EBL has been institutionalized within the Medical Library Assocation (MLA) Research Section. The journal *Hypothesis* regularly references EBL and the Association's committee structure reveals that more than half of these committees are directly or indirectly focused upon making EBIP a reality.

Co-operative publishing initiatives such as the 'International Research Reviews' column in *Hypothesis*; a *Health and Information Libraries Journal* Special Issue, and jointly authored articles in key health libraries journals (Booth and Eldredge, 2002) are widening the debate and embedding the principles and practices of EBIP.

Community access and discussion

A discussion list ('evidence-based-libraries') provides a forum for discussion and information sharing. It is complemented by a web site domain (www.eblib.net) with initial content developed primarily from the two EBL Conferences. The EBL website and discussion list have helped to promote the movement internationally and to encourage librarians from all subject areas to learn more. However, limitations to such an approach still remain: 'Despite attempts to use the mailing list there is as yet no natural forum for international discussions on EBL ideas, philosophies and techniques, and it is disappointing that the same names come to mind when planning conference presentations/articles/book chapters. There is no obvious source for funding for the establishment of a Centre for Evidence Based Librarianship, and in some areas a lack of central support for EBL initiatives' (e-mail correspondence between authors).

Involvement of senior and high-profile librarians in the early stages of the movement has signalled that this is an important and influential area for the profession, as well as offering vital leadership and direction.

Policy development

In the area of policy development, the UK HeLICON task group has modelled a unified approach to EBIP (bringing together seven previous groups), and has attempted to co-ordinate activities in all these areas. HeLICON has sought an outward-facing dimension in order to engage all information practice sectors, and has promoted and encouraged participation through the Research in the Workplace Award.

In the US, EBL/EBIP is firmly on the agenda of the Medical Library Association (MLA), being discussed, referenced, and debated in a variety of venues, and included in key strategic planning documents. Leadership is seen as key, and MLA presidents since 1997 have made direct or indirect references to EBL in their goals for MLA. Advocacy of EBL takes myriad forms, including the MLA Research Awards, which recognize relevant, practical and rigorous research projects.

Improving the knowledge base

One of the biggest challenges, if research is to be put into practice, lies in improving the scope and quality of the knowledge base together with its output and dissemination. In the US educational initiatives have focused on improving the understanding of, and participation in, research studies, leading to increased awareness and involvement.

The development of review methodologies has also focused attention and improved awareness on their benefits for practitioners. The development of small but critical masses of EBIP researchers in academic units in Sheffield, Salford and York has impacted on the quality and relevance of the research output, and also provided vital outlets for the development of new skills.

As mentioned in Chapter 4, much library literature appears in conference proceedings. In Canada, Bayley (Bayley et al., 2002) has led work, for the Evidence Based Librarianship Implementation Committee of the MLA Research Section, on the development of structured abstracts. It has been shown that research objectives become more recognizable and the outlines of paper presentations are more standardized when such abstracts are provided. Structured abstracts have been required for submissions to the Canadian Health Libraries Association conferences since 2002. Moves are underway to adopt this practice in other settings, including the MLA Conference in 2004, and future UK conferences.

Teaching and learning and practical tools

Getting research into practice, however, requires relevant skills to be built into professional development and educational initiatives supported by the development of practical tools and techniques. In the UK the production of the CriSTAL checklists (Booth and Brice, 2003 (see Chapter 9)), led to the development and piloting of CriSTAL, EBL and Research Methods workshops, short and online courses, which have met with a large measure of success.

In Canada, teaching has become a key strategic goal, and a health librarianship course for Masters' students at School of Library and Information Studies has generated interest among new librarians. In Australia the concept of EBIP has been piloted in an academic setting. Here, rather than teaching a separate module, the principles of EBIP have been integrated into a specific module of a Masters' library programme. Embedding EBIP skills within specific project work encourages students to practice EBIP within the learning environment (Partridge and Hallam, 2003).

In Canada, EBL is expanding rapidly both within and beyond health sciences librarianship. For instance, in Edmonton, workshops have been organized for University and other librarians and an EBL project presented at the Canadian Health Libraries Association (CHLA) 2003 conference. Librarians in the CHLA have become more aware of EBIP and the Special Libraries Association chapters in Canada are also becoming interested in research. To date, Canadian librarians are beginning to learn about, and to incorporate into their practice, EBIP through a range of educational and practical activities.

International collaboration and achievements

Collaboration with international colleagues, through committees, conference planning, and, indeed, the planning and production of this book have achieved much and promise more. The first EBL conference provided a focus for international dialogue, and led to further joint work on structured abstracts, guideline development, and the planning of the second EBL Conference (with the international programme committee including, for the first time, a representative from the developing world) (Eldredge, 2001). The Edmonton conference was the first to focus upon librarianship as a whole and to comprise a planning committee composed of librarians from all types of organizations. It has triggered a great interest in EBIP and librarians from various subject areas and institutions were in attendance.

An international collaboration, the Evidence Based Librarianship Implementation Committee (EBLIC), loosely organized by the MLA Research Section, has collected and published EBL questions important to the profession generated by health sciences librarians around the world (Eldredge, 2001). It has also convened two working groups, on guideline development and, as previously mentioned, on structured abstracts.

What is evident from developments across the three settings is that common achievements together with idiosyncratic skills and focuses make collaboration and co-operation both challenging and vital. Identification of what is best done at what level, when to do globally and when locally, is core to understanding the drivers for development and change. For instance it seems inevitable that we will witness collaborative EBIP research across national boundaries. Already various organizations are collaborating over policies and guidelines yet endeavouring to preserve a mutual respect and remain sensitive toward differing local circumstances. This is exemplified by the co-operation of international collaborations of groups of practitioners involved in the development of information retrieval methods research, such as the Cochrane Information Retrieval Methods Group (Pritchard and Weightman, 2003) and the HTA-i information specialists group.

The importance of a breadth and depth of sincere dialogue amongst colleagues about EBIP issues on an international scale should not be underestimated. In fact, it suggests that EBIP is gathering momentum among an informal community of colleagues. Trust is vital if communities are to move forward from passive and reactive forms to ones where real work is achieved and sustained. There is evidence that each national constituency has made a unique contribution without duplication of effort, although this may have been achieved more by chance than good judgement. This leads naturally to analysis of the challenges that the movement faces at this critical juncture on our journey, if we are going to arrive at our destination.

The challenges

Challenges identified within individual countries share many similar features, and highlight the potential benefits of shared development and learning.

EBIP for all

A key challenge for all collaborating countries involves understanding the context for all sectors of the profession, and responding to their needs – getting the message out to all librarians, not just those in the health sciences. Explaining the history of EBL and enabling non-health librarians to practice EBIP in their environment in a way that is relevant and accessible can be considered vital:

I do have some disappointments with regard to how the larger profession views EBL. While I am delighted that EBL is on the minds of my colleagues, I sometimes flinch when I realize how casually and inaccurately some colleagues have used the EBL term. As a peer reviewer for a recent program on the subject of EBL I was astonished by the inaccurate use of the term EBL by a large number of colleagues who had submitted abstracts. Situations like this present a challenge to all of us to ensure we are communicating clearly and to as wide an audience as possible as to what we mean by EBL.

(e-mail correspondence between authors)

What's in a name?

For some the 'evidence-based' label still causes concern with its strongly medical overtones. Whether to use the 'L' word, or to broaden the focus to 'Information Practice', as with the title of this book, is a second issue that generates much heat, if minimal light. What about health informatics, knowledge management? As reported in Chapter 2, this process mirrors that in other disciplines, not least in healthcare where definitions, as evidence-based medicine migrated to healthcare and onwards to practice, have been fiercely debated and are likely to continue. For those unfamiliar with the prehistory of evidence-based practice the concept of 'reflective practice' may strike a more resonant chord. As Ross Todd (2002), a foremost proponent of evidence-based school libraries, states: 'A profession without reflective practitioners willing to learn about the advances in research in the field is a blinkered profession, one that is disconnected from best practice and best thinking, and one which, by default, often resorts to advocacy and position as a bid for survival'.

Depth and spread

A further challenge lies in spreading EBIP beyond the keen enthusiasts in regional and national centres to the grassroots. Complacency poses a threat to innovation and development in many contexts. Practitioners need to apply EBIP principles and research to making decisions in their workplaces, and to do this need to be convinced that EBIP matters to them, that it is not just a concept for academics. It is not enough for the topic to be on the organizational agenda and to presume that someone else is sorting it out – responsibility is to be held at every level; individual, organizational, professional, national and international. Many believe that 'someone else' can make EBIP a reality.

A further major challenge is to ensure that all professional membership associations become interested in participating in EBIP and making it a major goal. It may be not only individuals, but also organizations, that do not understand how research can be of benefit to them.

Skills base

Specifying generic skills required for the development of EBIP at all levels (individual, organizational and policy), and allowing for flexibility in augmenting these with additional specialist skills, would be a major step forward, both in formal and in continuing education. What are the knowledge, skills and attitudes that an evidence-based practitioner needs, and how might such competencies be measured? Inconsistent approaches to teaching research methods in library and information studies departments and an absence of skills in implementing research findings provide a formidable obstacle if students are to be aware of the importance of research from the onset of their librarianship career.

Major differences exist in core educational programmes and in the content, structure and funding of continuing professional development programmes. Tools and products are urgently needed to make it easy for practitioners to apply research findings on a day-to-day basis. Publishing such outputs will require innovative models of dissemination together with considerable international effort. It also carries, at least for some, a considerable opportunity cost: 'spending so much time on the 'D bit' of R&D means that I have little time for research (evidence production)' (e-mail correspondence between authors).

Challenges for international collaboration

EBIP must be adapted to fit the context of all countries, most specifically within the developing world. Language and terminology issues can hamper skills and knowledge transfer across sectors and between cultures. Similarly, we need to agree a shared definition and vision of EBIP and of priorities for development (Eldredge, 1999). As members of an international movement, many different people are involved with a variety of opinions to be taken into account. In the absence of a formal committee overseeing the development of the movement, theoretical growth and diverse leadership come at the expense of unity:

> The fact that we have not come together to form a consensus of some of the issues; many of us are still publishing materials about EBL that really have little consensus and no input from an international committee. This is excellent from a theoretical point and to generate debate about where EBL is going, but there is enough literature to begin putting the pieces together. EBL is still mainly in developed countries so involving other librarians from all types of environments and situations would enable us to develop the concept for all librarians.   (e-mail correspondence between authors)

As mentioned above such diversity is not necessarily a disadvantage, but a structure for the further progress of EBIP that accommodates creative thought and inspiration would be preferable. It is vital to focus on making EBIP a reality, and superficial national differences should not distract from the many shared values or goals.

What makes people get involved?

Todd (2003) surveyed 11 teacher-librarians on evidence-based practice and respondents identified six key benefits:

1   It provides evidence at the local . . . level that library initiatives make a visible contribution to learning, and that [stakeholders] can see the real impacts.
2   It convinces administrators and . . . funders that the money invested in the . . . library is worth it.
3   It demonstrates the . . . librarian's commitment to learning outcomes.
4   It helps . . . librarians plan more effective instructional interventions and information services.
5   It contributes to job satisfaction.
6   It moves beyond the anecdotal, guesswork, hunches, advocacy, and the touting of research findings.

These findings are echoed in the comments of many innovators of EBIP. For those from healthcare, however, came an added impetus stemming from their prior involvement in the evidence-based healthcare movement. They were keen to see the principles and practices applied to the information profession, if not actually embarrassed that the profession was not already operating in this way. Taking on the librarian's role within EBP/EBM had taught librarians a structure for how to solve problems based upon research evidence. High-profile questioning of decision-making processes within librarianship instilled a desire to ensure that they were making the best decisions based upon their own experience *and* the research evidence.

What other motivations have drawn together the innovators of the EBIP movement, and does this offer any insights into how to engage the wider community?

Self-reported identifying factors and motivators include an interest in skills development and continuing professional development, interests in research mobilization and use, and in achieving change through personal and organizational development. External factors also provide a stimulus, for instance, requirements for professional re-registration, or the above-mentioned need to demonstrate value for money and effectiveness to funders. Several of the advocates of EBIP shared a desire to practise what they had been helping to preach, or modelling what they teach, to health practitioners. This was supported by an ambition to be able to improve the status of the profession by pointing to the evidence base behind professional practice. As evidence-based practice spreads to sectors other than health, information professionals could find themselves in a unique position in which to enhance their visibility and status.

Aspirations and frustrations

Have personal aspirations for EBIP been realized? Those who have committed time and effort to the early stages of EBIP hold mixed feelings about achievements to date and the distance yet to travel. For instance, in the UK, the core skills needed by practitioners have been outlined, but a sustainable continuing professional development policy and funding has neither been achieved nor implemented. Otherwise successful tools and educational activities have, disappointingly, not been recognized by commitment and funding at a policy level. In respect to the research agenda, the work of international working groups identifying the need to produce structured abstracts (Bayley, 2001) and guidelines (Booth et al., 2001) has been successful, but robust methods for disseminating research findings to practising professionals are yet to be achieved. Personal commitment and energy is not sustainable without an underpinning infrastructure and a critical mass of activity.

Some feel that there has been less progress with meeting personal aspirations. The following personal reflections from contributors to this book illustrate key themes highlighted in this chapter:

> To bring research to the forefront for librarians is important and it is slowly being done in all areas of librarianship whether under the umbrella of EBL or because librarians have a general desire to improve our profession. We feel good about the forward direction to date, but there is still a long way to go. To fully be where we would like EBL to be will take time and many hours of discussion among international colleagues.

> I am very hopeful for the EBL movement, since I feel it is the most important thing happening in librarianship today. My only disappointment would be that EBL is currently still stuck in health sciences librarianship, and therefore librarians outside health sciences may dissociate themselves from the movement because of this.
>
> (e-mail correspondence between authors)

Short-term priorities

Short-term priorities are required to sustain momentum and to engage new activists. These might include those listed below:

Policy and debate

Continued international exposure, more EBIP discussions, and presentation of EBIP projects at conferences would increase awareness and depth of spread. In order to gain wider support, suggestions include:

- publishing more articles about EBIP in mainstream library journals
- setting up an international association of evidence-based information practitioners
- establishing an international consensus on priorities and goals.

These initiatives would allow the movement to go forward and accomplish more than can be done by individuals or within individual countries. A joint international statement of policy and intent would be an important first step.

Research and dissemination

Mechanisms to improve the production and dissemination of good quality research might include:

- increasing the number of higher-level research evidence studies such as systematic reviews, randomized controlled trials and cohort studies
- ensuring that important, answerable questions are addressed through effective research policies
- the rapid dissemination of EBL conference proceedings
- using the EBL website as a short-term publishing medium.

The replication of the same studies in different locations would improve the generalizability of results. The viability of the systematic review, randomized controlled trial and the cohort design has been illustrated and more work to adapt these methodologies in relevant and unique ways would be highly visible. Although systematic reviews reveal serious gaps in our evidence base, we now have an accurate assessment of what kinds of future research need to be pursued as a profession.

Education and skills

EBIP practitioners need to continue to educate colleagues on EBIP methods and to demystify some of the theoretical concepts so as to demonstrate that EBIP need not be as complicated as some fear, even where statistics are concerned! Suggestions include:

- lobbying educational institutions to increase research and appraisal skills teaching in the curriculum
- roll-out of educational interventions such as the appraisal workshops
- continuing the development of e-learning and distance-based courses to increase access.

Where are we now?

The diverse and complex range of activities and themes described above, culminating in the successful running and completion of a second International EBL Conference, provides us with both opportunities and choices about where to travel next, both metaphorically and literally. We need to maintain momentum and visibility, and we may need to consider some 'quick wins' as strategic markers. What are the tipping points for EBIP?

Might they include:

- the development and dissemination of the first evidence-based guideline
- an evidence-based digest placed on the web
- an interactive version of the CriSTAL checklists on the web alongside other learning materials
- structured abstracts adopted internationally for journals and forthcoming conferences
- EBIP workshop sessions piloted on undergraduate and postgraduate library courses
- an international online EBL course re-run on a regular basis
- online virtual journal clubs
- a complete set of user guides to the library literature commissioned and published
- plans for a regular conference circuit but, more importantly, regular inclusion in mainstream conference programmes.

Longer-term priorities for the EBIP movement

What should the movement aim for in the longer term, and what sort of vision can we articulate? Incorporating all library sectors into the movement and revising the definition of EBIP to capture the different aspects of librarianship must be a long-term goal. The establishment of an EBIP filtered database, containing references to high quality research articles, categorized by domains or areas of common interest in librarianship is necessary if the effects, demonstrated throughout this book, of a diffuse and scattered knowledge base are to be overcome. This is a large task, but will give practising librarians a confident starting place when looking for evidence that will help them make better decisions.

Once we have attained a critical mass of rigorous studies such as randomized controlled trials and cohort studies we can then graduate to conducting more systematic reviews (Booth, 2001). We would need to ensure that all quality research, regardless of how unremarkable or controversial the results, can be communicated to the colleagues who need to know these results for their work.

Some specific longer-term objectives might include:

- a common international EBL curriculum
- an international research strategy and funding
- scholarships/fellowships
- a secondary journal of evidence-based information practice
- an international register of rigorous librarianship studies
- an international collaboration (Booth, 2001)
- large-scale international multi-centre prospective studies
- co-operative work with the information systems and informatics communities
- a safe space on the web to encourage mentoring research and applied skills
- an international group to represent all parts of the world.

Using the list-serv as a moderated discussion forum would be useful where specific items need to be debated as has been the case for such discussions in the past. Having an international working group and creating guidelines or systematic reviews on common topics would enable librarians to see tangible outcomes and move forward with implementation of EBIP in their practice.

We have come a long way in a short period of time but achievements have been driven by individual enthusiasms and energies supported by marginalized groups. A strategy for rectifying this situation might thus be summarized as:

1 Identify the most important and answerable questions facing our profession.
2 Devote appropriate resources to answering these relevant questions and making the results available.
3 Ensure that there are the individual skills and knowledge, and organizational policies and environments within which to apply the results where appropriate.

And finally – success in extinction! Maybe the most important longer-term aim, and critical success factor, would be the abolition of an international association of evidence-based information practitioners (because it has become so widespread and commonplace that *everyone* strives to be evidence-based).

The future

EBIP is a new movement providing an exciting opportunity to be proactively shaping the future of our profession. There are always going to be 'growing pains' and differing opinions about the direction it is taking. An international working group would provide an excellent forum by which to develop EBIP and yet not restrict the creative growth and debate that is already underway. Working with colleagues and librarians from many different backgrounds has yielded significant advantages in developing EBIP and one can only look forward to future instances of international collaboration. This would naturally include considering carefully what is happening in mainland Europe, Asia, South America, and in Africa in order to grow a truly international movement. Engaging with both stakeholders and activists is essential for success.

That EBIP has come thus far without its advocates playing the 'political game' is remarkable. However, future success will come only when EBIP becomes mainstream and is supported by those who are grounded in the organizational cultures of international, national and professional library associations and groups. In short the innovators have done their bit – now is the time for the early adopters to step forward and be identified: 'We've made the first faltering toddler's steps but we are a long way from adolescence and maturity' (e-mail correspondence between authors).

References

Bayley, L. (2001) Evidence-Based Librarianship Implementation Committee Report: report of the Research Results Dissemination Task Force, *Hypothesis*, **15** (2), 6–7.

Bayley, L., Wallace, A. and Brice, A. (2002) Evidence Based Librarianship Implementation Committee Research Results Dissemination Task Force recommendations, *Hypothesis*, **16** (1), 6–8.

Booth, A. (2001) Research Column: systematic reviews of health information services and systems, *Health Information and Libraries Journal*, **18**, 60–3.

Booth, A. and Brice, A. (2003) Clear-cut?: facilitating health librarians to use information research in practice, *Health Information and Libraries Journal*, **20** (Suppl 1), 45–52.

Booth, A. and Eldredge, J. (2002) Evidence Based Librarianship: a Socratic dialogue, *Bibliotheca Medica Canadiana*, **23** (4), 136–40.

Booth, A. and Haines, M. (1998) Room for a Review?, *Library Association Record*, **100** (8), 411–12.

Booth, A., Harris. M., McGowan, J. and Burrows, S. (2001) Submitted on behalf of the Evidence-Based Librarianship Implementation Committee Task Force on Practice Guidelines Recommendation/Position Statement, *Hypothesis*, **15** (2), 7.

Eldredge J. (1999) International Research Reviews. Evidence-Based Librarianship (EBL) needs international collaboration, *Hypothesis*, **13** (2), 14–16.

Eldredge, J. (2001) First Evidence-based Librarianship (EBL) Conference, *Hypothesis*, **15** (3), 1, 3, 8–11.

Eldredge, J. (submitted on behalf of the Evidence-Based Librarianship Implementation Committee) (2001) The Most Relevant and Answerable Research Questions Facing the Practice of Health Sciences Librarianship, *Hypothesis*, **15** (1), 9–17, http://gain.mercer.edu/mla/research/hypothesis.html.

Koufogiannakis, D. and Crumley, E. (2002) Evidence Based Librarianship, *Feliciter*, **48** (3), 16.

Marshall, J. G. (2003) Influencing Our Professional Practice by Putting our Knowledge to Work, *Information Outlook*, **7** (1), 40–4.

Partridge, H. and Hallam, G. (2003) Practising Evidence Based Practice: the impact of a Queensland University of Technology Teaching Model on a Culture of EBP in Librarianship, *Improving Practice Through Research: Current Perspectives, Future Prospects. 2nd International Evidence Based Librarianship Conference, June 4–6, 2003*, University of Alberta, Edmonton, Canada.

Pritchard, S. J. and Weightman, A. L. (2003) Towards a Cochrane Information Retrieval Methods Group: a progress report, *Health Information and Libraries Journal*, **20** (Suppl 1), 69–71.

Todd, R. (2002) Evidence-based Practice I: the sustainable future for teacher-librarians, *Scan*, **21** (1), 30–7.

Todd, R. (2003) *Keynote Paper: Learning in the Information Age School: Opportunities, Outcomes and Options*, International Association of School Librarianship (IASL) 2003 Annual Conference, Durban, South Africa, 7–11 July 2003.

Index